Why Christian Kids Rebel

Trading Heartache for Hope

DR. TIM KIMMEL

W Publishing Group
A Division of Thomas Nelson Publishers
Since 1798

www.wpublishinggroup.com

Published by W Publishing Group, a Division of Thomas Nelson, Inc., P.O. Box 141000, Nashville, Tennessee 37214.

Library of Congress Cataloging-in-Publication Data

Kimmel, Tim.
    Why Christian kids rebel : trading heartache for hope / Tim Kimmel.
    p. cm.
Includes bibliographical references.
ISBN 0-8499-1830-8
    1. Christian life. 2. Parenting—Religious aspects—Christianity. 3. Parent and teenager—Religious aspects—Christianity. I. Title.
    BV4529.K555 2004
    248.8'45—dc22

2004017378

Printed in the United States of America

04 05 06 07 08 PHX 9 8 7 6 5 4 3 2 1

Dedicated to
Cammie VanRooy

You never rebelled.
You never wanted to.
You never needed to.

Other Resources
by Dr. Tim Kimmel

BOOKS

Grace-Based Parenting
Little House on the Freeway
Raising Kids Who Turn Out Right
Homegrown Heroes
How to Deal With Powerful Personalities
Basic Training for a Few Good Men

VIDEO STUDIES FOR SMALL GROUPS AND CHURCHES

The Hurried Family Video Series
Raising Kids Who Turn Out Right Video Series
Basic Training for a Few Good Men Video Series
Grandparenthood: More Than Rocking Chairs

Dr. Tim Kimmel does keynote speaking and also conducts parenting, marriage, and men's conferences throughout the United States.

To obtain any of these resources or to contact Dr. Kimmel:

Family Matters™
P.O. Box 14382
Scottsdale, AZ 85267-4382

www.familymatters.net
1-800-467-4596

Contents

Acknowledgments

It's nice when you have so many people who believe in you and in what you have to say. This book enjoyed a great supporting cast.

Bill and Ann Epley—you provided the setting and the encouragement to get the creative wheels turning.

Steve and Barbara Uhlmann—There's something about a cabin in the woods that makes me want to get a lot of writing done. Thanks for the access to such a nice view and so much solitude.

The W Group—every last face in the team picture. You're beautiful.

Laura Kendall, David Moberg, Susan Ligon, and Debbie Wickwire—an author's "Dream Team." Thanks for your faith in me, your wise counsel, and your belief in this message.

Steve and Cheryl Green—I love the way you cover my front and back.

Mike & Karis, Cody, Shiloh, and Colt—you chose not to rebel. You chose wisely.

Riley and Lydia—Your parents are giving you so much to live for. You make your grandfather proud.

Darcy—You created a home where a kid would be crazy to want to rebel and a husband who would be crazy to take any of the credit. Thanks for a passionate Christian faith that we always wanted to emulate.

When That "Gleam" in Your Eye Makes Your Heart Hurt

A friend recently gave me a CD of classic Christian hymns sung by contemporary artists. I became enamored with this collection of songs because hymn after hymn reminds me of how completely I am forgiven and how certainly I am loved. I put it into my CD alarm clock so that at five, five thirty, or six o'clock in the morning, a quiet synthesizer slips in through the back door of my sleep and a woman's voice begins to sing about an encounter she has with Jesus each morning. As my mind begins its shift from the depths of sleep to the awareness of a new day, a calming lyric reminds me that . . .

> *He walks with me, and He talks with me,*
> *and He tells me I am His own.*
> *And the joy we share as we tarry there,*
> *none other has ever known.*

Beautiful music and meaningful lyrics can soothe us, encourage us, and give us hope. And I wish so much that I could have a small CD player installed in this book—one that would play songs of reassurance in the background as you read about why kids in Christian homes often rebel. I'd want to provide themes that evoke a confidence in God's great faithfulness and His amazing grace. I feel certain that our discussion about why kids rebel would be a lot easier to process if you could work through it while hearing a familiar melody that reminds you, no matter what your lot, that it is well with your soul. That's because the issue of rebellious kids has a way of slipping over us like the shadow of a thunderhead that has suddenly blocked out the sun.

FACING OUR FEARFUL EMOTIONS

The subject of why kids from Christian homes rebel isn't the punch line to some lighthearted joke, unless maybe you're into *sick* jokes. It's a subject that occupies the sober, tender, and often discouraging corridors of a parent's soul. Our children's rebellion trips circuit breakers in our emotional system—the ones labeled "panic" and "fear." Kids who are living a life of rebellion often inspire our blood pressure to seek record heights. It's the reason some parents buy Tums and Pepto-Bismol in "big box" quantities at Sam's Club or Costco.

Besides scaring us to death, our kids' rebellion can make us angry, too. It's like a slap in the face to moms and dads. After all you've done to give your child's life a good Christian jump-start, they just throw it right back at you as if you've done them some moral disservice. It kind of makes you want to stand on their air hose . . . if they had one.

The problem with all of these emotions—sadness, discouragement, fear, and even anger—is that they might define how we feel, but they don't give us much help when it comes to dealing with the problems that caused them. And they certainly aren't great travel partners if you have to ride side by side with them through an entire book—regardless of how helpful the book might be. But to ignore them or treat them as if they aren't serious factors could trivialize the severity of the problem you are dealing with.

The last thing you need in the middle of this discussion is someone giving you pipe-dream assurances that don't honestly address the reality of your situation. It would be so easy to soft-pedal your son's or daughter's rebellious actions with empty statements like, "It's not that big of a deal," when in reality it might actually be a bigger deal than either of us thought. Since feeling good is more important to most people than doing good, it would be tempting to beguile you with promises that everything is going to get better. But an honest assessment of the facts tells us that, in reality, things may get far worse. As I write to you, I need to be forthright and honest. Still, I don't want to steal any sense of true hope.

DEGREES OF DIFFICULTY

Fortunately, for many of you there is no need to offer reassuring promises sung with soft voices in the background. Your children seem to be responding well to the Christian training you are giving them. You're just checking in to see if there is something you need to do or keep doing so they don't take a nosedive into rebellion. I'm glad for you. I hope this book will not only encourage you but also help confirm things you've already incorporated into your parenting philosophy that may have minimized your child's inclination toward rebellion.

But there are others of you who have children that have taken their rebellion to discouraging and even dangerous depths. The impact of their bad choices has a choke hold on you. The problems they are making for you, your spouse (if you're married), and the other kids in the family are nothing short of a road trip through the suburbs of hell. You feel like the tag line of one of those old Roach Motel commercials when it comes to your child's rebellion: "You've checked in, but you can't check out."

AVOIDING CLICHÉD RESPONSES

In the face of your discouragement, I'd rather set a tone that, while not necessarily upbeat, is at least *positive*. Obviously, no one questions that rebellious Christian kids have a way of sucking the joy and confidence out of their parents' lives. But there's got to be some hope to cling to, even though you're walking through the valley of the shadow of rebellion.

There is.

Let's make sure, however, that we don't get confused at the outset. The hope isn't wrapped up in ingenious people or clever formulas. It's especially not found in the writings of authors, no matter how much insight they might bring to the discussion. Writers of books are human beings who walk on feet of clay just like you. Your hope is going to be found in your relationship with Christ and how you let Him work through you when it comes to dealing with your rebellious child.

I'm a father of four, a grandfather of two (and counting), a youth worker for fifteen years, and a family advocate for the last twenty. If anything, I'm just one beggar telling the other beggars where the food is. But I'm passionate about this subject. I've watched so many nice Christian families have the spiritual rug pulled out from under them as a result of one of their kids rebelling and, frankly, I'm tired of the devastation it creates. And I'm saddened when decent people hear the same old clichés dragged out when it comes to solving their problem. You've heard them:

- You need to discipline that kid more!
- Get her out of that heathen public-school environment and put her in Christian school.
- Maybe if you had been reading your Bible more . . .
- You should try having family devotions.
- If you'd just sit together as a family in church . . .
- Are you praying for that child at least three times a day?
- Get those kids busy memorizing Scripture.
- You need counseling, and . . .
- That kid needs medication!

It's not that any of these suggestions are necessarily bad. In fact, one or more of them might play a role in the final equation you come up with for helping your child. But in reality, everything on this list is just a *thing*; each item is an isolated action that may or may not have an influence on your child. Your child's rebellion is not a problem like crooked teeth or bad eyesight that can be corrected with prescribed external actions. It's an offshoot of an attitude or a series of conclusions your child is embracing about himself or herself, and you, and life, and love, and God. So, for example, reading your Bible more, regardless of how much comfort it might bring you, won't necessarily change anything in your child's heart. Meanwhile, hearing someone recite these worn-out suggestions just compounds the guilt, misery, and frustration you're already dealing with. Besides, you've probably already done everything on the list, and then some. And nothing has changed.

In reality, that list of typical suggestions doesn't address the real *problem*. Most parents think the problem is their child's rebellion. That's where they get sidetracked and why they turn to the isolated items on the "cliché" list as solutions. Our children's rebellion is not the problem. It is the symptom. *Why* they are rebelling is the problem. And unless we address the "why," the external things we do in reaction to their rebellion will not make much of a difference.

We want to address the *why* in this book. Why do kids turn their backs on the favorable and even enviable spiritual environment they were brought up in? Understanding the underlying reasons puts you in a much better position to do something positive to correct them.

THE HOPE BUSINESS

Most books that address the issue of teen rebellion march out the "usual suspects." They assume the problem is the peer group, the public schools, the Internet, television, movies, sex, drugs, and rock-'n'-roll. They also assume there's hope in the solutions we mentioned earlier: more Bible, more prayer, more camp, more discipline, a Christian education, etc., will counter these problems. What they fail to consider is that the Christian subculture we have chosen to raise our children in might *precondition* them to spiritual apathy or antagonism.

Most books address a change *in the child*. This book is going to suggest a change *in the parent*. If you think about it, this is the only thing that makes sense. The one (and possibly only) person you have any true control over is yourself. You can change *you*. If you could change your child, you would have done it already. A genuine change in you is the best way to create a change in your rebellious child. Changed lives change lives. Willingness to change also puts you in a far better position to transfer authentic faith to your child.

Prodigals cause panic. They break parents' hearts. They trigger endless self-doubt and second-guessing. In their desperation, many parents simply increase the passion with which they do the same ineffective things. Some even start to question their own faith.

I want this to be a book that helps you get a better glimpse at the source of your child's rebellion. I hope that before you are done, you will understand the vital role your child's rebellion may actually be playing in his spiritual pilgrimage.

You may have unwittingly taken up residence inside an evangelical ghetto, thinking it somehow offers a safer and healthier environment in which your children can develop their relationships with God. It doesn't. My hope is, if that is your case, this book will help you move out of that ghetto and take up residence closer to the front lines of the battle for the cross.

Too many parents feel helpless and hopeless when it comes to their children. They assume the powers of evil have the high ground. Indeed, in many family scenarios the powers of evil *do* seem to be in control. I want to show you how to turn these odds around. Jesus Christ is, among so many other things, in the *hope* business. He wants to help you with your rebellious son or daughter by first giving you an authentic love for Him as your Savior and then a grace-filled heart toward your boy or girl who may be careening seriously off course. He loves you more than you can imagine. He knows just what you're up against. He wants to walk with you and talk with you and tell you you are His own . . .

Even more, He wants to help you lead your son or daughter out of the clutches of rebellion.

QUESTIONING THE STATUS QUO

Don't freak out on me here, but I think we need to take an honest look at the things we do as "typical" Christian parents and ask some hard questions about their effectiveness. I'm not suggesting we turn our backs on the things that make up the checklist of the standard, conscientious Christian family. But there just might be something wrong about the way we are applying these things. More than that, our presuppositions about the *role* or the *impact* these Christian activities actually have on our children just might be flawed.

I watch parents raise their children in Sunday school and church from the time they are born. They educate them at home or send them to a Christian school. They have regular devotions with them and pack them off to church camp. They seem like cutting-edge Christian parents. The sad truth is that many of them, who faithfully do parenting that might seem to point kids in the right direction, are often the most disappointed with the results. That compliant, Scripture-quoting, chorus-humming child sometimes turns into an apathetic or antagonistic adolescent.

We need to be willing to slip past the veneer of our Christian lifestyle and take a hard look at the heart of our faith. This may require us to question the status quo, but it might also pump some fresh air into our approach to raising our kids.

KIDS REBEL AND PARENTS SELF-REFLECT

There's one other issue we need to address at the outset of this discussion. It's one of the true "joy stealers" when it comes to dealing with the reality of our children's rebellion. I'm referring to the inescapable sense that we played some role in it. Kids acting out against their family's faith and moral value system have a way of drawing their mothers and fathers to mirrors—to study themselves with the haunting sense that somehow they are to blame. And the cold, hard fact is that we *may be* somewhat to blame. We know we can play a positive role in our children's lives, and because that is true, we also have to admit we might equally play a negative role. In an honest discussion of why kids rebel, we have to assume that a healthy assessment of our part in the equation is in order.

Therefore, this discussion cannot be held without some possible discomfort to you. I wish I could guarantee that it won't be that way, but that would be naive on my part. And it would be naive on your part, too. We are parents. We make choices and carry out actions that sometimes have negative effects on our children. Our sons and daughters are unique individuals. What works well with one can blow up in a parent's face with the other. On top of that, we all make mistakes—sometimes lots of them. Our kids make mistakes—sometimes lots of them. We don't always see the big picture, either. In fact, we seldom do.

In the midst of all this, times change. We change. Our kids change.

What worked for our parents may not go over as well with our children. The pressures we are processing now may be quite different from what we were contending with when our kids were younger. And we all have blind spots—those enigmatic voids in our perspective that handicap our ability to see our children gracefully.

Most likely, you aren't too threatened by the possibility of reading some ideas that might be convicting. That's why most of us choose books like this. But that is not why I write them. I don't want to beat you up. I want to encourage you and give you hope. I want to suggest some lines of thinking that could actually set your child free from the tyranny that may have taken over his or her heart. Still, you may have to turn a few pages that are painful to read in the process. Try to keep in mind that it will be worth it, because there might well be a new relationship waiting for you and your rebellious child. You could end up seeing her through a whole different set of eyes—gracious eyes.

In any case, it's got to be better than what you've had to contend with so far.

You see why I wish we could play some soothing songs of hope in the background? It's easy to feel that the picture is bleak and the future is grim when you are assessing the cause and effect of a rebellious child's behavior. But you need to know at the outset of this discussion that there is hope. And that's not some empty Sunday-school promise.

Hope is ours for the taking.

Like the voice that serenades me each morning, I'm reminded that regardless of what awaits me today, I'm not alone. The song reminds me that no matter what ails my soul, it is not beyond the healing touch of the God I serve. My days are like your days. They are filled with scenes that aren't always easy to look at, decisions that aren't enjoyable to make, and people that aren't always easy to love.

Because of what I do as a minister, I have been face to face with some extremely angry kids—some of whom are living in the middle of textbook Christian families. I've seen the devastation. I've felt the despair. And over the years, I've also noticed some common denominators within many of these Christian homes. Similar patterns keep appearing in the backdrop of the crises because some aspects of the most popular Christian parenting models actually *incite* our children to rebel. It's a bitter pill for many Christian parents to swallow. When it comes to your philosophy of Christian parenting, before you've finished reading, you may have to honestly reassess what you are doing. You may have to ask yourself whether what you are doing is helping or hurting your rebellious child.

But again, whatever the answer you come to, there is hope.

A MESSAGE OF HOPE AND GRACE

This book is written to parents who are frustrated or discouraged with the results of their spiritual efforts with their children. You've done it all when it comes to the checklist of a good Christian parent, only to see your son or daughter turn away and embrace some frightening lifestyle choices. Some of you are near panic as you assess the human toll of your prodigal child's rebellion. Others have an opposite but equally serious dilemma: you have a child who is merely going through the motions of Christian behavior but is indifferent to the work of the Holy Spirit in her heart.

In either case, this book is for you.

It's also for any parent who wants to lower the possibilities of his or her children turning their back on their faith. Some of you with younger children are waiting in fear at the rapidly approaching teenage years and figure it's just a matter of time. Many parents see the rebellion in young people around them and assume it is a foregone conclusion for their own girls and boys.

It's not.

I want to show you how to increase the chance that your child will develop a vibrant faith early in life and stick with it into adulthood.

This book, like every other book I've written about parenting, is a book about grace—God's grace to you and the grace you can bring to your role as a mother or father. The amazing grace of God is the greatest gift you have to offer to children who may have lost their way. The wonderful thing about God's grace is that before you can give it, you first have to receive it. Before we're done, I hope both will happen.

CHAPTER 1

The Sheer Weight of Rebellion

There's nothing that hurts a mom's or dad's heart quite like having a child who is going astray. It is a constant ache, and sometimes it's worse than the pain you feel for a child who is seriously ill or contending with some kind of disability. Those problems aren't of the child's choosing. But when your son or daughter is consciously turning his back on God or is hellbent on rejecting the value system you have tried so hard to give her, it's like a sucker punch to your faith. To think that your son or daughter would *deliberately* choose a path that can only lead to disappointment and regret—well, it's a hurt that can seep its way into the deepest crevices of your soul.

And it tears you up to see what kids' rebellion does to them personally—to their relationships, to their health, and to their potential. They lose credibility as fast as they are losing emotional and spiritual momentum. Many of the kids who take on a mantle of rebellion put together a series of bad choices that place them in bondage to their mistakes—bondage they often can't get out of on their own. Yet when you try to help them, they react like a cat stuck in a tree, snarling and striking out at you as you attempt to coach them out of the mess they are in.

Most of the time these young people are unresponsive to your reasonable ideas. Sometimes they are closed to talking at all. They won't let you inside their hearts long enough for you to get a decent glimpse

1

of the contradictions that are tormenting them. When they finally do speak up, you not only face their hostility, but you often hear them spewing out philosophies of life that bear no resemblance to the one you thought you gave them. It hurts to see them making 180-degree turns away from the direction they were going during most of their childhood. It's as though the little cherubs who sat on your lap and basked in the Bible stories you read to them have suddenly enrolled in Osama Senior High.

Wendy's daughter serves as an example.

A GOOD GIRL GONE BAD

She couldn't decide which distressed her the most: the hurt, the resentment, or the fear. Each was fighting for mastery of her heart as she watched her daughter disappear across the front lawn. The screen door still quivered from the power with which the girl had slammed it as she stormed out of the house. It was so hard to believe that the fifteen-year-old who had just fired those F-bombs at her was the same girl who, only a few months earlier, had arrived home from a mission trip with her high-school youth group ready to change the world. How could one child regress so far in such a short time?

This teenager had thrived on her family's church activities. She had loved her youth group, her youth leaders, and her friends from church. Now she wanted nothing to do with any of them. While she was at it, she had decided she wanted nothing to do with her parents, either—and she especially didn't want to hear any of her mom's spiritual insights. "Save your homily for someone who gives a (expletive)," was the last thing Wendy heard before her daughter rushed out of the house.

The only thing Wendy's daughter seemed to be concerned about now was her boyfriend—a young man who was the polar opposite of everything their family stood for. Wendy's heart sank as she considered what all of this meant. How could this girl, who had been handed Christianity on a platter, suddenly reject everything? What kind of horrible path would her daughter's antagonism lead her down?

THE PROFILE OF REBELLIOUS KIDS

Rebellious Christian kids often share many similarities. They are blocking God out of their lives, parents annoy them, and family life ticks them off. They are capable of being stubborn, obstinate, argumentative, aloof, and moody. They often seem embarrassed by your outward commitment to God and are disinterested in your spiritual advice. They are no longer fans of church and Sunday school. These kids have no problem making a series of dumb decisions that will get them into trouble. When you inquire about their thinking, it seems almost as though someone has sneaked in and erased most of the spiritual programming from the hard drives of their souls. And it's not uncommon to hear them offering the most illogical and irrational reasons for their behavior.

Some Christian kids' rebellion is a short-lived parenthesis of stupidity that they get through rather quickly. It's just a brief little jaunt down the wrong side of the spiritual street and then they're over it. It's an isolated "My kid got suspended from school for being a bonehead"–type rebellion (an exercise I put my parents through twice), or a "My seventeen-year-old daughter bought a thong bikini for the church pool party and can't seem to understand why I, as her mother, can't stop hyperventilating"–type of spiritual crisis. These are the kinds of incidents that jump-start our relationship with God. It's as though, during these crises, God puts two spiritual cardiac paddles on the sides of our hearts, yells "Clear!" and gives us a jolt of reality. As difficult as they are, these incidents can be used to create a greater bond between struggling teens and their flustered parents.

Other than causing parents to temporarily wonder if they are losing their minds, these brief excursions usually do little long-term harm and leave everyone slightly better off for the exercise. They are like mini pop-quizzes on what you believe and how sincerely you believe it. Parents that grade a C or above on these little tests of their faith learn that God indeed *is* who He says He is, and that His grace is truly sufficient.[1] Most families go on to live happily ever after.

But there's another brand of Christian rebellion that has the potential to sear a hole in the entire family's belief system. This more debilitating brand of rebellion has, among other things, the potential of wrecking a child's view of God for the rest of his life. As serious as that consequence is, it's just the beginning of many things that can have a long-term negative effect. Debilitating, toxic rebellion can set up young people for relationship nightmares that can dog them for decades. I'm talking about the kind of rebellion that can create babies or destroy them, create marriages or destroy them, or plunge kids into deep financial debt, depression, and even jail time. It can permanently rob young people of their future earning potential in the marketplace.

It can even kill them.

I buried a young man whose poor choices led him to take his own life. My children buried a dear friend whose rejection of God's best for him ended in an overdose. In both of these cases, the abrupt end to these young lives was like putting a period before the end of a sentence. Both were bright, decent young men whose spiritual choices cost them everything. There was great potential for a better story to be told, but death stole that story from them and from us. When it comes to these more serious incursions into the world of rebellion, there's nothing funny about where some of them can lead. Martin can testify to that . . .

A BOY WITH A FIRE IN HIS SOUL

He sat alone at his son's desk. With his face buried in his hands, he fought his conflicting inner urges to either explode in anger or implode into the sense of helplessness that churned inside him. His visit to his son's dormitory had been unannounced. The boy's roommate was nice enough to invite Martin to wait until his son returned from class. They exchanged the obligatory small talk for a few minutes before the roommate came up with a polite reason to leave. Then, in the privacy of his son's dorm room, Martin had enough time to validate all that he had feared.

The alarms had actually started going off in his (and his wife's) heart a year and a half earlier. It seemed to them that their son had put his spiritual life on autopilot somewhere around his junior year of high school.

He wasn't antagonistic to the things of God, although he didn't appear to have the same spiritual passion he'd demonstrated in his early teenage years. But when he came home for Christmas break from his first semester at college, it seemed he had shut off the autopilot, slammed on the brakes of his spiritual life, and had actually shifted into reverse.

For a kid who had left home with a lackadaisical attitude toward Jesus, he seemed to have arrived back home with a clear ax to grind with Him . . . and with them, too. Martin and his wife had assumed their son would change a little when he went off to college, but they never figured he would change so dramatically in one semester. During Christmas break they encountered a boy who had no interest in calling or connecting with any of the close Christian friends he'd left behind. He responded with a deliberate, glazed-over look the few times either one of them mentioned anything about God or church. He seemed annoyed by his mom and dad, as though they had suddenly morphed into alien entities with which he shared no common ground.

Now, in this tiny room that served as a microcosm of his son's value system, Martin could see the evidence of a boy who was heading down a road that bore no similarity to the one his parents had encouraged him to take. The woman on the screen saver of his son's computer was probably scanned from one of the pornographic magazines neatly stacked on his nightstand, next to an opened box of condoms. Martin's supposedly virgin son had been busy. He'd taken up drinking, too. The sculpture of beer cans that covered half the window wasn't just dorm-room decoration. There was enough evidence in this room to indicate that a fire was burning in the boy's soul. But it wasn't the fire of spiritual passion. Not now.

Martin had seen this same thing happen to a few of his friends' children. He had heard the excuses they made and the blame they passed around. They tried to put the responsibility at the feet of the universities. In one case, it was an ironic accusation, since the daughter had enrolled in an elite Christian college. Other parents had felt that the lack of adequate programming in their church during their children's teenage years was the reason their children had fallen away from their spiritual moorings. Martin wouldn't make that foolish mistake. He felt three specific people were responsible for what was happening. One was somewhere in a class across campus, the other was back home waiting for Martin to call and give her a report, and the third was sitting in his son's dormitory room, wondering where he'd gone wrong.

SMOKE-SCREEN REBELLION

And then there are those textbook Christian kids who go through all the right motions, learn all the right truths, make all the right choices, and appear to be great candidates for becoming excellent Christian parents themselves. Yet they never seem inclined to make any spiritual difference in the world once they become adults. The fact is that rebellion isn't always outward and hostile.

Sometimes an adolescent's rebellion reveals itself as a lack of passion, a lack of concern, a lack of motivation. These can be the symptoms of kids who have been raised in a spiritual greenhouse. They've heard the truth and accepted it. They've learned the principles and believed them. They've seen God work in many miraculous ways and enjoyed it. They just haven't invested these gifts from God into a life that shines for Him. They've put their trust in a God who would actually sacrifice His Son's life on their behalf, but for some reason His gift of love hasn't motivated them enough to be a living sacrifice for Him in return.

This attitude invariably leads to indifference or even a low-grade cynicism, attitudes that pollute the child's view of God and his attitude toward the Christian community around him. It reminds me of a scenario I heard from a Christian school principal . . .

BAD NEWS AT GOOD SCHOOLS

Dr. Evans stood in the hallway just outside his office as one of his high-school students passed by. The boy wore the uniform of the Christian school, and if you looked at his report card, you'd see that he had given all the correct biblical answers and theological responses to the tests he had taken over the years. He had even represented the school at a Bible memory competition and had brought home a huge championship trophy that stood in the glass case in the gymnasium entrance.

But as he watched this young student stroll by, the question, What's wrong with this picture? kept repeating in his head. This young man may have known all the answers to the Christian belief system his school taught, but there was nothing about him that reflected any appreciation for what Jesus had done for him on the cross. He was dead center in the daily sports, social, and academic lives of this Christian school, but his attitudes and actions reflected that he was really just a walking contradiction of everything for which the school was established. There were no signs of a genuine heart for God—just a bunch of carefully rehearsed answers that had been drilled into his head.

Dr. Evans knew how much this young man teased and taunted the handful of students on campus who were seriously trying to live out their faith in God. He was a spiritual "Eddie Haskell"—saying the right things around his teachers, then mocking them behind their backs. His mannerisms reflected the behavior his parents had put him in Christian school to avoid, and his conduct outside the school indicated that he was devoid of spiritual direction. The principal understood that, in spite of all this young man knew about God, his unvarnished actions were evidence of where his heart really was. *What a shame*, he thought. *His parents have tried so hard and spent so much money, and all they are getting back is a son who couldn't care less about God.*

Dr. Evans couldn't expel the young man, even though he was poison to the rest of the students. The boy wasn't breaking any stated rules of conduct; in fact, he was turning in excellent academic work. Besides, the principal didn't want to throw him out. He wanted to help him. But he just couldn't get the equation to add up. How could someone who had been given so much embrace so little? He'd had his faith spoon-fed to him, but all his parents and this Christian school got in return was an overindulged Christian brat.

As the student disappeared around the corner, the principal wondered whether the word *Christian* was little more than an adjective in his life—a mix of biblical platitudes and spiritually canned behavior that had never taken its position as a noun in his young heart.

LIFESTYLE REBELLION

There's something about a Christian environment that can actually set a child up to become a spiritually mediocre adult. Kids from Christian homes often grow up going to church only if it's convenient. They serve others if it doesn't put them out too much, they tip God with the leftovers of their money, and they remain mute about their beliefs. These homegrown Christians can go for months, even years, on end without deliberately studying their Bible. They never graduate from an elementary understanding of what they believe. They may be Christians for fifty years and still feel unprepared to lead a Bible study or explain to those around them the hope within them.

After preaching to some congregations, I have found myself confronted by an older adult who chastises me for not using the right translation of the Bible or for using a tattered, dilapidated Bible to speak from. This adult assumes these things mean I don't respect God's Holy Word. Or an elderly woman might suggest that because I didn't wear a tie, I failed to dress appropriately for a sacred hour of worship. When these types of incidents happen, I always like to gently inquire about my critic's belief in Christ, and how long they have held those beliefs. It's not uncommon to hear they've considered themselves to be Christians for twenty, thirty, or forty years. Yet, for all the time they have supposedly been "walking by faith," they come across as small, petty, and spiritually underdeveloped.

You can't help but wonder if people like this are merely "technical Christians" who don't understand what it truly means to be a *follower* of Jesus. They may be able to find the book of Obadiah in their Bible but can't find the time to take their gay neighbor out to lunch to figure out how to pray for him. Jesus saved them so they could someday walk the "streets of gold." Meanwhile they seem satisfied to live holed up at the spiritual Sesame Street address they had when they first came to know Christ.

Rebellion doesn't always have to be ugly. Sometimes it's just lazy.

It's also contagious. Most people have heard about "the sin of the fathers" curse in the Bible.[2] But sometimes, as we've seen, the sins of a rebellious Christian kid can plague the youth group or the Christian school. Rebellious boys and girls can become a negative fungus to the Christian kids around them. So much of a child's life is "reflective" rather than "original," and too many fragile kids have a tendency to mirror the attitude of the people they gravitate toward, rather than being the force that fuels others' faith.

WHEN TRUTH IS STRANGER THAN FICTION

You might be wondering, "Are the people in these stories real or did you just make them up?" Yes and no. Yes, they are real, but no, their names aren't Wendy, Martin, or Dr. Evans. When you are writing a book about children who make utter disasters of their lives as well as their parents' lives, you've got to change names and locations to protect the innocent and to avoid embarrassing the guilty. But these scenarios are real. In fact, they are some of the tamer examples I could have shared with you.

They remind us why we need a Savior.

They also remind us why we need to have a keen and accurate understanding of our own propensity to break God's heart. Within the heart of every human being is a desire to do our own thing and to go our own way.[3] Rebellious Christian kids are following that inclination, which rages inside them. There are a lot of reasons why, and we'll get into them later. There are also some specific things we can do to help them get safely back into the fold. But none of the explanations make sense and few of the solutions work if we maintain a choke hold on our pride and refuse to see our own inclination to make dumb choices, too.

When we can't see our own capacity for rebellion, we are blocked from being part of the solution to our children's problems. Our kids see us as haughty and arrogant and envision themselves as being some-where far beneath us. Pride causes us to make excuses, blame others, and refuse to search our own hearts for any part we might have played in the choices they made.

Of course, if you are a parent looking down the barrel of your child's rebellion, you probably have very little pride left intact. Rebellious kids do that to you. There's nothing like a child turning his or her back on your Christian lifestyle and value system to help you develop accurate and balanced theology. A kid's rebellion knocks us off our holy high horses. It gives us a street-level view of life and an attitude that is far more savvy, sympathetic, and forgiving than it might have been before. Actually, that's not so bad.

These scenarios not only remind us of why we need a Savior; they also remind us of why we need grace in our homes. It would be so easy to give up, to write off your rebellious daughter or troublemaking son as a lost cause, and to wrap yourself up in self-pity. Grace helps us rise above these faults in our weak human nature. Grace keeps us going, keeps us believing in a greater good for our children, and keeps us focused on God rather than on ourselves.

A sober swig of reality teaches us that there's a bit of the prodigal in all of us. You were born with it,[4] and your ability to admit it is one of the best tools you have for minimizing your child's likelihood of making wrong spiritual choices. Your willingness to acknowledge your own feet of clay is one of the best starting points when it comes to helping your children, especially when they have chosen to embrace an attitude of rebellion against you, or God, or both. A realistic view of ourselves forces us to lean on God and helps us look at our rebellious children through His loving and grace-filled eyes. It also comes in handy when we are forced to pay the piper for our children's rebellion. When our kids need help, we need grace.

THE HIGH COST OF LOW-CLASS CHRISTIAN LIVING

When Christian kids rebel, a lot of times there's hell to pay for the parents. You'd think I'd say few pay the price the rebellious child pays. But in reality, most of our children's rebellion is more expensive for us than it is for them. After all, they are *choosing* the path they are taking; we are not. For the most part they not only want to rebel but often enjoy it. It's just the opposite for parents. Some kids actually come out the other side as better people. That's not always the case for the parents who had to walk through the valley of rebellion with them. The consequences of children's rebellion against their parents reads like a checklist for a nightmare.

Rebellious Children Frighten Their Parents

Sometimes the fear comes from dark shadows that lurk in some corner closet of parents' memories. They recall some of the choices they made as young people, choices that carved serious scars into their emotional systems. Some even carry physical scars that remind them of their young and foolish pasts. Because they are painfully aware of how devastating rebellion can be, these parents want to do everything in their power to spare their children the regret they've had to live with.

Many of these parents didn't have the privilege of being raised in Christian homes. Their choices were the standard operating procedure of kids coming up through a home with either too much dysfunction or too few boundaries. When they finally became Christians, they wanted to create an environment they felt certain would spare their children the same mistakes.

Parents who have been around the block know that cause creates effect—every time. Insolence, laziness, disrespect, deception, crime, drugs, and sex aren't stand-alone events. They have a malignant impact when they are the outgrowth of a rebellious heart. Parents who have faced the consequences of their own youthful rebellion are chilled to the marrow of their bones when they see their children following in their footsteps.

Rebellious Children Frustrate Their Parents

Our children's poor choices and disrespectful attitudes put us off our game and have a bad habit of wrecking the rhythm we're trying to maintain in our family's daily routine. Rebellion draws inordinate focus on one child when we need to be sharing our time equally with other family members. A rebellious child is like an out-of-control sports fan that has stormed the outfield of a baseball game. Everything has to come to a stop until he can be subdued. In the same way, rebellious Christian kids are first-class joy-stealers. They suck the wind out of your everyday life, your confidence, your personal goals, and sometimes your relationship with God. It's really frustrating when you are trying everything you know to do, yet seeing few positive results.

Rebellious Children Embarrass Their Parents

Our kids' rebellious behavior can give us a bad reputation. As you know, bad reputations live on long past the time they were established. Decades later, your son is now the understudy to take some great evangelist's place, and people still refer to you as "the dad who had that boy who got that nice little girl pregnant." Sometimes the bigger challenge after our children have passed through their rebellious years is to forgive them for the emotional damage their actions still inflict. The smaller the town you live in or the church you attend, the greater problem this is.

Most parents unconsciously feel that their children's behavior is a report card on their effectiveness as parents. But even if we're mature enough not to fall into that foolish trap of turning our kids into parental scorecards, many of our acquaintances and "friends" aren't necessarily as accommodating. When our children behave badly, it can make going to church or showing up for Thanksgiving dinner with the extended family extremely painful.

There's an old saying, "Christians are the only people who shoot their wounded." Actually, they *eat* them. Too many Christian circles connect the skill and spiritual sincerity of us as parents to the behavior of our children (even though our children are individual agents, underdeveloped emotionally, immature, naive, and born with a bent toward sin). As a result, it's easy to end up ostracized at church.

Praise God, there are many wonderful, grace-based churches and fellowships that *respond* rather than *react* to children who may be working out their salvation with less fear and trembling than we would prefer.[5] These are churches that understand basic theology about the nature of man and also realize that rebellion is often part of a child's spiritual journey. But even in an environment of grace, it's hard not to feel that your rebellious son or daughter is going to be the centerfold of the church bulletin, a postscript in the notes of the next elders' meeting, and at the top of the list of your Sunday school class's emergency Internet prayer chain. Your insecurities make you feel that everyone in the church wants to come up to your offspring, place their hands on his or her little forehead, and yell, "Demon, come out!" Whether the source of the embarrassment is real or imagined, its net effect is the same. It's no fun having a rebellious kid.

Rebellious Children Injure Their Parents

Sin costs money. Paying for counseling, moving kids to another public school or into a private or Christian school, and paying for damages, legal fees, and the cost of medical bills and rehabilitation can exact a huge chunk from a family's reserves. Too many parents of rebellious Christian kids have watched their savings evaporate. It's not uncommon for our children's behavior to leave us in financial debt long after they have found their way back to a balanced lifestyle.

Rebellion at home can also cost us professional productivity. Kids who are acting up often require you to miss work or leave work early, to take more personal phone calls, and to operate at a distracted level for long periods of time. A rebellious Christian kid can take a huge bite out of your efficiency and cost you a bad work review, a bonus, a raise, or a promotion.

A problem child can actually cost you your job. If you are in a management position, problems with your children can cause you to second-guess yourself as a leader of others. Even if you don't see it that way, your subordinates may. Eyebrows can be raised and whispering campaigns can be held at the office coffeepot. It's easy for people to wonder, *If he can't keep his children in line, is he the right person to be leading this crucial part of our company?*

A child's rebellion can cause our Christian marriages to pay a high price. Since every mule thinks his load is the heaviest, it's easy to feel that you are bearing more of the responsibility for the consequences of your child's problems than your spouse is. Blame comes easily. Rebellion also has a way of attacking a couple's ability to stay close, maintain a sense of romance, and feel comfortable being intimate. It's hard to feel free to enjoy each other when someone you love so much is busy ruining her life. Many times children's rebellion has contributed to their parents' divorce.

One child out of control can also do a lot of harm to the other children in the family who are walking the straight and narrow. Siblings can easily feel slighted by their parents because of the inordinate amount of attention one rebellious child requires. A misbehaving brother or sister can ruin an event that was supposed to be enjoyable for the entire family. Vacations, day-outings, going out to dinner, friends coming over to the house, and even the joy of attending church can be stolen from innocent brothers and sisters by rebellious ones. Good and godly children have watched their inheritance disappear into the coffers of their rebellious brother's or sister's rehab clinics. Regardless of how you draw the lines or do the math, when a child rebels, everybody pays.

RECIPE FOR REBELLION

There's nothing new about kids from religious homes rebelling. They've been doing it since Adam and Eve gave birth to their first child. As you might recall, Cain, their firstborn, was quite a piece of work.[6] If anything, Cain is the patron saint of rebellious children. He caused his parents incredible grief. He cost his brother Abel the highest price that can be exacted from any individual—his life. Fortunately, most of what the average Christian parent has to put up with today is mild by comparison. But it isn't necessarily less painful. And even though there's nothing new about rebellious Christian kids, there are some dynamics in today's contemporary Christian movement that can increase a Christian kid's *inclination* toward rebellion.

When I was a teenager, we were dead center in the middle of a decade that knocked the mainstream church on its rear. I was a teenager in the 1960s. Standard, denominational Protestantism and classical Catholicism didn't know what to do with all that was happening around them. The church had been enjoying a position of "tradition" in the average American family. The traditions wore well, like a broken-in pair of work boots. Then all of a sudden, teenage boys started to grow their hair as long as girls', teenage girls started to burn their bras, and both genders started to burn a lot of marijuana.

Contemporary music took on the themes of uninhibited sex, protest toward government and authority, and the questioning of the status quo. In those days, the traditional church stood in clear contrast to everything that was going on around it. Programming was locked in and inflexible. The liturgy or form of worship was the same as it had been for almost a century. The music was either classical or sacred hymns that had been written by songwriters long since dead.

Meanwhile, the life we were experiencing outside the church was changing faster than most of us could process. It was the front side of the technological revolution. Special effects were starting to make their way into the movies. Television was in color. News via satellite from Vietnam was instant. Meanwhile, we'd come to church and listen to a Sunday school teacher give us a Bible lesson using a flannel graph.

Our culture posed questions that demanded answers. The mainstream church, for the most part, was caught off guard. It didn't know how to deal with questions like . . .

1. "Why should we go off to war and possibly lose our lives to stop the 'domino effect' of communism in Southeast Asia when we have a heavily armed communist country ninety miles off the coast of Florida that we are doing nothing about?"
2. "How is it fair that a woman, doing the same job as a man, gets paid less money?"
3. "Why is it that a hundred years after the Civil War, black people from our community still aren't welcome in our churches and our schools?"

To question number 1, we heard lectures that could be summarized with the cliché "America, right or wrong!" To question number 2, we listened as biblical hairs were split to somehow justify the superiority of the male gender and the devalued nature of the female gender. To question number 3, we heard ridiculous attempts to justify a separation of races and the inferiority of certain races. (I actually heard a Bible teacher use the curse of Ham—one of Noah's sons—as a justification for keeping Blacks in a position of subjugation.)[7]

Bottom line, the mainline church movement was blindsided by that era and didn't offer thoughtful responses to all that was going on around it. To many young kids in the midst of that tumultuous decade, the church came across as irrelevant and out-of-step with where the world was heading.

As a result, there was wholesale rebellion among Christian kids during the 1960s. When the parents turned to the traditional church for help, the church defaulted to its "traditions." It suggested that parents get their children back in step with the time-tested customs that, in the past, had brought meaning and a sense of well-being. In practical terms that meant: get those kids to cut their hair, attend church (whether it had anything worthwhile to say or not), carry Bibles to church (whether they were reading them or not), sit together as a family (whether they could stand one another or not), strive for a "perfect attendance" Sunday school pin (whether the lesson had any relevancy to where they were or not). And for my Catholic friends: go to confession (whether it had any bearing on how they behaved after they came out of it or not). None of these things necessarily made a person a better Christian; they simply made him a better member of the traditional church.

Obviously, there were exceptions—lots of them. There were wonderful pastors and cutting-edge churches that were stepping up to the challenge of the changing times. Despite some of the dated methodology, many strong and soothing lessons were delivered in Sunday school classes throughout the country that helped the new generation get a grip on all that was going on around them. And frankly, there was something comforting about the tradition of the church as the young people tried to process an era where change had become a constant. After all, the church is the extended family of God. It is the primary place—outside our immediate family—where He can be counted on to connect with people.

The church has always struggled with cultural relevancy because of the way it operates. For the most part, it is underfunded and staffed by volunteers. It's usually administrated by committee. This always keeps the church several steps behind culture. This method actually works quite well as long as the church's singular foundation is Jesus Christ and it is fueled by the power of the Holy Spirit. Unfortunately, during the 1960s too many churches were letting tradition rather than the Holy Spirit lead the way through all the cultural upheaval. This attitude didn't provide much help to parents whose children were writing off all kinds of tradition, no matter where they found it.

But as I look back on that wholesale decade of spiritual rebellion, I smile. Many of those same kids who turned their backs on Christian tradition turned their faces to God. They may have taken an end run around the mainstream church, but many did not abandon their faith in its Head. Also, God raised up some of the finest parachurch ministries of the twentieth century to come alongside churches and help fill in the missing pieces of their messages. In spite of it all, that season of rebellion produced some of the finest parents, couples, pastors, teachers, leaders, and thinkers our country has ever known.

Spiritual rebellion isn't the worst thing that can happen to your child. And that's good, because as I take the pulse of the Christian movement today, I think we are in another era of wholesale rebellion. But this time it is not because the church is out of step with the culture. Now, churches are so much in step with everything going on around them that there is no attractive distinction. Perhaps in our attempt to become more relevant we've become a reflection of our society instead of a remedy to its ills.

Many churches, in trying to connect with the culture, have felt it necessary to temper their theology. There has been a subtle airbrushing of classical biblical doctrine to make it more appealing. Many churches have caved in to pressure when it comes to what the Bible clearly teaches about marriage and divorce, masculinity and femininity, motherhood and fatherhood, sexual purity, money, and celebrity. Whereas the mainstream church of my childhood lacked a sense of relevancy, today's churches lack a sense of authenticity.

This is a recipe for rebellion. Our children, in an attempt to be honest with themselves, are inclined to reject a lifestyle that is defined by the conventional brokers of God's truth—the people in the "business" of church. That means there is some good news in the midst of the bad. Some of your children's rebellion against your spiritual lifestyle might be a necessary step in their finding an authentic relationship with God. But beware: If they find it, it might look quite different from what you've always thought it should be.

And more good news, some of the greatest congregations ever in the history of the church are rising to the challenge of a need for authentic Christianity. The church movement will always have its cultural competition, but there are lots of terrific works stepping up to respond to the need. These churches are helping to fill the void that often *incites* Christian kids to rebel.

LETTING OUR FEARS GET THE BEST OF US

There is one other pervasive problem, however, that is plaguing a large segment of the Christian movement today and is responsible for a significant chunk of the rebellion among Christian kids. This is less a problem of the local church and more a mind-set among the parents of the local church. It has to do with the reaction to the evils inherent within our culture.

Parents today realize they've got a lot of competition for their value system. It's not just the evil that has raised its ugly head in the shadow of September 11, but also a *wickedness* that seems to have hijacked a generation. If you watch MTV or slip into one of the popular PG-13 or R-rated movies kids are drawn to today, it's not uncommon to feel like you need a bath afterward. Prime-time television has also sent decency packing, and wherever you look, it is standard fare to be confronted with a hedonistic world-view.

And there's the issue of education. Public education, in particular, has adopted many philosophies that compete with belief in God, the existence of truth, and the authority of the family. In the political arena, there has been a battle waging over the literal interpretation of the Constitution as well as an attempt to rewrite our national history. Any evidence of Christian influence on the early stages of our history has been slowly edited out of our textbooks and teaching in the name of academic integrity. These realities frighten many Christian parents. And in their fear, there has been a large-scale movement to create a safe haven in which to raise our children. As a result, we evangelicals have got our own music, our own entertainment, our own school systems, and our own network of safe Christian families. But I want to give you a little peek at something we're going to go into detail about later. *Our frightened reaction to the serious moral crises within our culture may be the very thing that turns our kids off to our faith.*

How so?

Let me answer by asking you a question. Are you a believer in Jesus Christ? If so, do you realize that, technically, followers of Jesus really shouldn't be afraid of much of anything? Especially the degraded climate of our culture. What did Jesus mean when He said, "I have told you these things, so that in me you may have peace. In this world you will have trouble. But take heart! I have overcome the world" (John 16:33).

Should we be concerned? Of course. But frightened? No, not really. Otherwise, our fears communicate a false message of what we believe to our kids. The fear that drives the choices we make about how we church our kids, how we educate them, the fellowship we provide for them, and how we entertain them may well be why so many Christian kids want little to do with what we are selling.

To make matters worse, our fears about our culture have helped guarantee its further descent into the depths of despair and indecency. The more we pull away from "the world," even for the protection of our children, the more that world is left in the dark. Meanwhile, the artificial world in which we are trying to raise our children is tailor-made to create spiritual apathy at the core of their souls. In the following chapters, I hope to show you how we can counter this built-in drawback to raising strong, culturally relevant kids.

CHECKING OUT OF THE CHECKLIST

I want to flip my cards straight up for you. This book is going to give you a deep understanding of why kids brought up in Christian environments often rebel. It's also going to show you some things you can do to minimize some of their *need* to rebel. But if you aren't open to honestly assessing the built-in liabilities of their Christian upbringing, you probably aren't going to gain much help from this exercise. If you are certain that doing more of the things on the "Parental Checklist" is the real answer, then I can't help you.

Maybe a reminder of some of the items on that checklist might be appropriate here:

❑   Church attendance
❑   Sunday school
❑   Summer camp
❑   Family devotions
❑   Good manners
❑   Christian school
❑   Home school
❑   Scripture memory
❑   Tithing
❑   Service
❑   No bad movies
❑   No bad friends
❑   No bad music

Frankly, ramping up the intensity of any of these things might be the very trigger that makes your son or daughter want to rebel more. Is that because there is something inherently wrong with anything on the list? Of course not. Everything on the list can benefit a child's spiritual life. But they are just items on a list if they aren't bathed in grace and motivated by a deep and sincere relationship with Christ. Because of this, grace is going to be our starting point, our map, and our destination when it comes to dealing with this issue of why Christian kids rebel. If you are not interested in utilizing God's grace when it comes to dealing with your errant child, not to mention dealing with yourself, there is little help I (or anybody else) can offer you.

A Taste of Things to Come

You need to know some things at the outset: If you have a child who is up to her nose in rebellion, the world isn't over for you. It's not even close. You might think you can see the end of the world from where you are standing, but it just isn't true.

As we've already seen, kids have rebelled against God from the beginning of time. Just about every family has at least one child who wants to take a "different" path from what the parents would prefer. None of us do our job perfectly. All families face pockets of resistance when it comes to raising their children. So don't feel like you are some first-class failure as a mom or a dad because of your child's mutiny. Just get in line with innumerable conscientious parents who are trying to figure out what to do.

And that's not to trivialize the severity of what you are facing. It bears repeating: it's a deep-down hurt when one of your kids is running from God. And some bigger-than-life problems can accompany this time in your child's life. But none of them are bigger than our God. As much as you are concerned for your child, He is concerned far more. As much as you want to help, He wants to help more.

He knows your fears. He knows your hurts. And although you might feel as though your child has abandoned Him, He has not abandoned your child. He loves you, He loves your kids, and He will be with you throughout your entire ordeal.

And here's something else you need to know: God does some of His finest work in the midst of our worst crises. He's in the business of redemption. He's a good shepherd who pursues His lost sheep. And He knows how to comfort the bruised and the battered.

This might be hard for you to accept right now, but you may actually come to a point where you look back on this season with your errant child as holding some of the finest moments of your life. It is during these times when we need God so much that we get to know Him better and better. These times may test your resolve as a parent, but they are also custom-designed opportunities to demonstrate to your wayward son or daughter the true depths of your love. You may come to realize, as so many parents have before you, that this time of rebellion is the very time when your children's love for you and for their Savior is galvanized.

So stop whatever you're doing. Look around. Listen carefully. And to quote the most frequently given piece of advice from our Savior, "Don't be afraid."

DISCUSSION QUESTIONS

1. Were you rebellious toward God or your parents when you were a kid? How does the fact that you were (or weren't) rebellious affect your attitude toward your own child rebelling? Does it better equip you, or handicap you?

2. Tim gave the example of the rebellious student in Dr. Evans's Christian school. Even though this student isn't aggressively rebellious, Tim sees his lack of concern for spiritual things as a form of rebellion. Do you think spiritual indifference or passivity should be considered a form of rebellion? Why? Why not?

3. Tim said that rebellious kids frighten, frustrate, embarrass, and injure parents (and other family members). If you've dealt with a rebellious child, which one of those four effects has been the hardest for you to deal with? Why?

4. Do you think your church is a safe and supportive place for your son or daughter to work out their issues with God or with you? How about your extended family?

5. Tim says, "Spiritual rebellion isn't the worst thing that can happen to your child." What are some of the "good things" that could come out of their rebellion for them personally? For you?

6. What do we communicate to our children about God when they see us afraid of the culture that surrounds them? Do you think our being afraid could contribute to their rebelling?

7. Tim mentioned the standard "checklist" of things people sug-
    gest we do to get our children back on track when they
    rebel. Why do you think these actions have very little effect
    on turning them around?

8. What is one thing God has taught you through this chapter?

CHAPTER 2

An Overdose
of Bad Behavior

Stephen Covey tells a powerful story, reminding us that it makes good sense to find the true cause of a problem instead of just reacting to it. In his book *7 Habits of Highly Effective People*, he relates an incident that happened one Sunday morning on the New York subway. A father with two young children boarded a subway car that only had a few passengers on board. One of these passengers was Stephen Covey. Up to that moment, the feeling inside that subway car had been subdued. The handful of travelers were either lost in thought or preoccupied with reading the Sunday newspaper. When this father and his kids boarded, however, the mood was turned upside down.

The two children ran up and down the car yelling at each other, climbing on and off empty seats, even knocking newspapers out of people's hands. Meanwhile, the father sat quietly in his seat, staring straight ahead, seemingly oblivious to the pandemonium his children were creating and the "hostage situation" the other travelers suddenly found themselves in. Finally Covey felt compelled to get the father's attention. He pointed out the behavior of the man's "rebellious" children and encouraged him to get them under control.

Like being awakened from a deep sleep, the father suddenly focused and realized his kids were annoyingly frustrating to the other people in the car. He said, "Oh, I'm sorry. We just came from the hospital. Their mother just died this morning. I'm not sure what I'm going to do."[1]

It's amazing how gaining a little perspective on a particular situation helps us know how to react. Stephen Covey suddenly changed the way he viewed this man. Instead of writing him off as a negligent father, he immediately switched to seeing him as a young husband devastated by the loss of his best friend, his lover, his soul mate, and the mother of his children. Covey's view of the two children immediately shifted, too. They weren't two obnoxious brats that needed a good spanking; they were a brother and sister whose world had been suddenly and permanently devastated.

LOOKING AT CAUSE AND EFFECT

Human nature reacts to the moment. Grace looks for the deeper explanation, the big picture. Consider a crying baby on an airplane—this little noisemaker might be nothing but a nuisance to rank-and-file travelers, but the grace-based passengers think about *why* the baby is crying. Traveling is tiring and it has a way of knocking children off their sleeping schedules. Exhausted babies are often cranky (like exhausted adults). Altitude is tough on the tender ears of infants. There are many reasons for the "nuisance," and the more grace you can bring to understanding why a person is behaving a particular way, the more likely you can be part of the solution.

Similarly, when your children behave in ways that are contrary to everything you've taught them, it's important to look for a deeper explanation before attempting to deal with their rebellion. I'm not saying that understanding the deeper reasons behind a child's rebellion absolves that child from responsibility for bad behavior. Nor am I suggesting that a grace-based response would preclude discipline. What I am saying is that gaining a clearer understanding of why a child is rebelling puts us in a better position to respond in grace.

Grace is more apt to administer *proper* discipline—if that's what children need. It also gives us a greater heart connection to our kids in the midst of their rebellion. Young people can figure out pretty quickly whether you really want to understand where they are coming from.

Your concern may not cause an immediate about-face in their behavior, but it ultimately makes them more inclined to trust you and respond to what you are trying to do for them. Discovering the "why" behind the "what" increases our patience, makes our prayers more specific, and helps our response to rebellion to be a little more strategic.

THE REAL MEANING OF REBELLION

I've been throwing around this word *rebellion* as though its meaning were clearly understood by all. That's probably not a wise assumption. One parent's idea of rebellion might be considered benign or even *entertaining* to another parent. Kids living out the normal nuances of childhood with the goofy ways they talk, dress, and act aren't necessarily rebelling. That is one of the key points I made in my book *Grace-Based Parenting*. Just because kids annoy us doesn't mean their actions are evil, nor does it necessarily indicate a deeper problem—at least not with them. As we learned in that book, the problem might actually be with us.

And your children aren't rebelling just because they don't adhere to some superficial standard determined by a committee-of-one in a pulpit, or some busybody perched on one of the obscure limbs of your family tree. There is no set biblical way for children to behave or dress or talk or play. God has called us to create an environment for our children where they can get a clear sense of the love, forgiveness, and grace of God. On top of that, He has given us the mandate to build qualities like respect, honor, decency, fairness, and modesty into the core of their character.

God allows children a lot of latitude in how they live out their personality type within the boundaries of these wonderful values. God is too much into original thoughts and ideas to create some mold that produces the "perfect Christian kid." He's also not the architect of *any* of the straitjacket models of parenting that float throughout the Christian movement. These arbitrary styles of parenting never have and never will pass the Bible's litmus test.

Some parents who are convinced their children are rebelling might be surprised to find out that God wouldn't agree with them. When parents compare what their children are actually doing with what the Bible really says children are to do, it could well be that their children aren't rebelling at all. They are just great kids having a good time completely within God's moral boundaries, but not the way some onlookers think they should. Once again, my book *Grace-Based Parenting* helps parents filter out the strident voices around them, and figure out how to measure their children's progress by God's standards, not the opinions of others.

I know people who consider a teenage boy wearing his hat backward an act of rebellion. Let me add to this superficial list a sampling of the other things I've heard over the years . . .

- Kids who play a lot of video games
- Kids who listen to rap music
- Boys who wear their pants low
- Kids who don't say, "Yes, sir" or "No, sir," "Yes, ma'am," or "No, ma'am"
- Kids who do just about anything "different" with their hair—especially boys
- Girls who have more than one piercing in a particular ear
- Girls who have their bellybuttons pierced
- Any older teenager with any kind of tattoo—even a "Christian" one
- Kids who aren't excited about church services that are primarily geared to older adults

In and of themselves, these things do not indicate that a child has a problem with God or you or anybody else. They are just "things." True, some of them have the potential of causing harm, but not as a general category. Video games aren't a problem—bad video games are a problem. Rap music isn't a problem—bad rap music is a problem. Shrewd, grace-based parents don't get trapped into writing off an entire category of entertainment just because part of it is toxic. That's what lazy parents do. They don't want to take the time to work with their children and coach them on how to discern between good and bad. Lazy Christian parents, by the way, have a much higher percentage of rebellious kids.

Some of the things on the list may make our children look foolish to older adults and may annoy us. Some will also look foolish to our kids when they are older and looking back. But God has made childhood a time of intense transition. It's a corridor where boys' and girls' primary identification changes radically in a brief period of time. Kids start out with their identification almost completely wrapped up in their family. In less than two decades, their identification is wrapped up in their individuality, their belief system, their friends, or their school. During this time every little thing they do may not pass muster with older adults. That doesn't mean the kids are rebellious. But when we treat our children like rebels who are somehow at odds with God because of our arbitrary list, we can actually incite a rebellious attitude that would not otherwise have been there.

When I was a young child, in the 1950s, Hollywood made a few movies that were meant to capture the look of a rebellious teenage boy. He wore cuffed blue jeans, Chuck Taylor tennis shoes, and a white T-shirt with a pack of cigarettes rolled up in the sleeve (whether he smoked or not). His hair was thick with grease, combed back in a ducktail with a little lock of hair curling down over his forehead. He had a comic book rolled up in his back pocket. The next thing you knew, every other kid in the outback of America was dressing like that, and their parents were certain that the Great Tribulation had begun. Many of these kids were just normal teenagers who were attracted to the teenage look of the day. The overreaction of the parents and the church unnecessarily antagonized many of these kids against God.

Then came the Beatles and all the other members of the "British Invasion." The look of youth took on an even greater contrast to the look of adulthood. The "Fab Four's" hair and all the other trappings of the 1960s caused near-panic in Christian homes throughout the land. Kids who were extremely serious about their faith—like me—were growing their hair long and listening to Beatles albums nonstop. The *coup de grâce* was when John Lennon said in an interview that the Beatles were more popular than Jesus. Pastors popped blood veins. People started trying to figure out if John Lennon's name had some numerical code that added up to 666. Some even went so far as sponsoring huge record-burning bonfires in their church parking lot.

Fortunately for me, my parents were more focused on what was going on inside me rather than outside. My pastor heard John Lennon's words as John meant for them to be taken—not that the Beatles were more powerful than Jesus. Even misguided John Lennon wouldn't make so foolish an assumption. He wasn't even saying that they were more loved than Jesus. He was saying that kids all over the world were more focused on the Beatles than they were on Jesus.

My pastor parleyed John's statement into one of the best Bible studies my church youth group ever had. He asked why we thought more kids were enamored by the Beatles than Jesus. After we responded to his question, he went on to tell us how we could be the light of the world and the salt of the earth, how to see our friends through Jesus' eyes, and how to love them the way Christ loves them. My young, grace-based pastor didn't react negatively to John Lennon's statement. He wasn't intimidated by it. It didn't frighten him or send him on some kind of witch hunt. He saw it for what it was, and he leveraged it for God's glory. In the process, he helped some longhaired boys and stringy-haired girls in our youth group sort through the idiosyncrasies of their youth culture.

This is how grace can save the day. Grace doesn't make issues out of the arbitrary standards that Christian voices use to define either a "rebellious kid" or a "good Christian boy" or a "sweet Christian girl." Grace has room for unique—even weird—kids. Grace gauges rebellion by where a child's heart is with Jesus Christ and how a child's choices align with the clear moral standards outlined in the Bible.

RULES IN THE NAME OF GOD?

Let me throw a monkey wrench into everything I've said. There are some people and organizations within the Christian movement that have every right to embrace arbitrary standards. A Christian school, for instance, has the right to establish a standard of dress or deportment. Their purpose is to educate their students. They have to define the right parameters (in their opinion) that best create a positive environment for learning. They may choose to not permit tattoos, or extreme hairstyles (as defined by them), or certain clothing styles (even styles that are not immodest). All schools, public and private, have the right to do this, too.

A Christian school is even within its right to have students sign on to certain standards of behavior that do not necessarily have moral connotations (like not allowing them to attend *any* and *all* movies or permitting them to engage in *any* and *all* types of dancing—even ballet and tap). These issues may unnecessarily complicate matters for them, but independent Christian schools have every right to impose arbitrary standards on nonmoral issues.

Where they create huge problems for themselves is when they give these arbitrary standards "spiritual" weight. By trying to use the Bible to defend their position on nonmoral issues (like goatees, sideburns, or nail polish), they drive an unnecessary wedge between them and the student as well as between the student and God. Shrewd Christian schools do not make this mistake. They simply state their school policy and give students the option to take it or leave it. They do not present policies as "Christian" standards but as school standards. If parents and students do not wish to sign on for these standards, fine. But if they do sign on, they are responsible to abide by them, regardless of how arbitrary or even silly the standards appear to be.

Christian camps, Christian businesses (like a bookstore), and churches have the same right to create these arbitrary standards for people who work within their systems. As long as they don't spiritualize them, these standards can serve them well. But the moment schools, camps, businesses, or churches place some kind of moral or biblical weight on arbitrary standards, they establish a legalistic system for the people within their authority. And legalism is one of the most toxic mind-sets any Christian ministry can embrace.

All this said, the question begs to be asked, "But, Tim, couldn't some of the items on your list be indications of a deeper problem inside the child?" The answer is obviously "Yes." But even so, let's get to the heart of the problem. For instance, suppose a young man is dressing like he was dragged to school behind the school bus, he has a staple in his eyebrow and a rivet in his tongue, and he doesn't want to go to church because of a deep-seated frustration with Christianity . . . or maybe he just wants to make life miserable for his parents. Or let's say a girl got her bellybutton pierced, has five rings in each ear, one ring in her nose, and has taken on a total "Gothic" look because of an intense anger within her toward the things of the Spirit. Does it make any sense to declare war on these "things" in their lives when they are only the outward symbols of the inner turmoil? Wouldn't common sense suggest that we concentrate on getting the fire in their souls under control? When we do, these outward things tend to take care of themselves. To fight with our children over external expressions of internal problems only makes matters worse.

DEFINING REBELLION

For the purpose of clarity, I am defining rebellion in the life of a kid brought up in a Christian environment as deliberate antagonism toward God, God's standards, or the people God has placed in authority in a child's life. This rebellion can show itself aggressively in a whole host of negative behaviors as well as passively in indifference and a lack of enthusiasm for the things of the Spirit. By defining rebellion this way, we are automatically eliminating some of the more "edgy" activities from the rebellion list that I outlined a few pages ago.

When we refer to a "rebellious kid" in this book, let's agree that by "rebellious" we are referring to *actions or attitudes that contradict the core spiritual beliefs the child claims to embrace.* We are talking about deliberate decisions to do things, say things, or believe things that are contrary to the heart of God. We are concerned about actions and thoughts that bring diminishing returns to just about every aspect of the child's life.

A second way kids fall into the "rebellious" category is if they are maintaining an obstinate or disrespectful attitude toward the people in authority in their lives—especially their parents. These are children who may indeed love Jesus, but for some particular reason are choosing to turn their backs on what He says about respecting their elders. This is what I like to call "compartmental" rebellion. In a narrow area of their lives, they are being obstinate; otherwise, they have a genuine relationship with God—albeit a disobedient one.

We'll also be using the word *prodigal* as an adjective to describe certain rebellious kids. The thing about prodigals is, they have embraced rebellion as a lifestyle and are in a position to live out their rebellion disconnected from their parents. Prodigals are usually older. Sometimes they are adults.

THE PROFILE OF A GENERIC SINNER

All humans are born with an antagonistic attitude toward God. The Bible says that "there is no one righteous, not even one."[2] The good news is that children exposed to the gospel within an environment of grace can come to know God personally. That's why God gave them parents, and it helps if those parents allow God to work on His own timetable. Even after they have given their hearts to Christ, however, there will be an ongoing struggle with inclinations toward sin and selfishness.

It's easy for parents to make the mistake of considering anything the child does wrong as an act of rebellion. In one sense it is. But that is not the kind of rebellion we are addressing in this book. I want to caution you against putting your child in the "specific" category of a rebellious kid when he or she merely falls into the "general" category. In a broad sense, all sin is rebellion toward God. But what we are addressing here is a bold antagonism that shows itself in out-and-out aggressive defiance or in passive indifference.

Things like sibling rivalry, getting frustrated or angry with Mom or Dad, occasionally lying or stealing, laziness, and the myriad list of kids' day-to-day infractions do not call for the adjective *rebellious* before their names. Kids that display these normal characteristics of sin may simultaneously be developing tender and contrite hearts toward God. They may dearly love and respect God and dearly love and respect you. They are just young believers who are living out loud their ongoing battle with sin. These kids need a gentle but steady touch of spiritual leadership from you.

For the most part, kids mature spiritually over time and learn how to appropriate God's internal power to help them live a more righteous and consistent life. Calling a child "rebellious" has the equivalent effect of calling a child that is struggling in school "stupid." It becomes a self-fulfilling prophecy. Instead, normal children need to be given ongoing correction for their infractions along with ongoing encouragement for their spiritual efforts.

EIGHT REASONS KIDS REBEL

People love lists, even a list of things they wish weren't true. I want to use the rest of this chapter to catalog the standard reasons why kids in Christian homes may rebel. Usually, rebellious kids in Christian homes demonstrate a combination of the reasons on the list. I offer you these options to help you identify the cause behind your child's rebellion and to free you to concentrate on the causes rather than on the resulting effects.

1. Kids in Christian Homes Rebel Because They Are Actually Lost and Don't Know Christ Personally

It's easy to make the assumption that because children grow up in a Christian home and make an early profession of faith in Christ, they are followers of Christ. These kids can pass the basic "I know I'm a Christian" test. Throw in a baptism and you feel that you have an almost ironclad case that they are true believers.

Not necessarily.

We're going to take a deeper look into this issue in the chapter called "Bridges of Hope," but for now let's understand that not all kids who go through the motions of going forward in church (if that's how your church encourages people to come to salvation) or praying the "sinner's prayer" with a parent or Sunday school teacher are necessarily bona fide followers of Jesus. They may know the truth, but it hasn't necessarily set them free.[3] What they may be doing is putting their faith in the faith of their *parents*. Their parents' faith won't save them once they get old enough to be accountable to God for their own sins. In the meantime, it can give them the temporary illusion of being a true "born-again" Christian and can inspire a long-term delusion that they are spiritually secure.

No matter what a person's age may be, only time will tell if his repentance and contrition are genuine or not. Jesus addressed this very issue in His famous parable of the sower. You can find the complete texts in Matthew 13:2–23; Mark 4:1–20; and Luke 8:5–15. There are four scenarios that He outlines:

1. Some seed falls on the pathway and gets carried away on the soles of the travelers' feet, or by birds that fly down and eat it.
2. Some seed falls in rocky soil, but the new life that sprouts up cannot be sustained because there is so little soil and moisture to keep it growing.
3. Some seed falls among the thorns. It takes root and grows, but thorns ultimately choke it out.
4. Some seed falls on good soil. It takes root and grows into a healthy plant that yields a crop a hundredfold.

As we read the way Jesus explained this parable, it's easy to see how a child—especially a young one—could go through the motions of salvation but not have a belief in Christ that truly takes root.

The first seed, the seed that fell on the pathway, falls victim to outside enemies that want to steal it. Jesus says, "The devil comes and takes away the word from their hearts, so that they may not believe and be saved."[4]

The second seed that falls among the rocks describes "the ones who receive the word with joy when they hear it, but they have no root. They believe for a while, but in the time of testing they fall away."[5]

The third seed, the seed that fell among thorns, represents the ones who hear, "but as they go on their way they are choked by life's worries, riches and pleasures, and they do not mature."[6]

Only the last scenario, the seed that fell on good soil, creates a true believer.

Just because our child has "accepted Jesus" into her heart or has prayed the "sinner's prayer," and just because our families go to church and read the Bible together, the work is far from over. Regardless of what kind of soil the word falls onto, the farmer doesn't just throw the seed once and stop. He continues to sow, season after season. In the meantime, things can be done to keep the soil healthy and receptive. Rocks can be removed. Thorns can be pruned back. An atmosphere of grace can counter the deceptive schemes of the devil.

What would be the signs that your child may not actually be a rebellious "Christian" kid but rather an "unsaved" rebellious kid? Let me give you a simple litmus test:

- Does he show any remorse when he does things that break God's heart?
- Does she have an inclination toward God's Word, and is she convicted by it when exposed to it?
- Does he long for and enjoy fellowship with other followers of Christ?
- Does he want to use his spiritual gifts to strengthen the church and reach out to lost people?
- Is she sensitive to the lost condition of the people she encounters at school and work?

If you answered "no" to most or all of these questions, there's a good chance that the Holy Spirit isn't dwelling in your son's or daughter's heart. Yet you could say, "But, Tim, based on that litmus test, half the people in our church may not be saved!" Unfortunately, you're right. Western Christians are too much into quantifying genuine faith by church attendance, biblical knowledge, and denominational affiliation. That's not how God quantifies it. Jesus says, "I am the good shepherd;

I know my sheep and my sheep know me . . . They too will listen to my voice."[7]

One of the things that can complicate the relationship between a parent and a rebellious kid is responding to them as though they are followers of Jesus when indeed they aren't. For one thing, a lot of the things we expect of them (responding to the Holy Spirit, reading their Bible, increasing their quiet times, etc.) don't even register. There is no reference point. Paul said, "The message of the cross is foolishness to those who are perishing."[8] We may be expecting spiritual behavior from children who are incapable of producing it. This doesn't mean we shouldn't talk with them about spiritual things or reference the Bible; we just should do it the way we would with someone who isn't a Christian.

By viewing our rebellious children as unbelievers, we have a tendency to be much more patient and understanding with them. It changes the way we pray for them. It even changes the way we view their sin— as an internal struggle rather than an outward display of spiritual insubordination. We see them more as people in the clutches of the evil one than as people thumbing their noses at God. We remove the false assumption that compels them to fill a role they aren't actually capable of filling, freeing them to honestly wrestle with the question of their eternal destiny.

So if you arrive at the conviction that your son's or daughter's rebellion is the result of their being unsaved, don't panic. Just start loving them the way God calls all of us to love unbelievers—with heavy doses of kindness, understanding, and grace. God will make His move when He is ready.

2. Kids in Christian Homes Rebel Because They Are Angry at God

A list of reasons why a child might be angry at God could go on for pages and pages. Here's a small sample. Some kids might be angry at God because of

- The early death of a parent
- The death of a sibling
- A sibling's birth defect or mental defect

- The divorce of their parents
- A string of unfortunate incidents that happened to their family (fires, theft, injury, etc.)
- Their perception of a limited IQ
- Chronic pain
- Certain physical features or body style
- Being left out of the mainstream on things like looks, athletic ability, or musical talent
- A horrific infraction against them personally (incest, rape)

You'll notice that the things on this list aren't little things such as not getting what they wanted for Christmas or not getting asked to prom. These are huge, life-defining issues. And they all have something in common: These are things over which the child feels no control. These are the kind of issues you either take to God or blame on God. When God chooses to do nothing about the child's prayer request, she may develop frustration with Him or even deny His existence. As for deaths, birth defects, or crimes committed against them, kids don't see why God permitted such a thing to happen or continues to allow it to cause so much pain.

Mature adults may understand that life isn't fair, but it takes a while for some kids to grasp this truth. They don't see the bigger picture—that God is working in their character to make them stronger or to mold them into His image. They don't understand why God allows parents to do things like get divorced. Regardless of the limited perspective or faulty thinking of the child, the result is a sense of betrayal or loss that he ultimately blames on God. He may know God, and may even love Him, but in the meantime he is angry at Him.

Many parents spend decades reacting to their child's rebellious behavior without ever realizing that the child is having serious issues with God. This lack of understanding on the parents' part only makes the child feel that much more frustrated. It behooves parents to consider rebellious behavior as a symptom of a deeper struggle. Start with the obvious. Look at that list. There might be one or more things that may be fueling a huge dispute between your child and God.

We have a dear friend who lost his wife after a prolonged illness. His youngest daughter was twelve at the time. The daughter never visibly grieved the loss of her mother. She put on a stoic face, held back her tears, and quietly moved on with her life. Outsiders applauded the "mature" way she handled everything. They aren't applauding her now as she moves into her fifth year of living in the depths of drug addiction. She wants absolutely nothing to do with God, even though prior to her mother's death she was a little girl madly in love with Jesus.

These bigger-than-life issues require a response of grace, not a re-action of anger or some Theology 101 lesson. It doesn't mean we con-done self-destruction. Nor does it mean we don't mete out consequences for bad choices. But our children need the unconditional love of their parents while they search for the unconditional love of God. In fact, your unconditional love may be the way they ultimately find His.

Besides needing our grace rather than our rage, there are kids who might also need some third party to help them walk through the deeper recesses of their pain. A youth pastor, a discipleship leader, a relative, or a friend may be the neutral person with whom they can work through their anger with God. This struggle might even require a professional touch. There are therapists trained and gifted in helping your child process this kind of anger. Your child may not want to go to a counselor, but some things are like emergency appendectomies: they aren't up for debate.

One thing that I think is very important when you are handing your child over to a counselor or therapist: never put them in the hands of someone who does not fear God, especially if your child is in conflict with God. There are qualified, believing counselors out there. Pray hard. Do your homework. You'll find one.

3. Kids in Christian Homes Rebel Because They Are Mad at Their Parents.

If the list of reasons kids are mad at God would stretch around the block, the reasons why they are mad at their parents would stretch around the world. Let me give you some possibilities to think about. Then we'll consider some things we can do about it. Some kids are mad at their parents because of

- Perceived favoritism
- The way you've mishandled your finances
- The way you've mishandled your body and your health
- Various ways you communicate how much of an imposition they are to you
- Your unavailability—"you never have time for me"
- Broken promises
- The way you trivialize their feelings—especially when it comes to their boyfriends or girlfriends
- The feeling that you don't respect their opinions
- Forcing them to move away from their friends
- Crimes you've committed or shame you've brought to them
- Screaming at them when they don't do what you want
- Your nagging
- Your perfectionism
- Comparing them to siblings or friends' kids in a negative way
- Your toxic, highly controlling ways
- Your lack of grace within the inner workings of your family
- Your divorce
- Feeling that they are being used to get back at your ex-spouse

Well, don't we all feel a lot better having read that nice little list? I know it's tough to face some of those things, and it would be hard to find a parent that hasn't done at least a couple of them. I know some who have done them all. Frankly, I'm amazed that their kids don't rebel more.

Our children do not exist as solo acts. They are completely at the mercy of the parents they have. We give them their DNA, their name, their reputation. We give them their start. They are like a blank white board, and we write on them the definition of their lives. We aim them; we pace them; we play the biggest role in how much meaning their lives will have—especially when they are young.

But here's the problem. We make mistakes. We don't know what we're doing in a lot of areas when it comes to raising kids. We don't know what we're doing in a lot of areas when it comes to ourselves, either. The good news is, our children are capable of granting us a lot of grace and forgiveness when it comes to our failures. But that's assuming two things: one, we first grant them a lot of grace and forgiveness when it comes to their own failures; and two, we are quick to take responsibility for our mistakes and ask for forgiveness.

Here's the bigger problem. A lot of parents have a hard time doing "the grace thing," owning up and taking responsibility for wrongs. We either deny we're responsible (when a jury of our peers would unanimously say that we are), we make excuses for our actions, or we trivialize the severity of our mistakes' impact on our kids. When you look back over the above list, there is only one thing on the list that you may have no choice in: when you have to move your family away from familiar places and friends. Even so, some parents have made career moves for lifestyle reasons during the most crucial times in a child's relationship to his or her friends. These children are plopped into a new neighborhood or school system feeling naked and disconnected. They may be treated as outcasts for the early months after the move. These are serious issues that can cause kids to vent a lot of anger in our direction. It doesn't mean we can't move. But before we ask our family to sacrifice on our behalf, we've got to factor in the enormous impact a move can have, and then do everything we can to minimize it. And even after we've done that, we've got to be patient as they work through the grief they feel in having lost childhood friends and a lot of their sense of security.

Everything else on the list is mostly of our doing. We might not be able to do anything about some of them after the fact (like our health, our immediate finances, our divorce, or our criminal record), but we can step up and take full responsibility for the pain they have caused our sons or daughters.

We are the adults. We create adult dilemmas. We make adult mistakes. We can't slip into a child's mentality and say that because of our own problems (divorce, financial ruin, etc.) we can't help our hurting children. I'm not diminishing the severity of the pain you might feel after something like a divorce, a job termination, or a jail sentence, but I think we need to consider our children's needs. Too many times, we buy into the world's mentality that when we mess up we have every excuse to become absorbed with ourselves and our pain.

No, we don't. Not when our children's relationship with God hangs in the balance. And here's something that the voices of the world don't tell you: when you unselfishly own up to your mistakes and take full responsibility for the pain and anguish you have caused your child, you not only help relieve a lot of her hurt, but you actually speed up your own ability to heal and to change.

Right now you may be thinking about something you need to do or say. Don't let the earth make another complete rotation between now and the time you sit down with your son or daughter and confess. Don't spiritualize it. Don't minimize it. Don't try to justify it. Just confess. Call it what it is—horrible, hurtful, and debilitating. Then ask your child to consider forgiving you when he is ready. He may have been processing this pain for a long time, so it might be a while before he gets around to forgiving you.

In the meantime, continue to take responsibility for your actions, and do so for the rest of your life. In the process, you remove your arrogance and selfishness as an ongoing excuse for your child's rebellion. Once she can no longer blame you for her behavior (because you've owned up), she is forced into a position where she has no one to blame for her rebellion but herself. This puts her on a shorter path to repentance. Like parent, like child.

4. Kids in Christian Homes Rebel Because the Strengths of Their Personalities Are Pushed to Extremes

Every person has personality strengths. You might be naturally talkative, charming, complimentary, or inquisitive. God might have hard-wired you with an acute attention to detail, a natural ability to lead, and a stubborn streak. Every personality trait I've just listed is a wonderful trait—when used in balance. But each one can become a toxic trait in a relationship if it is overexercised.

And then there are the strong-willed personalities. These are people who have the same wonderful traits, but it's as though those traits are on steroids.

It's a shortcut to rebellion when we fail to see particular traits as assets in our children and don't teach them how to use them in balance. Instead, we may mock our children for being nitpicky or opinionated or cerebral. We may shame her for being extremely sensitive or quiet or shy; we may fault him for being determined or aggressive or confident. We push their wonderful qualities to extremes until they are either extremely suppressed or extremely expressed. The conflict that follows increases the child's frustration, and the next thing you know you've got full-scale rebellion.

Our job is to see our kids' traits in a positive light, and then turn them into valuable tools within their personalities. Is your child argumentative and stubborn? I know some people in the Bible who were like that: Moses, Elijah, Peter, and Paul (to name a few). When those traits were tempered with grace, God used them to do mighty works. Is your child nitpicky and particular? That sounds like Joseph and Solomon. Stubborn people steeped in the skill of argument make great lawyers. They know how to draw lines in the sand and not surrender. Come to think of it, they make excellent officers in the military. Those nitpicky kids can grow up to be superb organizers, accountants, and troubleshooters.

If you are unsure about this process, it may be worth getting some outside assessments. Talk to your children's teachers, relatives that have a lot of exposure to them, or their youth workers. What do they think your children's strengths are? If you are still wondering, study how they are rebelling. Where do they get the best of you? It may just be their strength pushed to an extreme.

It's never too late to start recognizing and applauding children for their strengths—especially when you see them used properly. But even when they are not, you can still recognize the strengths. After an argument over some issue, you might say something like, "Son, I hate it when we argue like this. It hurts me inside, and it doesn't look like you appreciate what it does to our relationship. But one thing I've noticed in spite of all this pain we've just been through . . . you are *very good* at holding your own. You are articulate, quick, and resourceful. You are so fluid on your feet that it is sometimes astonishing to see just how gifted you are verbally. Obviously, we can't go on fighting this way. We both need to figure out how to talk to each other more respectfully, and I want to work overtime to do my part on this. I also want to do my part to understand where you are coming from. In the meantime, I just want you to know that I'm impressed with these gifts and skills God has given you. I'm not excited about how you use them on me, but I'm excited that you have them. As you learn to use them more and more for good, they could become huge assets to you professionally and as a leader of others."

There's an old saying that what you got in trouble for at school is what you end up doing for a living as an adult. Obviously, I got bad conduct grades for talking too much. And now . . . I get paid to talk.

The more we can help our kids ratchet back the extreme use of their strengths, the sooner we can bring some relief to their rebellious patterns. I know what some of you are thinking right now. *How? How do we help them ratchet back these strengths?*

I want you to use the things God has already given you to figure this out. He's given you a mind and experiences, mistakes, the Bible, prayer, shrewd friends, and common sense. Use them. Don't be afraid. Don't let Satan tell you that you are a loser and incapable of figuring these things out. God assigned you this rebellious child because He knew you were capable of being part of the solution. Trust in Him. Lean on Him. And watch what happens!

5. Kids in Christian Homes Rebel Because They Are in a State of Confusion or Disillusion

Children go through awkward periods in their lives that cause them to get more anxious and edgy. These periods may include

- Adding siblings to the family
- Starting kindergarten, junior high, or high school
- Puberty
- When they first notice or start to get involved with the opposite sex

- Firsts: dates, kisses, breakups, betrayals
- Getting ready to leave home for good

All of these have something in common. They are unavoidable passages that all kids go through. But they bring a high level of anxiety that can lead to rebellious behavior.

Children from Christian homes may also rebel when a pastor, youth minister, or Christian schoolteacher is caught up in scandal. It is hard to watch when leaders fail to live up to what they have required of others. And that includes us as parents. When we do something that demonstrates a huge disconnect between our beliefs and our actions, it can put our children into a tailspin. Children look up to their moral teachers in an almost irrational way. When sin brings one of these icons to ruin, it can cause kids to doubt a lot of what they've been taught.

Confusion is part of childhood. People we trust occasionally let us down. Children might be behaving badly, but some dialogue with them about incidents of betrayal can help them process the situation until it is safely in their rearview mirror. If we've caused the tailspin, we must start with disclosure, responsibility, and repentance. But assuming the person in question is some moral/spiritual leader they've looked up to, we can help by being candid about the frustration we have felt during similar dilemmas in our youth. It helps them see us in a different light—as someone who understands the pain of confusion and betrayal.

6. Kids in Christian Homes Rebel Because They Are in Bondage

When it comes to getting people into a state of bondage, Satan has no equal. The enemy can put a child in a lockdown that turns him into his polar opposite, spiritually speaking. And he uses methods that are as old as time. His methods are similar to the warfare we use today. First, Satan weakens a child's defenses with a constant barrage of images, ideas, and temptations that get him second-guessing what he believes. He knows kids' three most fundamental driving inner needs—the need to be secure, to be significant, and to feel strong. He knows most of their parents are oblivious to these needs, so he carpet-bombs the kids day in and day out with counterfeit ways to meet these needs. For security he offers money, sex, and materialism. For significance he offers popularity, sex, and applause. For strength he offers control, sex, and abuse.

Once he's gotten our kids' guard down, he establishes a beachhead in their lives. He might get them to cheat in school, or get into pornography, or sleep with their boyfriend or girlfriend, or start drinking, or try drugs. Sometimes he manages to get them to do all of these things. Once the beachhead is established, he can hold the other parts of their life hostage. From that beachhead he is able to completely destabilize them. When this happens, it's not uncommon for children to do a 180-degree turn from everything they've lived for and stood for. I've seen parents with the equivalent of shell shock, stunned by the sudden and radical change that has taken place in their son or daughter.

I remember a girl who came back from an exciting summer mission trip to Spain. It was the apex of several years of careful spiritual choices. But two weeks later, she met a guy who told her all the things she wanted to hear; she slept with him and turned into a spiritual nightmare for her mother almost overnight. It went on for the next two years. There were other factors in her life that made it easier for Satan to trap her. Her father had abandoned her and her brother when they were both very little. Her single-parent mom left the kids alone a lot because of work demands. Obviously, there was a clear father-wound in this young girl's heart. Satan simply used all of these things to get her trapped and then held her hostage with guilt and shame.

A quick, radical shift in children's behavior, when they change from committed Christian kids to spiritual terrorists, often points to some area of life where they are in bondage. They react negatively to their parents out of guilt and disgust in themselves. They are also embarrassed before God and figure they have let Him down so much that He is utterly ashamed of them. They are also fearful of what will happen to them should they be found out. And, in fact, the issue isn't really whether they will be found out, but when.

These areas of bondage can cause phenomenal fear in parents. Cheating, promiscuity, drugs, and alcohol are some of the most debilitating problems a young person can get involved in. Lifelong scar tissue to a child's emotions, spirit, and relationships are often the by-products of these vices. Parents' fears are legitimate.

These areas of bondage can also incite an unusual amount of parental anger. That's because they are unusually embarrassing. Parents also feel insulted when they compare these activities to all the things they've done to build good qualities into the child. Behaviors that lead to bondage cost families immeasurable losses of cohesiveness and joy.

Regardless of how much sorrow these areas of bondage give us as parents, they do not mark the end of hope for our children. Hope ends only if everyone else around them gives up and writes them off. God won't do that. And that's why He gives children parents. Regardless of how hurt, embarrassed, and angry they are, there's something about parents' love that helps them get past their personal pain in order to help their children.

But there are also mistakes that can make matters worse. The standard mistake is to work overtime trying to control your image at the expense of the best interest of the child. A pregnant daughter is spirited overnight to a relative across the country to avoid public embarrassment for the family. It's done under the guise of protecting the daughter, but she can figure out fairly quickly whose image is being guarded.

Kids on drugs or in trouble with the law aren't the kinds of things we like to bring up at church or work. But when they become a reality for your family, the best way to address them is head-on, out in the open, with a ton of grace. While you are getting counseling yourself with regard to embarrassment, anger, and guilt, you need to communicate to your child what God communicates to him in His Word. He or she is *loved*. Nothing can separate your child from your love, just as nothing can separate him or her from the love of God. Reading between the lines of Romans 8:38–39, you can see every possible type of bondage your child could get caught in. This passage assures us there are no problems that are not covered by the love of God: "I am convinced that neither death nor life, neither angels nor demons, neither the present nor the future, nor any powers, neither height nor depth, nor anything else in all creation, will be able to separate us from the love of God that is in Christ Jesus our Lord."

There is not one area of bondage that will cause God to turn His back on your child. No matter how miserable our kids make life for us, when they see unwavering love emanating from us . . . love ultimately wins. You may be in doubt. I don't like to be a name-dropper, but God said it Himself (through the apostle Paul): "Love is patient, love is kind. It does not envy, it does not boast, it is not proud. It is not rude, it is not self-seeking, it is not easily angered, it keeps no record of wrongs. Love does not delight in evil but rejoices with the truth. It always protects, always trusts, always hopes, always perseveres. Love never fails."[9]

7. Kids from Christian Homes Rebel Because It Is an Essential Part of Their Spiritual Pilgrimage

I'm not suggesting that God causes our kids to rebel. The Bible says, "When tempted, no one should say, 'God is tempting me.' For God cannot be tempted by evil, nor does he tempt anyone; but each one is tempted when, by his own evil desire, he is dragged away and enticed."[10]

But as we've seen, some kids wrestle with an internal dilemma about their faith. They don't feel it's original. It was simply e-mailed to their hearts because they were brought up in Christian homes. They primarily believe because they've been told that they need to believe. Their faith has not been forged through difficulty or testing. It's just part of the spiritual tradition of their family.

As they start to grow older, it is normal for some children to develop a spiritual wanderlust. Actually, I think all children must go through the process of moving from believing the faith of their parents to making it their own. For most kids in Christian homes, this can be done without a whimper. A grace-based environment makes the transfer from parental faith to personal faith almost an assumption, because a grace-based environment requires an authentic faith in order to be maintained. Children in this kind of environment are encouraged toward a deep and personal faith from the get-go. But there are some kids who have to touch the wet paint before they'll believe the sign.

The disciple Thomas wasn't going to buy into the resurrection of Christ just because his buddies said He was alive. It's fair to assume that Thomas was savvy enough to calculate that claiming Christ rose from the dead, whether He did or not, was probably going to cost them a lot personally. He was ready to sign up for whatever might happen if the Resurrection was true, but he wanted to see the proof with his own eyes. Jesus had already appeared to the other disciples and, interestingly, had encouraged them to "look at my hands and my feet. It is I myself! Touch me and see; a ghost does not have flesh and bones, as you see I have."[11] Thomas wanted to get the same substantiation the other disciples had already gotten (at Jesus' request, no less). Thomas said, "Unless I see the nail marks in his hands and put my finger where the nails were, and put my hand into his side, I will not believe it."[12] Jesus obliged Thomas.

Some kids have a hard time getting their arms around a relationship with God that has primarily been transferred "theoretically." It's especially tough if they are children of parents who were lost through their young adult years and then God did a mighty cleansing work in their hearts prior to their having children. They tell their kids of God's tender mercies, they tell them of His forgiving grace, but the kids would rather see it firsthand than merely accept it at face value. Like Thomas, they are simply saying, "I want to see for myself."

Do they think all of this consciously? No. I don't believe that all of this is going on in the forefront of their consciousnesses. But at a subconscious level, they realize that they simply don't have much of an affinity for a prepackaged faith. Other kids in the same family may have no problem embracing Christ without a gutter-to-glory testimony. In fact, Jesus mentioned them with honor when He said to Thomas, "Because you have seen me, you have believed; blessed are those who have not seen and yet have believed."[13] But some kids don't seem to realize how much they need Jesus until Jesus is all they've got.

I've got good news. Some of the most powerful voices for God in history have been people who questioned their faith for a period of time. And in the process, they sowed some wild oats and wheat and barley. But they ultimately made it through to a point of total confidence. And, just as He accommodated Thomas, so Jesus was glad to accommodate their concerns.

Your child's rebellion might be painful, but it might be part of a spiritual pilgrimage she is on. If so, you'll need to practice steady and bold prayer on your knees on her behalf. You might be surprised at the outcome. She could end up being the most passionate and compassionate warrior for the cross of all your children.

8. Kids in Christian Homes Rebel Because They Are Reacting to Flaws within the Brand of Christianity They Are Being Exposed To

It's time somebody called a spade a spade. There are many things we have been encouraged to do in the name of a "great Christian upbringing" that can press our kids over the edge into full-scale war against our beliefs. Many of the things Christian parents do have great merit in and of themselves. But too often these are good things done for the wrong reasons or, at least, for half-baked reasons that bring out the worst in our children.

Too much of what we are encouraged to do can actually create a spiritual anemia that weakens our children. Some kids wake up and say, "That's it! I've had enough! This isn't worth it!" Their rebellion is either spiritual anarchy or worse (and much more sinister): quiet but toxic indifference. They may say all the right things, but deep down in their hearts, they could care less about the things of the Spirit.

Of all the reasons for our children's rebellion, this last one—a reaction to the brand of Christianity within their spiritual environment—is actually responsible for most of the others. For so many of the families that are experiencing the pain of a child rebelling, the fact is, it wasn't necessary. Your kid could have come to a passionate conviction about Christ without having to put so many bad miles behind him. But there are inherent flaws within today's Christian parenting philosophies that actually set our children up for failure.

It is this issue I will address in the rest of this book. In the process, I will offer help and hope for those of you who are contending with a rebellious child and those of you who want to keep your child from becoming one. If we can just look past the familiar checklists and see our higher calling, I think we'll realize how business as usual in our Christian families is going to yield disappointing results. In the process, I want to take an honest look at the standard icons of Christian parenting. Maybe we have been expecting something from them they weren't designed to deliver.

I want to invite you to join me on a quest for passionate Christian parenthood—the kind that makes a kid *want* to follow Jesus. We might have to shoot a few sacred cows along the way. I think they need to be put out of their misery anyway. I've got to warn you, my primary target for a change of heart is *you*. You are the parent. You are the one who plays the biggest role in your child's faith. But don't worry; I'm on your side. And even if I weren't, God is. He wants to give you success in your job of raising kids who move into adulthood ready to make a huge difference in the world.

Before we start to look at some of the drawbacks inherent in our evangelical system, I thought we'd do well to stop by and visit one of my friends and take some notes from one of the finest fathers of all time. He also happened to have some problems with his kids. He's got a lot to teach us.

DISCUSSION QUESTIONS

1. Tim said, "Some parents who are convinced their children are rebelling might be surprised to find out God wouldn't agree with them." He followed this statement with a list of attitudes and actions that are seen as rebellious to some parents but in reality are not moral issues at all. How do the arbitrary judgments of our extended families and the broader Christian community add to our children's propensity to rebel? Why do you think we make these kinds of judgments? What should we do to correct them?

2. Why do you think we are so quick to assume that the styles and quirky behavior of childhood are rebellion? What effects do our overreactions to our children's styles and quirky behav-

ior have on their developing an intimate relationship with Christ?

3. Do you think that creating arbitrary rules (regarding hairstyles, musical styles, etc.) and then giving them moral, spiritual, or biblical weight unnecessarily sets your children up to rebel? Why or why not? What should you do if we have made the mistake of moralizing nonmoral issues?

4. Tim gave a specific definition of rebellion on pages 31 and 32. Based on this definition, do you think you have a rebellious child? Is that difficult for you to admit? Why or why not?

5. What are some of the acts of grace we can show our rebellious children if their rebellion is because they are mad at God or mad at one or more of their parents?

6. Some kids rebel because the strength of their personality is pushed to an extreme. If your child is rebelling, what are some of the strengths and assets of their personality that seem to be pushed to an extreme in their rebellion? How does your reaction to these either make the problem worse or better?

7. If your child rebels because he is in bondage (drugs, alcohol, cheating, sex), what are some typical reactions you have that make the problem worse? What are some things you can do to help him get released from bondage?

8. Why do you think some kids need to rebel in order to finalize their faith in Christ? What are some things you should do to help them through this time in their lives? What should you go out of our way to avoid doing during this time?

9. What is one thing God has taught you through this chapter?

CHAPTER 3

A Prodigal Primer

If you'll allow me, I'd like to take you on a little side trip to meet a man I met a long time ago. He was an amazing fellow with a touching story. As you'll see, he was a man who, like you, had a lot on his plate. But it wasn't just his success in the marketplace and his status in the community that kept him sitting up and paying attention. It was his two boys. It turns out that in spite of the fact that he was a great father, he still ended up with two sons who turned out to be prodigals. One took rebellion to the level of a self-destructive art form; the other had a different style. The first son also took some of the best years out of his young life and used them to see how much he could age his good father.

We can find him in the land of Luke, the fifteenth county, and his spread covers parcels 11–32.

You're saying, "Okay, okay. I know where you are going. It's the famous story of the prodigal son in the Bible."

Of course it is. How could we have a discussion about rebellious kids in Christian homes and not look at the one story in the Bible that speaks directly to the subject? This story makes you wish you had been there when it was told. Here is Jesus, that matchless storyteller, wrapping one of His most meaningful messages in one of the tightest packages of all time. It's amazing what we learn in twenty-one simple verses.

FOUR STYLES OF PARENTING

To set this story up, however, I'd like to get out my broad brush and paint some pictures of a couple of parenting styles. I want to contrast these parenting styles framed within the context of kids who rebel. We'll look at the three standard styles that pop up in varying degrees in families, and then suggest a style that represents the balance that works best—whether your children are rebelling or not.

Clueless Parents

This doesn't need much development since I seriously doubt that anyone reading this book would admit to being this kind of parent. In fact, I seriously doubt that any of you are in this category, since clueless parents rarely pick up a book to try to figure out what they should be doing. When things go well they're not sure why, and when things go wrong they are equally confused. That's why they are considered clueless. They parent more by accident than by intention. They are not bad parents; they are just unusually inadequate when it comes to the decisions they make.

To be fair (and gracious), there is usually some major issue in their lives that keeps them in a parental fog. It might be painful abuse in the past or a serious addiction in the present. They may be hooked on drugs or alcohol, or they may have one of those subtler yet serious addictions to work, pleasure, self, pride, beauty, status, money, or fame. For these types of parents, kids serve more as extensions of their ego needs or as neat stand-ins for the Christmas card photo. To clueless parents, their kids are more like plush toys in their lives. And when one of their children rebels, they view her like a Beanie Baby that has lost its tag: "Now what do we do?"

EMT Parents

EMT stands for "Emergency Medical Technician," but you get the point. You'll recognize these parents because they're usually on their way—with lights flashing and sirens wailing—to rescue their kids from the latest mess they've gotten themselves into. These are moms or dads who spend most of their waking hours shielding their children from anything that could result in emotional, physical, or spiritual duress. They run interference between their children and any teacher, playmate, coach, or spiritual leader that might actually assess their child accurately.

These are the moms that try to talk the teacher into giving a daughter extra credit to raise a borderline grade; these are the dads that browbeat a coach for not playing their son enough. These are parents who will move their child from one school to another because of unkind classmates. Rather than teach their child how to flourish in these true-to-life types of environments where girls are catty, boys are territorial, and kids would rather function within the exclusive confines of a clique, they grab their son's or daughter's book bag and take them to another school, which, it turns out, has girls who are catty, boys who are territorial, and kids who would rather function within the exclusive confines of a clique.

I know an EMT mom whose daughter was running for student council at her junior high. This mother not only made and hung all the campaign posters, she made all the campaign handouts, wrote her daughter's speech, and also called every kid in each of her classes, trying to convince them why they should vote for her daughter. She wasn't above using guilt and manipulation to get those votes, either.

You guessed it. Her daughter lost.

The mom took it harder than the girl. And that typifies the inner characteristics of EMT parents. They do a lot of these rescue operations because they actually have a huge need—they need to fix things for people. It makes them feel significant. That's because they also are primarily driven by their feelings. Since it hurts them so much to see their children lose or suffer, they do everything they can to protect their kids from life's harsh realities. They run interference in front, in back, and all around their children. These are the moms that make several trips to school in a week's time to bring French homework, a forgotten lunch, or a freshly typed research project. Most of these parents have this step-'n'-fetch lifestyle down pretty well before their first child is two years old.

EMT parents are convinced they do these things for their children out of love, but if it's anything, it's self-love. It is a twisted view of parenting that assumes love, protection, and caring are synonyms. They aren't.

Love is best defined as "the commitment of my will to your needs and best interests, regardless of the cost." It isn't in the best interest of children to accommodate their laziness, cover their mistakes, and shield them from the things that make them uncomfortable. Part of the price tag of parental love is that you sometimes have to watch your children fall flat on their faces or get knocked on their butts. And sometimes these are the greatest lessons kids ever learn.

Not, of course, in the EMT parent's opinion.

Protection. Obviously there is a time to protect our children—from circumstances, outsiders, and themselves. But there is a distinct line we need to draw between things that hurt them and things that harm them. You want to be careful protecting your children from things that may hurt them, because most improvement in life comes with pain. Hurt is almost always temporary, and often is the gateway to improvement, experience, and wisdom.

Harm is a different matter. Harm comes from things over which the child has no control; he is powerless to protect himself from it. Getting a lower mark in calculus because she keeps forgetting her homework won't harm her; it will just sting her—maybe enough to help her start remembering her assignments.

Caring. When it comes to caring for your kid, the line you want to draw is between a hand-up and a handout. A hand-up helps kids muster the courage they need to face their fears, the encouragement they need to face their enemies, and the wisdom they need to face their mistakes. A handout, on the other hand, is what you do when you want to keep your child fearful, weak, and irresponsible.[1]

EMT parents have an uncanny way of raising kids that grow up to be EMT parents. And Brother Love's EMT Parental Salvation Show rolls on.

What really messes up an EMT parent's rhythm is when one of his kids develops a rebellious streak. It's like Dumb and Dumber in the ambulance business. They pay speeding tickets, buy birth-control pills, fix wrecked cars, bail their kids out of jail, and attack the people who are trying to hold their child accountable.

One of the reasons they do this is because EMT parents, by nature, tend to grade their children far more favorably than the child deserves. What's interesting to me is that the best parents I know—I'm talking about the ones who are raising stellar kids who have a passionate love for God and are taking on life with enthusiasm—tend to grade themselves, as well as their children, realistically. They are quick to see their flaws and admit their mistakes. In contrast, EMT parents come close to falling into the "clueless" category when it comes to accurately assessing their children. An EMT parent might have a son who is hooked on drugs, is sleeping with his girlfriend, and drops the F-bomb every other sentence, and yet Mom says something like, "Yeah, but he's a really good Christian."

No, he's not. He's not even in the time zone of a good Christian.

And when EMT parents do try to discipline, it's not uncommon to find half-baked attempts. A son gets caught driving drunk, and they take away the car for a weekend. A daughter cheats on a test, and after getting her out of being suspended, they make her pay her own cell-phone bill for a month.

You probably figured out that EMT parents provide little incentive and direction that would help their kids find their way out of a rebellious lifestyle. Maybe that's why EMT parents whine so much.

Special Forces Parenting

I want to be careful here because there is clearly a time and place for Special Forces. They are vital to the war on terror. Their SWAT divisions come in real handy when some guy is holding a gun to your head in a hostage situation. But when Special Forces describes your style of parenting, rebelloius kids usually aren't far behind. They are those in-your-face, storm trooper, my-way-or-the-highway-type moms and dads that bark a lot of orders and like to throw their weight around. This isn't actually a bad idea if you are a platoon leader in some military hot spot, but it has a nasty way of backfiring when it's used on offspring. For the most part, families don't live in war zones. If there were any kind of zone a family should be living in, it would be a grace zone. Unfortunately, if

Special Forces–type parents aren't careful, they can create a war zone in their child's heart.

There was a time when this autocratic style of parenting actually worked. The gears of industry and the wheels of commerce turned under the inertia of an autocratic system. That's not the way it is now. Obviously, there are pockets of autocratic leadership, but they are more the exception than the norm. Even education—once a bastion of autocratic leadership—is more likely user-friendly and democratic in the way it oversees students. Because of this shift, autocratic leadership in the home stands in stark contrast to just about every other type of system the child is exposed to.

Special Forces parenting makes a lot of noise, offers up a lot of threats, and tries to rule by intimidation. When it's time to deal with a problem in a child's life, these SF parents love to pull out the heavy artillery and often turn to some form of punishment. Unfortunately, that tends to miscarry with overuse. That's because punishment is one of the least effective forms of correction. Why? Lots of reasons.

Punishment is more about getting even or balancing the score than it is about correction. It's also about communicating who is boss. But it is ineffective because it's not the way our world deals with shortcomings. If you're a baseball player and you fall into a hitting slump, the coach doesn't make you go stand in the corner of the dugout. He sends you back down to the minor leagues. If you don't live up to performance expectations at work, the boss doesn't take away your Palm Pilot. He fires you. Even prison isn't seen by our penal system as punitive as much as it is the proper consequence of breaking the law.

As we'll see in the story of the prodigal son, the most effective form of correction is *consequences*. And the more natural the consequences, the better. That's the way the real world operates, that's the way God operates, and that's the method most helpful to rebellious kids in figuring out why what they are doing is unacceptable.

Another reason why the autocratic control of a Special Forces parent doesn't work well over time is because it conditions children to respond to outside voices and forces in their lives. They get a little bigger and a little older and it's easy for them to start submitting to the barking orders of overbearing boyfriends or girlfriends or the outspoken voice of the crowd. I guess you kind of figured out that Special Forces parents make it easy for their kids to find their way into rebellious lifestyles.

Grace-Based Parenting

In grace, we find a breath-of-fresh-air balance between rules and relationships. Grace-based rules are realistic and attainable. The relationship between parent and child is personal and deep. Grace-filled parents don't whine or browbeat. They don't rescue and they don't punish. They treat their children the way God treats His children. You might have noticed that God never whines. He doesn't taunt, ridicule, and badger. He doesn't come swooping in to rescue us every time we do something stupid. And He doesn't bully or pester us.

The Bible says, "The LORD disciplines those he loves."[2] Later on it says, "God disciplines us for our good."[3] Punishment is primarily about payback. Discipline is designed to correct. Grace displays an attitude of honor, favor, and value toward the ones you love, regardless of how they are behaving. Grace-based parents aren't surprised that children sin, they aren't afraid to let consequences run their course, and they don't feel guilty when they have to correct them.

A great platform to stand on as a grace-based parent is one built with five strong planks:

1. Grace-based parents are committed to moral discipline in their own lives. They know they are far from perfect and they realize that every day is an ongoing struggle, but they make their day-to-day choices based on an absolute moral code. They don't question the moral standards of the Bible or complain that they are expected to live by them. If anything, they are grateful for the clear boundaries God has provided for their lives.

2. Grace-based parents are committed to fiscal discipline. They understand that every penny they make and every asset they possess is actually God's property. They steward their resources

so there's always enough to get by, a portion to store away, some to enjoy, and a generous amount to give strategically to God's work. They do this because they live their lives with an attitude of gratefulness. They are grateful for what they have because they understand who the Giver is.

3. Grace-based parents are committed to physical discipline. They realize that age, disease, wear, tear, and gravity all will have an influence on the bodies they live in. But in spite of these human realities, they aren't going to roll over and play dead before it's time. Since their bodies are tools they depend on to carry out responsibilities, they do their best to feed them properly, exercise them regularly, work them reasonably, and rest them religiously.

4. Grace-based parents are committed to intellectual discipline. They are never satisfied with what they know. Since grace keeps others' best interests in mind, grace-based parents are always learning with the goal of serving the people around them more effectively. They read, study, listen, observe, and ask a lot of questions.

5. Grace-based parents are committed to spiritual discipline. They take responsibility for their own intimate relationship with God. They aren't in a codependent relationship with Bible teachers or spiritual mentors. Grace constrains them to individually study the Bible, pray, worship, and serve the body of Christ.

A GOOD FATHER AND HIS REBELLIOUS SONS

Now I'd like you to take these four types of parenting styles and slip them into the background of the prodigal sons' story. I want these to be reference points as you see this wonderful father handle two extremely difficult situations with his sons. It will be obvious how Clueless, EMT, and Special Forces styles of parenting would have thoroughly undermined the process this family went through and would have ruined the wonderful outcome. To set the stage, I want you to read the entire story of the prodigal son, even if you're already quite familiar with it.

Jesus said:

There was a man who had two sons. The younger one said to his father, "Father, give me my share of the estate." So he divided his property between them.

Not long after that, the younger son got together all he had, set off for a distant country and there squandered his wealth in wild living. After he had spent everything, there was a severe famine in that whole country, and he began to be in need. So he went and hired himself out to a citizen of that country, who sent him to his fields to feed pigs. He longed to fill his stomach with the pods that the pigs were eating, but no one gave him anything.

When he came to his senses, he said, "How many of my father's hired men have food to spare, and here I am starving to death! I will set out and go back to my father and say to him: Father, I have sinned against heaven and against you. I am no longer worthy to be called your son; make me like one of your hired men." So he got up and went to his father.

But while he was still a long way off, his father saw him and was filled with compassion for him; he ran to his son, threw his arms around him and kissed him.

The son said to him, "Father, I have sinned against heaven and against you. I am no longer worthy to be called your son."

But the father said to his servants, "Quick! Bring the best robe and put it on him. Put a ring on his finger and sandals on his feet. Bring the fattened calf and kill it. Let's have a feast and celebrate. For this son of mine was dead and is alive again; he was lost and is found." So they began to celebrate.

Meanwhile, the older son was in the field. When he came near the house, he heard music and dancing. So he called one of the servants and asked him what was going on. "Your brother has come," he replied, "and your father has killed the fattened calf because he has him back safe and sound."

The older brother became angry and refused to go in. So his father went out and pleaded with him. But he answered his father, "Look! All these years I've been slaving for you and never disobeyed your orders. Yet you never gave me even a young goat so I could celebrate with my friends. But when this son of yours who has squandered your property with prostitutes comes home, you kill the fattened calf for him!"

"My son," the father said, "you are always with me, and everything I have is yours. But we had to celebrate and be glad, because this brother of yours was dead and is alive again; he was lost and is found." (Luke 15:11–32)

As we've seen, every child is born with three driving inner needs: security, significance, and strength. The best way to meet these needs is with a secure love, a significant purpose, and a strong hope. That's exactly what this father ultimately does. But notice that Satan is also aware of these inner needs and tries to entice the younger son into meeting his needs with counterfeit substitutes: money, power, sex, booze, popularity, drugs, and other diversions.

The younger son was loved. He was set apart from the hired help by the quality of his clothing and by the privileges that came with being both a son and an heir. He got to go into the main house at the end of the day and sit down with his mom, dad, and brother to the smorgasbord that was available from the kitchen. He was part of the brain trust of the operation and had both his father's attention and affection. He slept in the safety and comfort of the family's inner sanctum. He was being groomed for greatness. He had a hopeful future as his dad taught him the ropes of the family business and prepared him for the day he would take over his share of the estate.

But this boy didn't want to wait for that day. The call of the wild was too enticing and the calling to the family was too confining. He wanted his rightful share, now. This passage proves that even if parents are doing a good job, they still can have serious problems with their children.

Although I'm convinced that there are things we can do to minimize the possibility of our children being inclined toward rebellion, it is equally obvious that sometimes kids who are being raised well can still choose to go their stubborn, self-destructive ways. And that's exactly what this younger son did. He was tired of life around the house and bored with the banter around his table. He had heard that there was so much more excitement in the glitter and lights of the city. With that in mind, he asked his father to allow him to pursue his dreams.

In asking for his share of the estate, he was asking for what he knew he was ultimately entitled to. It is not uncommon for children to start positioning themselves for a life of independent rebellion by taking advantage of some rights or implied freedoms that they know they have coming in their homes.

Whether the father saw everything this precocious boy had up his sleeve is unknown. But we can assume from the passage that this father knew his boy was hellbent on getting his hands on his inheritance and that trying to stop him would only make life miserable for everyone. He had the wisdom of a man who had been around the block enough times to know that the only way some kids can come to their senses is by facing the full consequences of what they think they want. Like the dog that chased the car and caught it, many kids don't realize how unprepared they are to see some of their dreams come true.

In order to establish the property rights of the younger son, the father most likely had to define the property rights of the older son at the same time. Our children's rebellion often requires us to deal with other children in ways we weren't prepared to. We don't know how long he waited, but this young prodigal ultimately put the gears in motion to liquidate his assets. There are a couple of possibilities for how he did this. He might have offered his property back to his father at fair market value. Or he might have sold his part of the estate to someone else, thereby requiring his dad and brother to contend with strangers operating next to their estate.

Our kids' rebellion often forces strangers into our family circle. Often these people do not share our value system or our goals, but because of their connection to our children, we have to deal with them.

It might be a toxic boyfriend or girlfriend; it might be their parents—too often these people have a completely different moral and spiritual orientation. It is like suddenly finding that part of your property is being inhabited by troublemaking squatters, and you can't control what they say or do.

This young boy, with a chip on his shoulder and a bag full of silver under his belt, packed his suitcase and took off down a road that soon became quite familiar to his father. It was a road that the father gazed at every day, watching in anticipation of his son's return home. But for now, the boy was headed for Party Central. Imagine a teenager taking every last penny and heading for the strip in Reno, Las Vegas, or New Orleans. This young man was a sap in training and a sucker in waiting. And as his silhouette disappeared on the horizon, the father knew that his boy had no idea how to handle what was waiting for him. He was taking the shortest route he could find to the underbelly of society, about to become easy prey for the predators who work overtime setting traps for fools.

Benjamin Franklin said, "A fool and his money are soon parted." He was right. It's mind-boggling how quickly an idiot with money in his grip finds himself empty-handed. When you have money to spend, you can always find someone willing to help you spend it. It's amazing how, for the right price, financial parasites will say and do just about anything you want. We don't know how long the boy's money lasted: a couple of weeks, months, or years. We do know that eventually this boy had frittered away his entire inheritance. He found himself totally broke. Meanwhile, a severe famine had gripped the entire country.

Rebellion has a way of taking people from bad to worse. Rebellion at its core is a determination to do the selfish thing or the reckless thing. So even without a severe famine, foolish people can find themselves crossways with the forces of nature, and they get there all too quickly.

It's interesting that the young prodigal's home—the home he'd so arrogantly abandoned—seems to have been famine-proof. This reflects the fact that no matter how bad the economy gets, farmers typically have something to eat. They may struggle to raise enough food for others, but they usually figure out how to keep food on their own tables. During the Great Depression in American history, farmers were notorious for always having something cooking on their stoves.

God has a way of famine-proofing people who live according to His precepts. This boy had chosen a different path. As a result he began to be in need. His stomach started to growl and his soul began to howl. Even after hocking his jewelry and extra wardrobe, his financial state continued to deteriorate. This would have been an ideal time to head back home, but true repentance usually doesn't come until you've completely run out of options. As long as the boy had possessions to pawn or employment to gain, his stubborn pride stayed intact.

The passage says he hired himself out "to a citizen of that country." The prodigal sought employment within the foreign world he had entered, which was like being a busboy at a topless club or driving a car for a mob boss. Rebellion often leads to a dependency on people who have zero concern for your best interests. In this case, a Jewish boy was feeding pigs, and pigs weren't exactly part of a Jew's kosher diet. The rebel was working to accommodate an industry that was utterly distasteful to the family he grew up in. Worse, when he evaluated his situation, he realized that these animals, which were considered unclean, actually had it better than he did.

Apparently, he was being monitored. As much as he wanted to bury his face in the pig slop and satisfy his hunger, he was not allowed to help himself to any of it—not even the pods he was feeding to the hogs. It is so painful to see the depths of disgrace rebellion will lead a person to. This is where EMT parents completely freak out. They come flying in with their checkbook, their pity, and their excuses.

This prodigal's father didn't interfere. And it wasn't because he was unaware of what the boy was going through. You may have noticed as you were reading the story that his older brother wouldn't go into his younger brother's "Welcome Home, Prodigal" party because of all the shameful things the boy had done. How did he know what his brother had been up to? For all he knew, his brother could have gone to a foreign city to use his money to establish a charity or build a great business. But it seems that this family had more than a hunch about where this prodigal was going and why. Maybe the father had received regular reports from "the front" about his son's enterprises and knew the good, the bad, and the ugly.

That's the way it is with prodigals. Regardless of how far they stray, invariably their problems slip back home by word of mouth. So here was this young man, once the cherished prince of an affluent family, starving and working for minimum wage. He realized that his resolve and pride were slowly but surely imploding. There was no way he could get ahead. Every day his living conditions took him a little deeper into hopelessness and helplessness.

RETURNING TO THE FATHER

Despair is often the gateway to the sunrise of a new day—especially if the despair is the consequence of foolish choices. This is where most repentance takes place. And when this boy repented, he thought of home. More specifically, he thought of his father.

He thought, *How many of my father's hired men have food to spare, and I'm out here starving to death. These people I'm working for see me starving and couldn't care less. My father wouldn't think of having people working for him that couldn't develop some margin in their lives assuming they used what he paid them properly. I can think of so many of them that have leftovers after every meal.*

In this state of emotional, physical, and spiritual nakedness, when he had absolutely nothing to hide behind, he thought of the way his father treated even the lowest of his servants. It was an epiphany that made him want to throw himself at the mercy of his dad. Not only did his father treat his hired help with great respect, he had treated this young prodigal with grace as well. Ultimately, it was his father's characteristic love and wisdom that helped the young prodigal come to repentance.

"'I will set out and go back to my father' . . . So he got up and went to his father." Isn't that interesting? He didn't say, "I'm going to go back to my family . . . or my mother . . . or my brother." The son wanted to go back to his father. He wanted to return to the one he had hurt so much. Why? Because he realized that the way his father had treated him when he demanded premature independence gave him confidence that his father would deal fairly with him now. Sadly, some kids never go home because they can't recall their parents dealing with them in understanding, patience, and grace.

The prodigal doesn't blame his father for the mess he is in. He's mad at himself and realizes there is no one else to blame. This is a wonderful awareness. Many kids maintain their rebellion because they think it is a legitimate reaction to all that their parents have put them through. Sometimes, they actually have reason to feel that way. Fortunately, that wasn't the case for this young man. He came from a home of grace, and it was that home he wanted to get back to as soon as possible.

The fact that he prepared his speech tells us a lot. Maybe he wasn't careful about what he said when he left. He wanted to make sure he didn't misstate the true condition of his heart. He wanted to communicate sincere contrition to the one man who deserved it the most. His speech tells us about the lessons he learned from his experiences.

The first thing his prepared speech tells us is that he knows he has sinned against God. He recognizes that the mess he made of his life isn't just a smear against his family; it is an insult to the God who gave him such a great family in the first place. We know we are genuinely repentant when we regret how we have treated the love, generosity, and mercy of God. This boy had spurned, mocked, and belittled the good things God had provided for him.

Second, his prepared speech tells us that he also realizes the pain he has put his father through. He recognizes the insults, the embarrassment, the loss of reputation, the financial hardship, and the emotional hurt he has forced his father to experience. No doubt, his little romp through the back streets of hedonism put a strain on his parents' marriage, cost his father status with his employees, and clearly complicated matters between his father and his older brother.

The third thing his prepared speech tells us is that he no longer sees himself worthy to be his father's son. In a way, this acknowledges his respect for his older brother. In comparing his rebellious attitude to the obedient and respectful attitude of his older brother, he realizes that his sibling is the only one who truly deserves to be called "son." Biologically he would always be his father's son, but in practical terms, he has forfeited the privileges that go with "sonship."

In asking to be hired on, he is saying, "I am so sorry for what I've done. I'm willing to pass up the big house with the dinner table covered with bounty, the evening banter of a family, the cozy and comfortable surroundings of my own bedroom. I'm willing to give up the privilege of being able to call out from my safe, warm bed, 'Good night, Mom,' 'Good night, Dad.'"

Always before, his security, significance, and strength had been because of his father's attachment to him as a son. He is now willing to have these vital needs met from the subordinate position of a hired hand.

THE LONG AND WINDING ROAD HOME

The boy had lots of time to think about these things while he walked home. I doubt this boy was a successful hitchhiker. Life doesn't offer many rides to hungry, penniless, tattered, barefoot, dirty, and smelly sinners. That's just one of the trade-offs to a life of rebellion; it usually leaves you thoroughly spurned and looking your worst. For this repentant young prodigal, if he wanted to see his father again, he'd have to make the journey on foot. And so he set out. And each step he took got him farther from his folly and closer to his father.

As an aside, this story tells us a few interesting things about this boy's mother. She married smart. She trusted her husband's decisions. She wasn't into doing end runs around her husband in order to rescue her children from their foolishness. She, like her husband, allowed consequences to unfold.

"While he was still a long way off . . ." Jesus tells us this boy's father had been keeping an eye on the road leading back home. He had seen his son disappear on the horizon so long ago with a wallet filled with cash, and he had been checking for him ever since. He seems to have believed the boy would once again appear on that same horizon, closing the distance between his stubborn heart and his home. And sure enough, the father sees a figure on the horizon. As the silhouette gets larger, somehow the father can tell it is his son. Maybe it is his gait, or the way he holds his head. He is no doubt thinner and gaunter than when he left, but there is no mistaking who is heading his way.

For the father, the response began first in his heart. That's where the boy had always been, even when he was off sleeping, sipping, and snorting his life away. Regardless of where he'd been and what he'd done, the boy had left home as a son, and in his father's eyes he came back as one. This father didn't see a beggar or a vagrant or an eyesore coming down the road. He saw a son whose choices had put some rough miles on him. He realized how difficult it had to be for the young man. Most people have the luxury of swallowing their pride in nice little bite-size pieces. Not so with this boy. He had been force-fed his pride in a humiliating feeding frenzy. The father knew the boy was taking a huge step in humility by coming back in this condition.

Let's face it, when one of our children takes off in arrogance, he wants to come back in a cool car, with a beautiful girl in the seat next to him, and more money in his bank account than when he left. That's what the boy was sure would happen. He knew more than his dad. He'd show him. Now he was coming back just as his father knew he inevitably would. But the dad wasn't ashamed of him. He was proud of him. His son had figured it out; he had learned life's lesson. He was a better son coming back in ruin than he ever was leaving in wealth. All this father wanted to do was throw his arms around his boy, kiss him, and welcome him home. How long he had prayed and dreamed and waited for this moment!

The father took off at a full sprint to intercept his returning prodigal. In doing so, we discover another reason why he was not only a great father, but also why he handled this rebellious son so well. This father wasn't worried about what people thought of him. He was a successful landowner, businessman, and leader of the community, and surely knew that with his position came protocol and a certain expected level of public deportment. People were watching. But his love for his son relegated all of these other things to a subordinate position. His love for his son was more important than anything else—his reputation, his wealth, and his status.

No self-respecting man of stature in that Middle Eastern culture would cinch up the bottom of his robe and free his bare legs so he could sprint. But the father wasn't preoccupied with image. He wasn't caught up in his stature; he was caught up in the fact that his boy had finally figured life out and made his way back home.

Before the boy could get a word out of his mouth, his dad just about tackled him, smothering him with kisses. When he had money in his pocket, he could get beautiful women who smelled wonderful and whispered amazing words in his ear. But once he was out of money, no one wanted to touch him. Now filthy, smelly, and unkempt, his father is pulling him in close. He's transferring the body odor of his son's clothes, the dirt and mud and pigsty smell of his skin, and the ratty hair and knotted beard to himself as he buries his son in his chest in a joyful bear hug.

The boy starts his prepared speech. He gets the first part out that he had worked so hard on. "Father, I've sinned against heaven and against you. I am no longer worthy to be called your son." That was all of his speech the father needed to hear. His son was truly repentant. This wasn't one of those practical apologies of convenience: "If my actions have hurt you, then I'm sorry, but you know you had really made life so miserable for me and I just needed to get some distance . . ."

His son realized he had sinned against God. He realized he had sinned against his dad. And he realized that as a result of his sin, he deserved consequences. If he had gotten out the last part of his carefully written speech, the part about maybe being taken on as a hired hand, the reaction from his father might have been something like, "Hogwash! Don't even consider such an absurd possibility. You always have been and always will be my son."

Notice that he didn't say to the household staff, "Get him some decent clothes to put on." He told them to get the "best robe." Just as Jacob dressed his son Joseph in a robe that set him apart, this father wanted everyone to know this young man was highly valued. He also wanted his son to know his arrival back home meant he was clothed in the garments of an honored member of the family. The tattered remains of his sordid life were to be removed and replaced with the best the family could offer.

I love the fact that his father told the servants to put the robe on him. This wasn't, "Find some clothes and give them to the boy so he can go off and change." Instead, he wanted his son accorded the same accommodations from the servants that any highly esteemed child of this successful man would be given—a bath, haircut, shave, lotions, colognes, and the best clothing that could be found.

The father looked at his boy's feet. These were the feet that went stomping out of the house and racing down the road in search of lust and luck. Now they were bare, covered with sores and mud. In that culture, honor was shown in foot washing. And this son's feet not only needed to be scrubbed, but they needed to once again feel the wonderful comfort of a good pair of sandals. Sandals were not standard parts of people's outfits. They were a luxury item in the warmer months, and most servants didn't wear them. This father wanted his son to have sandals.

But clean, scrubbed, coiffed, and clothed was not going to be enough. There was still one thing missing: the ring. This was the unique item that finalized the son's reentry to the family circle. A lot of successful people wore nice clothes and sandals. But the ring identified him with this father. And were such rings just lying around the house in abundance? No, this ring had been in the wings waiting for this moment. The father had longed for this reunion and had made sure all the necessary arrangements were made in advance to welcome his wayward son home. There's a good chance that this ring was one the boy originally wore before he left. Perhaps he had thrown it at his father in anger as he set out on his reckless adventure. Or perhaps it was a replacement for one that had been left in a faraway pawnshop. Regardless, a family ring was placed on his finger, setting him apart as a son of great status.

CELEBRATE GOOD TIMES; COME ON!

The day had started like most days around the complex: servants and hired hands doing the many tasks of maintaining a successful estate. The older son was out in the fields supervising. Mom and her household staff had been about their routines. Then all of a sudden the prodigal returns, and Dad shifts the whole focus of the operation. "Forget the routines; forget the chores; forget your responsibilities. It's party time! Call the band, set up the dance floor, get out the best china, and cook up those juicy steaks we've been saving for an occasion like this. 'For this son of mine was dead and is alive again; he was lost and is found.'"

I love this last statement. It tells me so much about the wisdom and grace of this father. He could have said, "This boy," or "This young man"; but he said, "This son of mine . . ." He wanted everyone to know this boy that had been through so much and had made so many poor choices was *his* boy. He had been dead. Sin was starting to squeeze the life out of him even before he left, and this father knew it would simply be a matter of time until all the dimensions of his life—physical, intellectual, emotional, relational, and spiritual—would be, for all intents and purposes, dead.

Let me point out another lesson we learn from this father: he was quick to bring his friends and allies into the celebration. He was not pre-occupied with image control. He had grieved during his son's absence, and when the boy finally returned home, he wanted all his friends, neighbors, and staff to join him in celebrating. How often we hide our grief and socially position our problems to protect our fragile egos. This father was too secure in his love for his son to play that dead-end game. This is the kind of man you want as a mentor to you when your son or daughter is going through rebellion.

A CASE OF SIBLING RIVALRY

And then there's the older brother. He represents two different people in this powerful story. He speaks for all the siblings who have watched a rebellious brother or sister shame the family, mock the parents, tax the family resources, and then come slinking home with his tail between his legs looking for mercy. There is no doubt that siblings of rebellious kids pay a heavy price. Sometimes, they don't get a fraction of the attention from their parents that an out-of-control brother or sister gets. It's easy to compare, to resent, and to want to exact a toll for all they've had to go through.

And then when you see the sibling reestablished in his or her position as son or daughter, with all the status and privileges that go with it, it's a bitter pill to swallow. It's easy to want to reject the party inside so you can wrap yourself up in your own pity party outside. *Here's my brother, center stage inside our house, dancing with all the pretty neighborhood girls, being applauded, and basking in Mom's and Dad's affection, and what did he do to deserve this? He made a complete jerk out of himself. And in the process he brought our entire family heartache.*

The older son also represents a category of "prodigal son." Step back for a second. Look at the bigger context of this story. Why did Jesus even tell it? Whom was He telling it to? At the beginning of Luke 15, Jesus was hanging out with some of His favorite people—the social outcasts of the day. A handful of Pharisees, spiritual snobs that dominated religious thought at the time, had upbraided Jesus because of His choice in friends. The Pharisees were the champions of doing all the right things but doing them for all the wrong reasons. They were sticklers about the fine points of the ecclesiastical law but lived disconnected from the heart of the original Lawgiver. They were scorekeepers and showboaters. And when someone fell short of their ridiculous standards, they loved to pile on.

Jesus appealed to the Pharisees' hearts with three stories—emotional, real-life word pictures. He tried to show the Pharisees why He was reaching out to religious outcasts. Today, His stories are familiar. One is about a man with a hundred sheep who loses one sheep and leaves the others behind to find and rescue the lost sheep.

The second story is about a lost coin: "Suppose a woman has ten silver coins and loses one . . ."[4] Her desperation over her loss is seen in how she lights a lamp and won't rest until she finds the lost coin. And when she finds it, she does the same thing the shepherd who found his sheep did, she throws a party and celebrates with her neighbors and friends.

Then, in case the Pharisees still hadn't got the picture, Jesus slips past their greedy hands to put His finger on their empty hearts. He uses the parable of the prodigal son to illustrate why He was hanging out with notorious sinners and why they should be, too. In this third analogy, He appeals to them as fathers. He knows that they, with all their selfish ambition, still understood the connection between a father and his boy. These men were fathers and their lives were wrapped up in their sons. And so Jesus gave them an analogy they could all relate to.

But Jesus mentioned two things in the story that had to poke them right in the eye. First, He described a father whose behavior was the opposite of what theirs would have been. And then to make sure they didn't miss the bigger point of the story, He used the angry and selfish older brother to represent their true attitude. Jesus was saying to these Pharisees, "These may be sinners who have lost their way and truly have made a mess out of their lives. But when they come to their senses and repent, God can't wait to restore them to their rightful place in His wonderful family."

These stories relate perfectly to Christian kids who lose their way. The three illustrations He uses—a lamb, a coin, and a son—have something in common. They were all three originally part of a group. They were part of the flock, the financial statement, and the family. In other places in Scripture, Jesus talks about going after people who were never part of the original group (i.e., unbelievers). But in this case, He's addressing things or people that were once a vital part of the whole. Jesus wants these Pharisees to see the vital role they could and should be playing in dealing with people suffering from the wages of sin.

A servant informs the father that the older brother refuses to go into the party. He's incensed that they're even having one. The father doesn't simply ignore the behavior of his older son, dismissing him as a selfish jerk. He loves this son, too—just as much as he loves the younger son who has found his way back home. The father goes out to talk with his older son.

First, he lets the boy vent his feelings. "Look! All these years I've been *slaving* for you . . ."[5] What a contrast between the younger brother, who barely feels worthy to be a slave in his father's house, and his older brother, the model son who feels enslaved by his responsibilities and position. The older boy had walked the straight and narrow path of obedience, but he'd done it for all the wrong reasons. Deep down, he resented his father and was indifferent to his position as a son. He saw his dad more as his master than his father. He didn't see his father's desires as "requests" but as "orders."[6] He was more of an "Aye, aye, sir" son than a boy who was grateful for the role his father played in his life.

His father handles this so beautifully. He says, *"My son . . ."* He could have said, "Listen, you obstinate little twit." But he didn't. He knew where his son's heart had been all along. He knew his older son didn't obey out of love, but out of obligation. He knew this son had been brooding and jealous over his father's longing for the prodigal's return.

Now he reminds his older son of something he had failed to see. The grace that was being extended to his errant younger brother is the same grace that had been available to him, too, even though he had turned his back on it and wrapped himself up in his legalistic pride. He had been living by the letter of the law, completely ignoring its spirit. The father says, "Listen, Son. Every day you've been in my house, I was more than happy to celebrate you as I'm celebrating your brother. But you weren't interested. You've got to open your eyes to the bigger picture here. Your brother had been given up for dead, but he's alive. He was totally lost, but he's found his way back."

FIVE RULES FOR DEALING WITH REBELLIOUS KIDS

This good father is a model for us, whether our children have left home as prodigals, are still young but demonstrating a bent toward rebellion, or are the spiritual equivalent of the "elder" brother—ungrateful and unresponsive. Here are five rules we can learn from his example:

1. Avoid the Guilt Trap

When kids make up their minds to go against God or against you, it's easy to beat yourself up. But losing sleep second-guessing and trying to figure out where you went wrong doesn't help anyone.

The first step to avoiding the guilt trap is to acknowledge the mistakes we've made. It's impossible to get through the parenting process without doing and saying things that hurt our children.

The second step is to take full responsibility for the harm our mistakes have caused. We have to avoid trivializing, rationalizing, or defending our mistakes and own up to them with unvarnished honesty.

The third step is to ask for forgiveness. Even if our child isn't in the mood to forgive us, we need to go through these three steps at the outset. Otherwise, we leave the door wide open for Satan to torment us with guilt. We also leave issues in our kids' minds that could actually prolong their rebellion.

Guilt wrecks our ability to think clearly. It does damage to all the other parts of our lives that we are supposed to be maintaining in the midst of a child's rebellion. Guilt causes us to hide from the people who could be helping us through our ordeal. And the most important person guilty people hide from is God. Guilt can cause our trust in Him to evaporate.

The prodigal son story is one of the best messages in the Bible about not letting parental guilt overwhelm you. Jesus uses this tender story to illustrate the kind of father His Father is. This is wonderful comfort for parents whose children are rebelling. It's as though God slips from the background of this story to the foreground in order to make a powerful point. "Hey, stop beating yourself up because you have children who rebel. I'm a *perfect* Father, but guess what? My kids still rebel. If I can't keep My kids from rebelling—and I'm God—why should you be beating yourself up because your kids are acting up?" The father in the prodigal son story gives no indication that he's acting out of guilt. And nothing in the Bible indicates that God feels guilty for the stupid choices His children make, either. Phil Waldrep captures this point well in his book *Parenting Prodigals*:

> We must use both reason and faith to move beyond any oppressive guilt we feel to experience the joy of being forgiven and loved by God. Don't interpret your prodigal's behavior as an indictment of you. Others may believe that lie, but God doesn't. You undoubtedly did the best you knew how to do. If you

wronged your child, respond to the conviction of God's Spirit and experience His refreshing grace.[7]

2. Pray, Pray, Pray, Pray, Pray

The story of the prodigal son doesn't actually say the father prayed. But it's fair to assume he did. He needed God's wisdom in knowing how to handle his son's request for the early inheritance. He needed God's patience when the boy took off down the road in search of his prodigal adventure. He needed God's strength during those lonely days, months, and years of wondering and waiting. He needed God's grace when the boy finally showed up on the horizon. He needed God's love when talking to his indifferent older son. These things assume a passionate life of prayer.

When we seek the Lord through prayer, He often reveals His answers through His Word. In fact, Scripture is vitally linked to the process of prayer. It's hard to be committed to either one without the other.

When we're praying for our rebellious children, we need to ask God to start with us. It's hard to see change in our children until God brings about change in us. In fact, it is not uncommon for our children to be acting out attitudes they've seen in us. Our attitude needs to be brought under His authority. We need to ask God for perspective on how to respond. We need to ask Him for strength to persevere and not give up.

When it comes to praying for our rebellious children, we can ask God to use friends and influences in their lives to turn them around. We can also ask Him to bring about brokenness in the child. Watching that prayer be answered can be very difficult, but we must be willing to pray, "Lord, do whatever it takes to draw my child's heart back to Yours."

Finally, when our rebellious kids come to their senses, we can express our thanks in prayer and ask for guidance in our future relationship with them.

3. Don't Be Afraid to Let Sin Run Its Course

Kids invariably find themselves dealing with the natural consequences of their rebellion: they lose friends, they get in trouble with teachers, they get kicked off a team, they lose status, they damage their reputations, or they hurt themselves physically. It's natural to want to intervene and try to soften the impact of these consequences. If there is no sense of repentance on the part of your rebellious child, then softening the impact of their behavior only inspires them to continue it. Learning things the hard way is sometimes the only way rebellious kids learn at all.

As with the father in the prodigal son story, there comes a point with us where reasoning, rules, and restriction no longer work. That wise father teaches us to allow a rebel to feel the full force of his folly. Misguided compassion would have circumvented the work of God, who brought the boy to his knees in repentance. Savvy parents realize that pain is often the best tutor.

4. Be Careful What You Say

There are several places in the Bible where we are reminded of the power of our words. Our words can be used for good or for ill. Rebellious kids have a way of storing up emotions toward our poorly timed words that could easily spill out of them later in the form of hurtful overstatements. Parents dominated by the power of the Holy Spirit want to submit their tongues to God and use them to solve rather than incite.

Not only do we see words of love and forgiveness in the way this father welcomed his boy home, but we also see some careful use of words when he was called on to deal with the older brother. There are two things I see this father doing when it comes to what he says. First, he corrects sparingly. He could have used this moment to remind his boy what a cold and empty heart he actually had. He could have lectured him on his ungratefulness, really putting him in his place. Instead, he simply reminded him of facts that shouldn't be overlooked: "Your brother was dead and is alive again. He was lost and is found."

He also affirmed the older boy by leaving the celebration to help this other son process his anger. He let the boy make his point. And then he acknowledged his loyalty and allegiance: "My son, you are always with me." He gave him credit for sticking with him and not following his brother's self-destructive example. He reminded him that the party inside the house for his errant brother was a small example of all the wonderful things this older son will inherit. "All that I have is yours," he says.

5. Once They Repent, Forgive Them and Restore Their Status

When we see a prodigal child making her way home in the distance, it is difficult to avoid being angry. Prodigals hurt people. They beat up their parents' hearts. They take advantage of their siblings, they jeopardize a family's reputation, and they sometimes drain assets. A person can heap only so much pain on others before there is a reaction. A mom or dad can grow indifferent. A brother or sister can decide they don't need the headaches. When the prodigal shows up at the front door (or the dinner table), hoping to be restored to his place in the family circle, it's difficult to not make him pay for all the pain he has caused. There's a natural urge to want to get even.

In fact, that's how this story in the Bible was supposed to end. It might help if you knew that this story of the prodigal son wasn't original to Jesus. It had been around for centuries. Rabbis would tell the story to teach a lesson about standing firm for family standards, regardless of the cost.[8] The difference is that Jesus changed the ending. And His editing of the story exposed the huge contrast between the heart of God and the conventional wisdom of humanity.

The original story ended something like this: The prodigal son returns to his home and asks to see his father. Once ushered into his father's presence, he repents of his sin, acknowledges that he is not worthy to be part of the family, and asks if he can be hired on as a servant. The father says, "No! Are you out of your mind?" He explains to the boy how much he has hurt his parents, how he has used his siblings, and how he has shamed the reputation of his family. The father not only refuses to welcome him back into the family, he also refuses to give him a job in the family business. He shows his son the door and bans him from looking up his family in the future. In the end, people applaud the father not only for his "tough love" toward his undeserving son, but also for protecting the integrity of his family standards.

That ending found no place in the heart of Jesus. The father in Jesus' story was all about grace, about helping an errant child get back on track. Obviously, he had squandered his inheritance and wouldn't get another one. There are natural consequences to a rebellious child's sin, even after he repents. But you can still show grace. Jesus described a father who ignored public protocol, washing away the filth of sin, restoring the status of sonship, and then throwing a party to celebrate the great ending to an otherwise sad chapter.

I think if you had been there when Jesus told this familiar story with a new twist at the end, you would have seen tears start to gush from the eyes of many of the men and women who surrounded Him. They remembered being rejected when they came back from their own tour as a prodigal. Since then, they had been longing to be embraced and restored to their families.

They were exactly the kind of people Jesus' story is talking about.

"WELCOME HOME, MY CHILD"

You may feel you're in that Clueless category of parents we talked about earlier in this chapter. Your kids have gotten the best of you, and you simply don't know what on earth to do. You may be one of those EMT parents and desperately want to rescue your child from consequences, but know deep down inside you shouldn't. You might be one of those Special Forces parents and feel like using every bit of muscle you have to simply overwhelm your rebellious child with your power and authority. Please, choose grace. Take your cues from the perfect Father in the Bible. Avoid the guilt trap. Pray—spontaneously, specifically, and strategically. Don't be afraid to let your rebellious child's sin run its course. Be careful what you say. And once that happens, forgive freely.

God has a tough time keeping His own children in line. If you've struggled with the pain of a prodigal under your roof, take courage from your heavenly Father, who has clearly been there and done that. And learn from His lead when that prodigal finally makes his way home.

In reality, there's a little prodigal in all of us. Some day you're going to make your way toward your heavenly home. And when you do, don't be surprised if a gracious heavenly Father runs out to meet you with open arms. And don't cry too hard when His precious and faithful Son takes your face in His nail-pierced hands, kisses you, and whispers, "Welcome home . . . for good."

DISCUSSION QUESTIONS

1. Of the four types of parenting styles (Clueless, EMT, Special Forces, and Grace-Based) which kind was your mom? Your dad? Which kind do you tend to be?

2. Tim defines love as, "the commitment of my will to your needs and best interests, regardless of the cost." How does this definition help guide parents as they work with a child going through rebellion?

3. If the prodigal son were your child, do you think your style of parenting would have made this situation better or worse? Why? How?

4. The prodigal son's father let his boy fall flat on his face and feel the full consequences of his folly. Would this kind of response come easy to you or would it be extremely difficult? How does this either help or hurt your rebellious child's recovery?

5. What are some lessons you can learn from the way the father responded to his repentant prodigal son?

6. How important is it that a rebellious child see the sin they've committed against God (not just you)? Why?

7. The prodigal son's father bared his legs, ran in public, and threw a party for his repentant son. How much does the opinion of others affect you when it comes to dealing publicly with a rebellious child? Why?

8. If one of your children rebelled as this kid did, would you be inclined to greet him like the father or like the older brother? Why? What are some things you can do to develop more of the attitude of the father in this story?

9. The father in the prodigal son story illustrates God. God is the perfect Father, yet even His kids rebel against Him. How does this fact help you when it comes to the guilt you feel when one of your kids rebels?

10. What is one thing God has taught you through this chapter?

CHAPTER 4

A Lesson from
the Italian Stallion

It's hard to believe the Christian environment we've put in place to encourage our children to a deeper and holier faith could be the very thing that drives many of them away from God. Unfortunately, it's true. Whether they demonstrate outright hostility or toxic indifference, children within our Christian homes are often driven to one extreme or the other by what we thought were the right things to do.

We're going to discuss in depth the built-in drawbacks of raising kids in Christian homes to see what those drawbacks look like. In the process, we'll learn how to counter them. But to set the stage for that discussion, I'd like to get out my box set of DVDs of the "Rocky" saga and show you, from the heart of this classic American film series, how raising kids in what appears to be ideal surroundings can backfire on us.

So many of the most treasured stories of all time are loved because of the metaphors they represent and the bigger lessons they teach. The Rocky series is a good example of this. America has always loved "underdog" movies. These stories align with the spirit of what made our country great. Our country was built by men and women who dreamed huge dreams but often faced insurmountable obstacles to seeing those dreams come true. That's just one aspect of the Rocky Balboa boxing story. It's a love story, a story of family and friendship forged under great stress, and it's a powerful story that reminds us just how fleeting fame can be. Even people who can't stand prizefighting are able to get into the bigger message that threads through the odyssey of the "Italian Stallion." But for me, the greatest lesson of this series speaks to some of the built-in problems of transferring a faith to our children—a faith they actually *desire* to embrace.

SLY STALLONE'S SUNDAY SCHOOL LESSON

I realize it makes some people nervous when writers like me invite a person like Sylvester Stallone to put together their Bible lesson for them. But as you will see, he did a tremendous job illustrating the process that often leads many kids to rebel against their faith. The parallel will be clear, but if you nitpick the details of the story, you may see the illustration weaken a bit. Let's study the movie from the backseats of the theater where we can take it all in, and leave the scene-by-scene nuances to more sophisticated critics.

In the first installment of *Rocky*, we are introduced to a heavy-weight fighter named Rocky Balboa, who fights under the moniker "The Italian Stallion." If you want to see him fight, however, you'd be hard-pressed to find him in any of the major sports venues that serious contenders fight in. Instead, you'd have to hunt him down in some of the out-of-the-way bars, dumps, and dives of Philadelphia. And when you watch him, the phrase "Italian Stallion" isn't what comes to mind. "Italian Meatball" seems more fitting. He's a no-name heavyweight has-been who's going nowhere in his career.

If he happens to win one of his unsanctioned bouts, he might make $65. After he pays his corner man and the doctor who is required to examine him after the fight, he'll be lucky to walk away with $40. He lives in a second-floor apartment on the back streets of a tough Philadelphia neighborhood. His closets and chest of drawers are empty. There's no car in his garage. His primary mode of transportation is his two feet. To augment his income, he's a collector for a loan shark. Mickey, the pug-nosed owner of the gym where he keeps a locker, summarizes Rocky's career in three simple words: "You're a bum!"

Enter Apollo Creed. He's the reigning heavyweight champion of the world. He has a title fight set for a future date when, through a series of unfortunate circumstances, the man who is scheduled to fight him is forced to bow out. Apollo demands that his handlers get the next opponent in line. That guy is unavailable. They look at the next man in line, and the one after him, and find that either an inability to prepare for the fight or current injuries have put all these men out of the running. Realizing that without a contender no one will take the fight seriously, Apollo decides to turn the event into a publicity stunt.

It is here that Apollo and Rocky are brought together. Apollo decides to do something that many boxing fans have often wished could happen—namely, give a contender with great potential a chance to bypass the normal process of fighting his way to the top of the ladder, drop him in the ring with the reigning champion, and see what happens. Through a series of arbitrary decisions, Apollo decides to give "The Italian Stallion" a chance to fight him for the right to be called the heavyweight champion of the world.

ROCKY'S CONVERSION EXPERIENCE

What happens next in the story is what I like to refer to as Rocky's "conversion experience." Much like the impact of a spiritual conversion, the opportunity for Rocky to fight Apollo Creed for the heavyweight belt causes him to do a 180-degree turn in his habits. There's a radical change in the way he views his gifts and skills, too. Rocky decides that he not only wants to fight Apollo, he wants to beat him.

This is where *passion* is introduced into the story. Rocky gets up on that first morning of training—well before dawn—to do the endurance part of his regimen. He goes over to his refrigerator, cracks five eggs into a large glass, and drinks them raw. This gives him the sudden urge to run!

You can see, during his initial morning runs, that he is way out of shape. His legs seem rubbery. His lungs heave as though they were trying to extinguish a fire inside them. As he makes his way through the back streets of Philly, down the boulevards, and ultimately up the stairs to the museum, his poor condition leaves him sucking for air. He finally reaches the top.

Each day he slips out into the predawn streets of Philadelphia to force his body into shape, and each day his desire for victory enables him to get stronger and stronger. It doesn't hurt that he has that full orchestra following him through town playing that famous theme from *Rocky* that would make just about anybody want to strap on Nikes and sprint down the street. By his final run before the fight, Rocky has carved his body into a tremendous fighting machine. You see a potential champion as he bounds up the museum steps two and three at a time.

Rocky is ready.

The fight between Rocky and Apollo is classic David versus Goliath. The heart, the passion, and the determination of Rocky Balboa empower him to go toe-to-toe with Apollo for the entire fifteen-round bout. They pummel each other with a vengeance—keeping the crowd on its feet for the entire fight.

Technically, the fight is a tie. Ties always lean toward the reigning champion. So Apollo wins the right to keep the heavyweight belt. But Rocky's passionate performance also guarantees a rematch. In movie language, this is what is known as a guaranteed sequel.

In *Rocky II*, Rocky and Apollo fight a rematch, and this time Rocky wins. Now he is the undisputed reigning heavyweight champion of the world.

ROCKY III

The Rocky we meet in the third installment of this grand story is a different man from the one we met in the first two movies. Instead of living in a second-floor apartment in the back streets of Philadelphia, this Rocky now resides in a sprawling mansion in the suburbs. Instead of wearing one basic outfit, this Rocky has closets full of expensive suits, shelves crowded with the finest shoes in the world, and drawers stuffed with the nicest watches and jewelry wealth can buy.

In this movie we are introduced to a new contender named "Clubber Lang" (impressively played by Mr. T). Clubber has been carefully and ruthlessly dispatching every man along the ladder of heavyweight fighters that leads to the top. He has earned the right to fight Rocky, but

Rocky's trainer has refused to agree to the fight. Ultimately, Clubber confronts Rocky in front of his fans and asks why he is hiding from him. Why won't he agree to fight him? This, of course, is the first Rocky has even heard of Clubber, and he quickly agrees to meet him in the ring.

Rocky goes home angry at his trainer, Micky, for not agreeing to a fight with Clubber. And Micky gives Rocky a lesson that has huge ramifications for Christian parents trying to raise dynamic Christian kids. Pardon the grammar, but this is how the verbal exchange went:

Micky: "This guy will kill you to death inside of three rounds. He's a wrecking machine, and he's hungry. You haven't been hungry since you won the belt. He'll knock you to tomorrow, Rock."

Rocky protests and tries to explain why he feels confident he can dispatch Clubber without any trouble. Micky puts things in perspective for him.

Micky: "Three years ago you were supernatural. You was hard and you were nasty, and you had this cast-iron jaw. But then the worst thing happened that can happen to any fighter. You got civilized."

Micky was reminding Rocky that when he first fought Apollo Creed for the title, he was hungry for the victory. He was willing to focus and sacrifice in whatever way it took to beat Apollo. Since then, however, he'd taken on the creature comforts that can easily distract a true contender. On the other hand, Clubber wanted the title so badly he could taste it.

THE EYE OF THE TIGER

Before I discuss the parallel this series has with so many families trying to raise dedicated, motivated Christian kids, I want to give all of you movie watchers a peek at the rest of the story. Rocky makes a series of mistakes in preparing to fight Clubber.

The first mistake is not taking Clubber seriously. Rocky's familiarity with the boxing ring, along with his previous victories over contenders like Clubber, has made him overconfident. As a result, he has no clue what he's really up against. That makes him vulnerable.

The second mistake has to do with the environment he chooses to train in. Preparing for a major boxing match requires focus, isolation, and denial. Rocky decides to turn the lobby of a high-end hotel in downtown Philadelphia into the staging area for his training. He's more interested in mingling with his fans than doing the sweaty hard work required to get ready for a serious fight.

Besides turning his training time into a circus, he also gets sidetracked by marketing and merchandizing the fight. His trainer, Micky, just about pops a blood vessel in his frustration with Rocky. But Rocky tries to calm him with assurances that everything will be fine. He's doing what he's always done—just in nicer surroundings and with prettier girls cheering him on.

When the fight finally takes place, it takes only two rounds before Rocky finds himself semiconscious and flat on his back. The new heavyweight champion of the world, Clubber Lang, is glaring down at him.

Apollo Creed, Rocky's former nemesis, has since become Rocky's dear friend. He insists on joining Rocky's training team for the inevitable rematch with Clubber, but he wants to take Rocky to Los Angeles and train in the old gym where Apollo got his start. One of my favorite scenes in the entire Rocky series is when these two former heavyweight champions come walking unannounced into this gym, which is crowded with boxing wannabes. It would be like Muhammad Ali and Joe Frazier walking into a boxing gymnasium today.

One by one the different fighters stop what they are doing—skipping rope, hitting bags, sparring—and stare at these two champions. And it is here that Apollo shows Rocky something that is missing from his life. He has him stare in the eyes of these different fighters and then points out what he sees staring back at them. He calls it "the eye of the tiger." It's an almost mystical look of determination and confidence that seems to emanate from deep within the fighters' souls. His challenge to Rocky is that he wants him to get that "eye of the tiger" look back into his eyes.

You're going to have to rent the movie to see how it all comes together. For Rocky, regaining the championship doesn't come easily, or quickly. But when it does, it's on par with a spiritual rededication or some "revival" feelings you might have experienced in your spiritual journey. And it also gives way to another great musical theme that the Rocky series is known for. It's a song that has become a mainstay on nostalgia radio stations and for years was the soundtrack for innumerable aerobics classes. What's interesting about the song "The Eye of the Tiger" is that the stanza in the middle perfectly describes many kids who have grown up in Christian homes.

> So many times, it happens too fast,
> You trade your passion for glory.
> Don't lose your grip on the dreams of the past,
> You must fight just to keep them alive.[1]

You trade your passion for glory. I've watched this happen in Christian after Christian and family after family. The metamorphosis from hungry, passionate Christian to one basking in the "glory" of the Christian life can happen to parents and children alike. And it's a catalyst for rebellion.

REDISCOVERING A PASSION FOR JESUS

Whether you like boxing movies or not, whether you've seen the Rocky series or not, a profound lesson can be learned from Rocky Balboa. We can learn how easy it is for well-meaning Christian parents—parents like you and me—to unwittingly create an environment that leaves our children with few honest options except to resist our faith.

Like Rocky Balboa, many Christians start out with a singular focus. For Rocky, it was the heavyweight champion's belt and the bragging rights to an indisputable title. For us, it is Jesus—the author and perfecter of our faith.[2] Knowing Jesus, enjoying Him, conversing with Him, singing love songs to Him, confiding in Him, pleasing Him, and wanting to know everything we can about Him—these are the characteristics of many Christians who are on the upswing of their faith. Every day is like a training session for the ongoing conflict we have with the forces of evil. To the degree that we train in Christ's power, stand in the ring in His power, and ultimately fight in His power, we get to see God do marvelous things in us, through us, and for us.

And then we get civilized.

The eye of the Lion of Judah—the dazzling gleam that consumed our vision when we first came to know Jesus—is displaced by the many good things we focus on in place of Him.

We get some spiritual treasure in our lives, and we start to acquire the creature comforts that make the life of faith more predictable and less demanding. Some of the spiritual treasures we get to cash in on include things like a primary knowledge of the Bible, great Christian friends, a friendly church, and early spiritual victories. The problem is that living in the midst of an ongoing battle for the hearts and souls of men is demanding, risky, and often lonely. And it is so easy to gravitate toward the things that make our Christian lives safer and more comfortable instead of things that make our Christian lives stronger.

Within two or three years of becoming a Christian, most believers have taken themselves out of the fight. The vast majority of them have a whole new network of friends. For the most part, these are Christian friends who present little risk to the ongoing battle with the flesh. In fact, these friends can become so much a part of the formula for success that they end up being substitutes for the power of Christ working from the inside out. Instead of Jesus, these wonderful friends become our anchor. Our weekly spiritual workouts are more in tune with a trip to Starbucks than a trip to the gym. Although most Christians still have contact with the unbelieving world, it's more accidental or professional than deliberate.

In the early, enthusiastic days of our faith, we move from knowing nothing about the Bible to knowing things like the books of the Bible, its major themes, some specific verses, and the rudimentary outlines of the gospel. It's easy to shift from studying the Bible as a means to know Jesus more to studying the Bible as a means to know the *Bible* more.

The church, Jesus' bride and joy, is first seen as a hospital for new Christians. They take their broken and battered spirits there and find healing for the things that have hurt them so deeply. But after they start feeling better, it's easy to start using the church for a comfortable family getaway or, even worse, a family *hideaway*.

It doesn't take long to shift from having a passion for Christ to basking in the glory of Christian busywork. Volunteering, serving, and participating in Christian programs are all wonderful things when done as an outgrowth of a sizzling relationship with God. But it's so easy to end up doing all of these great things for their own sake. Our children watch us change. Where we once looked like contenders who *could* have the eye of the tiger, we now look like has-beens who *should* have the eye of the tiger. When our kids don't see genuine passion in us or in our spiritual activities, that lack of passion invalidates everything they are being taught about the true heart of a champion for Christ.

It's also easy to rest on our laurels. We become like soldiers at a reunion, reminiscing with their unit about battles long past. Once we've returned to the bunker, it's human nature to slip from the passion of the front-line conflict to the glory of the victory celebration. Too many Christians stop sharing their faith on a consistent and deliberate basis once they've gotten a few years of spiritual victories, Bible lessons, and church experience under their belts.

It's only *human* to want to make our spiritual lives more manageable. That's the problem. Our human nature isn't supposed to be calling the shots when it comes to the daily challenges we face. The Holy Spirit should be guiding our spiritual natures to do that. When we don't stay engaged in spiritual combat, quietly, subtly, and certainly the strength leaves our arms, the sting leaves the tips of our fingers, the dance leaves our steps, and the passion for the fight leaves our hearts. It explains how we sometimes end up like Rocky—flat on our backs, in a semiconscious state, with the pressures of life glaring down at us.

In Search of Peace and Prosperity

Whether it's the parents' spiritual pilgrimage or the child's, the fact is that routine, complacency, and predictability in our spiritual lives leads to rebellion. And the easier we make it for ourselves or our children to live the Christian life, the lesser the value we put on an authentic relationship with God, as well as the more at risk they become to developing an antagonistic attitude toward God. Trying to distill God down to an elementary equation, a network of nonthreatening friends, predictable behavior patterns, or an "insiders'" language is all it takes to remove the one thing we need to keep our spiritual passion alive—God Himself. Eventually our confidence and power shift from the Lord to our equations, friends, systems, and pat answers. Since we are our children's number one teachers, and our words of advice are mere substitute teachers, it behooves us to take a personal inventory to see how much our lives contribute to our children's frustrations.

Added to all of this, the challenges our children face can actually be more complicated and sinister than the ones we encounter as parents. They lack the chronological maturity and the ongoing experiences to help them process the spiritual fights they are facing. They are struggling with fragile emotions, unmet inner needs, and unpredictable hormones. They might actually prefer to be in the middle of the boxing ring of life, taking on all contenders in the power of the Holy Spirit, but they don't know how. It's tough to find their way into the battle when the people around them have long since surrendered their passion for the fight and instead are enjoying the glory of past victories.

The participants in the children's, junior-high and high-school departments in many churches are much like the wannabe boxers that Rocky and Apollo found in that gym in L.A. They are hungry, anxious, and spiritually determined kids, looking through the eyes of the tiger. They are young people working hard with their trainers to prepare for their next bout for their faith—which usually takes place in school on Monday morning. Meanwhile, the conversations around the coffeepot in the adult Sunday school classes or in the lobby after the worship service have the hollow ring of people who haven't been in a bout for the Lord in a long time.

Parents who want to truly understand the why and the what of Christian rebellion need to first be willing to gaze into the mirror and study their own eyes. Take a look right now. Do you see the eye of the tiger or the dim stare of a worn-out spiritual lap dog? The answer may be part of the explanation for why one or more of your children are rebelling against you or God.

Maybe you're saying something like, "Speak for yourself, Tim. You don't know me. You don't know my heart. You can't assume where I stand in my relationship with Christ." That's true. I don't know you, or your heart, or where you stand with God. Only God knows that. What I do know a lot about is why kids in Christian homes rebel. And although there are other reasons, one of the main reasons has to do with the way the average family goes about living the Christian life. The goal is often simply to live safely and successfully—in "peace and prosperity." Parents want to live that way, and they want their kids to live that way, too.

Unfortunately, we can experience a safe and successful Christian life without being passionate about the Lord. As Christians, how do we measure success? In our westernized view, success is measured in ways that are easily quantifiable: how much you know about God, how much you serve, what public policy issues you embrace, what kind of Christian friends you have, your spiritual reputation, the kind of money you make, the amount of money you give to God, how few hassles you have in life, how well your kids behave, and how consistent your spiritual routine is.

The problem is that all of these things can be enjoyed without having to passionately walk with God. But our kids, especially our most honest ones, are looking for something far more authentic. When it isn't there, it's easy for them to be drawn to other options that work against everything we've tried to teach them.

Here's the good news. Just as Rocky figured out how to get the "eye of the tiger" back in time to defeat Clubber Lang, we can figure out how to get the "eye of the Lion" back in us. There are more battles ahead and more opportunities for us to passionately live out our faith in Christ. And the same thing can happen to our rebelling children. We need to take some advice from a man who has been there.

King David rebelled against God. He lost that lovin' feeling for the God who had so powerfully used him early in his life. It cost him and his family dearly. In his repentance letter to God, he said:

> Create in me a pure heart, O God,
>   and renew a steadfast spirit within me.
> Do not cast me from your presence
>   or take your Holy Spirit from me.
> Restore to me the joy of your salvation
>   and grant me a willing spirit, to sustain me.

Then I will teach transgressors your ways,
        and sinners will turn back to you. (Psalm 51:10–13)

David realized that before he could have an impact in the restoration of others, he had to first get his own relationship with God back on track. We can learn much from his relationship with God—especially if we are dealing with people (maybe even ourselves) who have lost their spiritual "eye of the tiger." Let's help them get it back.

DISCUSSION QUESTIONS

1. Tim makes a radical shift in this book and starts talking about the inherent drawbacks of raising kids in a Christian environment. Do you think it is fair to put the Christian environment on trial when it comes to discussing why Christian kids rebel? Do you think the Christian environment your kids are exposed to encourages them toward obedience or incites them toward rebellion? Why?

2. How does your relationship with Christ either compare or contrast with the relationship you had with Him when you first became a Christian? Is what you are experiencing now more passionate or more predictable? What effect do you think this has on your children's faith?

3. What are some of the things typical Christians or local churches do that cause us to lose the "eye of the tiger" when it comes to our passion for Christ?

4. What are some things we need to do to either keep from trading our passion for glory, or to get our passion for Christ back?

5. What is one thing God has taught you through this chapter?

6. We prefer our Christian lives to be safe and comfortable. The Holy Spirit tends to lead us more into a wild and risky Christian life. Which message do you think your child is getting as a result of living in your home? Going to your church? How does this affect his/her faith?

CHAPTER 5

Compulsory Christianity

I once met a family of cloggers.

Up to that point, I didn't even know what clogging was. Once I found out, I was amazed that an entire family would actually want to define themselves by this activity. But they did.

In case you've been living in a choreographical cave most of your life, clogging is a form of folk dancing that is built not only around the style of the dance, but the sound of the dancers' shoes on the dance floor.

Clogging owned this family. Their lives revolved around it. And it wasn't just the nuclear family I met that was defined by this style of dancing. Their extended family ate, slept, and drank clogging. We're talking a family tree filled with cloggers. Frankly, I can't imagine many things more frightening. The grandparents were cloggers. The parents, aunts, and uncles were cloggers. The children, nieces, and nephews spent most of their free time clogging. They showed me pictures of various members of their family in their clogging outfits. Clogging.

You have to see clogging to appreciate it. The problem with a picture of someone clogging is that it's a *picture*. You can't tell by a photograph if they are really clogging or just standing there looking like they are. And you can't tell whether they're any good or not. It would be like me dressing up in top hat and tails and my wife, Darcy, getting a long, flowing gown, and the two of us posing for a photograph in a Fred Astaire/Ginger Rogers stance. Trust me; in that case, looks would be quite deceiving. So I didn't know whether these were pictures of people in a "clogging pose" or just people impersonating cloggers (although it's pretty hard to imagine anyone actually wanting to impersonate a clogger).

But lest I questioned their authenticity, this family had cupboards full of home videos to prove they were indeed the real deal. They traveled all over their area clogging. They planned their annual vacations around clogging. The parents had met and fallen in love as teenagers through their involvement in clogging. Several of the aunts and uncles had paired up the same way. They started clogging very young. You could almost say that clogging was part of this family's DNA. Regardless of any other interests they had, everything was subordinate to their overwhelming love for clogging.

CHRISTIANITY AS A HOBBY

Clogging was this family's hobby. As an outsider looking in, I couldn't figure out the attraction, but to each his own. I may not want to spend one minute of my life clogging or watching anyone attempt it, but more power to the person who does. God is a God of variety, and life's texture is made up of people's different tastes. Nor do I have a problem with people making something like clogging their entire family's hobby. People without hobbies usually aren't very interesting. My bigger problem is not about people having a hobby, but about their hobby taking over life so much that they end up one-dimensional.

Hobbies have a way of doing that—especially to people with addictive or obsessive-compulsive tendencies. A guy decides he likes hunting and the next thing you know he's got every type of shotgun, rifle, and handgun you can buy. His life revolves around his next hunt. He thinks about nothing but target shooting, reloading, and ammunition and talks constantly with other gun lovers about their latest kill or acquisition. Name the hobby: fishing, sailing, antiquing, collecting specialty items, photography, or bird watching. There's either a way to do these things that adds quality to your life or the hobby holds everything else in your life hostage. With all the psychological quirks within my family tree, I'm just grateful my parents weren't into the accordion.

People don't realize it, but Christianity can actually become a family's hobby. For the parents, it might be built on a relationship with God, but it can easily be embraced as a hobby by the offspring. That's because of the nature of hobbies.

Think about it for a second—what do hobbies have in common? They are interests that bring joy to the ones involved, but they usually demand a significant commitment of time, and they almost always require a financial investment. A family takes up boating and the next thing you know they have a garage filled with all the paraphernalia that goes with boating, such as skis, life vests, miles of nylon rope, and navigational equipment. The family adjusts to weather patterns that complement their boating hobby. They might join clubs or regattas where everyone fellowships around their boats. There are boating magazines on their coffee tables and in their bathrooms. And it's not uncommon for them to adjust their wardrobe and even the interior decorations of their homes to reflect their nautical pastime.

A family's hobby is often, in reality, one person's passion (usually Dad's or Mom's) and everyone else's interest. Other members of the family might get a lot of joy out of it, but if it weren't for the passionate one, somebody the rest of the family loves or highly respects, the others wouldn't have chosen that hobby for themselves.

Obviously, some hobbies are individual in nature, such as stamp collecting or playing a musical instrument. The hobbyist can enjoy her interest within her larger family without expecting anyone else to accommodate it. But many hobbies, by their very nature, require perfect attendance from everyone else in the family circle. It might be because of the outlay of cash involved, or it might simply be that some pleasures are greater when they are shared.

With that in mind, maybe you can see how one person's commitment to Christ can be embraced by other family members as if it were a hobby. Church, Sunday school, even discussions about God can be an interesting part of the parent's (or parents') life, and the kids go along with it as much because of their commitment to their parents as because of their own interest. Besides, Christianity is not something you can easily ignore in a family. It's a belief system that has the potential of permeating every part of the home. If parents believe in it, kids just about have to be involved in it.

But just because something is the focus of a family while the kids are growing up doesn't mean it will be embraced by the kids when they get older. My boating example hits close to home for me. I grew up on the Chesapeake Bay. Many of my friends' families had waterfront property and the boats that usually go with it. The kids were involved in boating mostly because it was an inescapable part of their family life.

When storms came, the children had to go out in the middle of the night to help secure the boat. In the wintertime they had to assist with boat refurbishing. Throughout the summer they had to participate in the upkeep of the boat. But as they grew older, during their teenage years, many of them drifted away from their family's boating hobby. Other things became greater priorities. Inevitably, the father would complain that they never wanted to go out in the boat with him anymore, and the kids often caved in to his guilt trips and spent the day with him on the water.

That's how kids in Christian homes sometimes respond to their parents' faith. Since to them it's like a spiritual hobby for their parents, their interest in it might be more temporary than permanent. The good news is that although Christianity can be treated like a hobby, an authentic relationship with Christ can't.

What would cause a family member to embrace Christianity as a hobby rather than Christ as a Savior? Some families are enamored by the wholesome and pleasant activities of Christianity. They enjoy the fellowship, the music, and even some of the service opportunities. But they don't necessarily connect to Christianity through Christ. They are more drawn to God's people than to God Himself. Church is a great moral and social activity they do together as a family.

Let me list some questions that might help you discern whether your faith is a hobby or an authentic relationship with Christ:

- Do you go through your day thinking of all the things you could do that you know would make God smile?

- Do you have a passion for worship that goes beyond the time set aside for it in your church service?
- Do you go through your normal day with a mind-set of wanting to walk closely with God?
- Do you enjoy the people you go to church with, think of them throughout the week, and pray for them on a regular basis?
- Do you want more than anything else to be transformed more and more into the image of Christ?
- Do you feel hurt when you sin? Do you ache when you know you've acted unkindly toward God or toward one of His precious creations?
- Are you conscious of ongoing spiritual battles and constantly appealing to God through prayer for the Holy Spirit's power over them?
- Do you have an insatiable appetite for God's Word? Do you look forward to spending time with Him in the Bible every day?
- Do you consistently take responsibility for your wrong actions, make no excuses, and ask the people you've wronged for forgiveness?
- Do you serve in areas of God's work that stretch you and force you to function outside all your areas of confidence, doing things that don't come easily to you?
- Do you give money sacrificially, offering to God more than "tips" that can be easily spared?
- Do you have an ongoing love for the lost people that surround you, especially those whose sin has an impact on you?
- Do you live and long for opportunities to tell people how your relationship with Jesus started?
- Are you quick to tell others about the life lessons you've learned from walking with Jesus?
- Do you have special areas of passion God has placed in your heart that you go out of your way to meet, such as the hungry, the homeless, the sick, the disenfranchised, the unborn,

moral public policy issues, youth, divorced people, single parents, or foreign missions?

- Do you know how to tell someone how to become a Christian and look for opportunities every day to share the gospel?

- Is your concern for God's influence in the world bigger than your immediate family and local community? In other words, are you concerned about getting God's message of the good news of salvation out to the entire world, so much so that you are willing to do more than just pray about this issue?

If you couldn't answer "Yes" to the majority of those questions, then don't be surprised if your children's attitude toward Christ is more like a hobby than a life-changing relationship. As we saw in the last chapter, if we trade our passion for Christ for a convenient Christian experience, it's going to be very difficult for our children to develop a deep intimacy with God—at least not through our example. In these types of Christian families, rebellion is usually not a case of *if* but *when*.

The problem is compounded when parents unwittingly assume that their children's interest in Christianity is based on a genuine relationship with Christ, when in reality it is more on par with a spiritual lifestyle. They see the child participating in church and showing a positive attitude toward the things of the Spirit, and they draw the assumption that this child has indeed embraced Christ in a personal way.

Not necessarily.

Embracing Christianity as a hobby can so easily masquerade as a commitment to the real thing that parents can allow years of their children's lives to pass before they realize that the kids don't really have a heart connection to Christ. Usually, it's rebellion that tips them off.

CHRISTIANITY AS A TRADITION

Tradition is an inescapable part of family. For the most part, tradition adds a wonderful dimension to family dynamics. Just think of all the traditions that surround your family's celebration of Christmas. You may open your presents on Christmas Eve or Christmas morning. You always open them in a certain order; perhaps you save your most prized gift for last. You probably eat certain foods, visit certain people, and watch certain movies year after year. These traditions add to your family's sense of security and closeness.

I've had friends who, because of their nationality, embraced unique traditions. Whether they were Italians, Poles, Greeks, or Irish, there were certain occasions that drew them into time-honored traditions, many of which were deeply connected to their religious beliefs. We all now know about big fat Greek weddings. But my Italian friends enjoyed a lot of traditions around Columbus Day, and my Irish friends on Saint Patrick's Day.

But no one embraced tradition quite like my Jewish friends. Whether it was articles of clothing they wore or the way they focused in on celebrations like Hanukkah or Passover, I could always count on them to cherish their traditions. But here's the problem: Although they were Jews and passionate about their traditions, few of them were passionate about a relationship with the God of Israel. Most of them didn't believe in a personal God. If anything, they believed in their *traditions* and they believed in *Israel*.

These Jews loved the Torah and they loved to read the Hebrew. But few of them could tell you the actual stories in the Torah or—more important—what they meant. Often they were surprised how, as a Gentile, I knew more about the history of their faith than they did. They shouldn't have been surprised. That's what happens when you're wrapped up in tradition.

In a similar way, it is extremely easy for the children of Christian parents to connect to God through the traditions surrounding their beliefs rather than through an authentic relationship with Christ. Tradition places a lot of emphasis on symbols. Religious families tend to honor the symbols of their faith over the substance of their faith. Some of the symbols of Protestantism are church attendance, praying before meals or at bedtime, carrying your personal Bible to church, enthusiastically singing, and wearing Christian jewelry. Mom and/or Dad may have a living, breathing relationship with God, and one or more of their kids may be embracing passionately the symbols of their parent's faith. Unfortunately, these symbols cannot sustain them. Furthermore, Christianity, at its core, is not just something we do or something we know; it's Someone we love.

If kids are relating to Christ as a spiritual hobby or as part of the family's tradition, as they grow up it doesn't take long before they find themselves at odds with what's going on around them. Suddenly there's an incredible disconnect between what we assume they believe and what they actually embrace in their hearts. When this happens, a rebellious attitude can surface. They start to revolt against Sunday school, church attendance, family devotions, or having to pray out loud before meals. They might roll their eyes when you try to bring Jesus or the Bible into a discussion about them and their life. When you see this happening, it could be because they are relating to Jesus at a hobby level or traditional level more than a substantive level. Interestingly, their rebellion might actually reflect a yearning for spiritual authenticity in their family and an attempt to find it.

Keeping the Family Faith

Some children are simply functioning in a Christian default mode. They were born into a Bible-believing, church-attending family, and it's a foregone conclusion that Christianity will play a vital role in their lives—just not necessarily a life-changing one. It's a lot like being born into a family that loyally backs Democratic candidates and votes Democratic. The kids in these homes tend to think and respond the way their parents do. When they are older, their political convictions might lean more to the right than to the left. But for the corridor of time that they are under their Democratic parents' roof, they tend to share their political convictions.

You really see this in people's denominational preferences. If a young man is brought up in the Pentecostal tradition, he may never feel comfortable in a Presbyterian church with a more formal and conservative worship style. Church of Christ kids grow up to attend Church of Christ congregations; Baptist to Baptist, Bible church to Bible church. In fact, denominationalism contributes to the mind-set of Christianity as a hobby or as a tradition because children are taught to see Jesus through filters that their denomination has placed over Him. There are many inherent problems with this, but one of the biggest is the tendency for people to develop a love for their denominational uniqueness rather than a deep and personal love for Christ.

Think about how much Christians differ over styles of worship. Some go so far as to part company and condemn one another because of denominational preferences. Churches sometimes raise a certain point of doctrine to the top of their list, prioritizing it over all others. They do this at the expense of the full counsel of God. It might be the method of baptism, speaking in tongues, divine healing, world missions, evangelism, or the intense study of biblical doctrine. All these are wonderful aspects of the Christian faith, but when emphasized above all else, they can eclipse a close relationship with Christ.

Parents unwittingly incite their children to rebellion when they push them toward the spiritual hobby or the traditions of Christianity at the expense of a personal relationship with Christ. I recall a single mom who grew up in a Pentecostal church. I was a youth pastor in a Bible church at the time, and her daughter was involved in our high-school youth group. We were a nondenominational congregation that didn't emphasize any one spiritual gift over another.

This young girl was in the middle of her career as a teenager. She was pretty, with a bubbly personality. Several boys at school were interested in her, but none of the ones she liked wanted anything to do with her Christian beliefs. Her mother caught her sneaking out a couple of times to rendezvous with one of these boys. In her desperation to rescue her daughter from falling into a sexual trap, she started to almost browbeat her about how she needed to receive the "second baptism" (i.e., speak in tongues). The mom was convinced that if her daughter experienced this New Testament phenomenon, it would pull her out of the free fall she was in. This mother was looking at one aspect of her belief system as though it had supernatural power to reform character apart from a deep relationship with Christ.

Around that same time, I met a couple whose answer for everything their children did wrong were things like: "You need to read your Bible more." "You need to be in church more." "You need to get back in the church choir." All of these were symbols of their beliefs but could be done without any connection to the substance of their beliefs.

Kids are the first to see through this foolishness. It particularly frustrates them if they've been doing all these things yet not experiencing the kind of true closeness to the Savior they long for. When we make ridiculous statements to a rebellious kid like, "You need to read your Bible more," it simply incites a deeper level of rebellion in them. It says to them, "My mother (or father) actually thinks that if I go through the motions of our family's religious beliefs, I will somehow be affected by them." It just doesn't work that way.

THREE FATAL FLAWS IN CHRISTIAN KIDS

It is a great thing for a child to be raised in a vibrant Christian home. But there are problems inherent in Christian family life that, if we aren't aware of them, can draw our children into rebellion against God. The rebellion might be out-and-out anarchy toward the standards of God, or it might take the form of indifference toward the heart of God. Kids in full anarchy against their Christian family's standards can do a lot of damage to everyone concerned. But kids who have lost their sense of passion toward Christ can be equally toxic.

I have observed that there are far more rebellious Christian kids in the indifferent camp than the anarchy camp. Because the child isn't giving her parents any specific grief, they don't realize she is actually rebelling toward God. These kids jump through all the right hoops, but deep down inside they don't really give a rip about Jesus. You can find the source of their attitude in the way their parents or their church measures spiritual conviction—usually focusing on the behavior of the Christian instead of on the character of the Christian.

For kids like this, Christianity is all about going "forward," getting baptized, saying creeds or catechisms, and being able to fill in the blanks on their Theology 101 quiz. It's about spirited worship, taking copious sermon notes, and serving in the nursery. These are all legitimate and even wonderful things to do, but they are not the Christian life. *Jesus* is the Christian life. Not stories about Him or songs to Him or service for Him. Just Jesus. When the environment of our Christian life draws our children to activities surrounding faith rather than to Jesus Himself, you can be sure they will rebel against that belief system. Unfortunately, it's easy for kids in this environment to develop three fatal flaws to their faith.

Flaw #1: They Don't Think God Is as Real as He Is

When you grow up from the first day of your life in a certain environment, it's easy to assume and presume things about that environment— things that you should take more seriously. It's all part of being so familiar with something that you take it for granted. There is little sense of discovery and wonder in the commonplace. And familiarity lends itself to laziness and procrastination.

It's like the people who live in Brooklyn all their lives but have never taken the ferry to the Statue of Liberty, or the people raised in Arizona who never see the Grand Canyon. Because these things are so close, they think, *Oh, I can always go see it. One of these days I will.* The problem is that, for many of them, that day never comes.

There's another problem regarding familiarity with God in a Christian environment. You can feel like you never have to get to know Him because you always have. This causes you to lean heavily on what He does for you instead of thinking about what you can do for Him, and you never get to know Him intimately.

Two analogies might help you see where I'm going. First, let's say when you were growing up, there was wallpaper on the bathroom walls. You saw it many times each day—every time you used the bathroom. This went on for years. Yet if I asked you to draw the pattern of that wallpaper, you might not be able to, even though you looked at it every day. It was so familiar; you never bothered to study it up close enough to memorize its intricacies.

Another analogy may be wrapped around your wrist. Try this: if you are wearing a wristwatch, without looking at it, cover the face of it with your opposite hand. Now let me ask you a question. Does your wristwatch have numbers, roman numerals, or slashes to mark the hours? Think for a moment, then look and see if you remembered correctly. People often get it wrong. You wonder how you could have a watch for years, look at it several times a day, and still not know what it looks like.

The same kind of thing can happen to kids raised in a Christian home. They may never develop an intimate and personal relationship with God because He's been too much of a backdrop to their childhood to be part of the forefront of their daily lives, and because of that, they don't think God is as real as He is.

Flaw #2: They Don't Think Sin Is as Bad as It Is

People who grow up in Christian homes are perfectly capable of committing heinous sins, but they are less likely to. Conscientious Christian parents usually put forth a concerted effort to live moral lives, make righteous choices, and keep evil at bay. That's good. Obviously, no family bats a thousand, but those who are diligent can do an excellent job of sparing their children the wages of serious sin.

The problem is that kids in this environment often fail to understand the true nature of sin. They haven't seen its ugliness at its worst. Many of these wonderful homes rightfully spare their children those dreadful trips to the wrong side of town. But they also can unwittingly fail to give them a true sense of sin's power to destroy. It's hard to build a strong set of spiritual antibodies when you live in a spiritually sterilized environment. And it's hard to appreciate the grace of God when you don't feel you have that much to be saved from. Jesus' dying on the cross seems like a huge price to pay to a kid whose worst sin was stealing some change off his dad's dresser. There are few from-the-gutter-to-glory testimonies for most kids brought up in the pristine confines of a Christian family.

Am I suggesting that you allow your kids to experiment with serious sin just so they can appreciate how much they've been forgiven? Of course not. Nor am I advocating throwing your kids into the filth of culture just so they can learn how bad it is. That would be reckless.

But living in a biosphere isn't like living in the forest. Holing up in a fort isn't like hunkering down near the front lines. Whether we like it or not, a lot of kids growing up in Christian homes develop a very naive attitude toward sin. Meanwhile, the war that wages within may cause them to want to fly closer to the flames. Sin looks enchanting and alluring. This could be the very thing that lures our children into trouble.

The first two fatal flaws of being raised in Christian homes are that our kids don't think God is as real as He is, and they don't think sin is as bad as it is. But even if these two things don't present a problem, the third fatal flaw of being raised in a Christian home can finish them off.

Flaw #3: They Don't Think for Themselves

One of the age-old problems of Christian parenting is that we have a bad habit of doing our children's thinking for them. Our churches, Sunday schools, home-school curriculums, and even our Christian educational institutions have the consistent tendency of giving our children answers to questions they've never had to wrestle with. It's easy to fall into the trap of chewing their meat for them.

Life is tough. Real life is tougher. Kids are fragile. Time is fleeting. It just seems to make sense that if we help our children reason things through by reasoning it through for them in advance, they'll be more likely to grasp it. That might work with some subjects, but it can backfire when it comes to spiritual issues.

The person of Christ doesn't transfer well through spiritually sterilized environments or rote memorization or catechisms. Giving our kids the answers to theological questions they never ask or to problems they may never face is an open-book test that yields little retention. Kids need to struggle with their faith. They need dilemmas that force them to their knees. They need to be forced to follow a path of discovery that allows them to fall passionately in love with God. That's hard when all the blanks on life's test are filled in for them in advance.

Many Christian families would like to think they don't do this. They say, "That's not the way it is in our family. Our kids face the crucible." Many churches and Christian schools would like to say they don't do it, either. But the fact is, they do. We all do. It's just about unavoidable in serious Christian homes and organizations because failure to give our kids the answers in advance invites huge risks into the equation. There are a lot of frightening things that can happen if we switch our kids from the spiritual "Food Channel" to an episode of *Evangelical Survivor*.

These three flaws don't have to be foregone conclusions in your family. But parents who want to show their children the path to a real-life relationship with Christ do themselves a favor by being aware of these flaws and developing the spiritual savvy to overcome them.

A Marathon, Not a Sprint

Having kids in rebellion is never fun. But whether your kids are barely walking, too young to drive, or too old to "ground," you can gain some calm in the midst of their spiritual calamity. Understanding why they rebel, grasping what led them into misbehavior, and finding counter-measures can be worth your journey through the outer banks of hell. You might feel that your child's rebellion is like running a marathon with no clear finish line. But then again, you just might be surprised.

Start by asking yourself two questions: *Has Christ become a hobby to me?* and *Am I more in love with the traditions of my faith than with the Savior of my soul?* How you answer these questions, and what you do about the answers, will play a huge role in whether your children's rebellion is a brief parenthesis or will become their way of life.

Discussion Questions

1. If you were brought up in a Christian (or at least religious) home, can you see any ways that your family's faith became more of a hobby to you or one of your siblings? Why?

2. Tim asked seventeen questions to help you discern if your faith is more of a hobby or if it is genuine. Do you think his list is realistic or overidealistic? Why do you think embracing anything less than the criteria on that list lends itself to turning our faith into a hobby in the eyes of our children?

3. What are some specific things you can do to counter the tendency to turn Christianity into a family hobby?

4. Traditions can be wonderful additions to our Christian experience. But sometimes they become substitutes for a genuine relationship with Christ. What are some specific ways you've seen this happen in your life? What are some things you can do to counter this?

5. Why do you think living in a Christian environment lends itself to taking God for granted? What are some things you can do to keep Christ authentic and real to your kids?

6. One of the ways to keep your children from developing a naive attitude toward sin is to cultivate close friendships with non-Christians and stay engaged in the lost culture around you with the goal of impacting it for Christ. Do you think this is a good idea? Why? Does the thought of doing this frighten you or excite you? Why?

7. Do you agree with Tim that doing our kids' thinking for them, especially when they are teenagers, lends itself to their rebelling? Why or why not?

8. What is one thing God has taught you through this chapter?

CHAPTER 6

Cliché Christianity

"This doesn't make any sense. I put her in a Christian school. She went all the way through to graduation. We handed her Jesus on a platter. How can she act like this?"

I've heard laments like this many times over in my thirty-plus years of working with Christian families. And every time I do, I can see why the child in this particular Christian home is rebelling. I think to myself, *If that were the mind-set of my parents, I'd probably rebel, too.*

PURPOSELESS AND POWERLESS PLATITUDES

It's very easy to turn Christianity into a cliché. When we do, the purpose and power of our children's faith are diminished to a level of banality. Things that are precious become things that are predictable, and the profound becomes the profaned. What may surprise you is that one of the greatest sacrifices many Christian parents make for their children may be the very means through which their children's faith is dissolved into a series of purposeless and powerless platitudes in their lives.

Perhaps before we go too much further into this discussion, we ought to define this clever-sounding French word *cliché*. A cliché is a trite expression or idea that becomes meaningless with overuse. Clichéd also applies to words or actions that lose their punch or impact as a result of having no substantive connection to the bigger and more serious context in which they appear. Let me give you an example of standard clichés. Two friends run into each other on the sidewalk, and they exchange a greeting that goes something like this:

"Hi, John. How are you?"

"Fine, Michael. How are you?"

"Fine."

What did these two men just say to each other? Nothing! They simply greeted each other with the standard American salutation, acknowledging each other's presence and breaking the ice. But for all intents and purposes (speaking of clichés), no actual information or authentic communication took place.

Suppose, however, after this initial exchange, John asks Michael how things are going at work and Michael tells him that he just got laid off. And what if Michael asks John how his wife, Cynthia, is doing, and John informs him that they just located a lump on her breast and she's going to have a mastectomy the next day. *Now* these two men are communicating. They have slipped past superficial dialogue to the deeper issues that engage another person's mind, heart, and soul.

In Christian homes, many of the religious ideas, biblical information, and acts of service we are involved in can become mundane and routine. Even the words we use to express our excitement about God can become predictable and lose their impact. Phrases like "Praise the Lord," "Do I hear an 'Amen'?" and "Hallelujah!" can become empty fillers in our worship experience. After a while they have the tendency to sound more like tired exclamation points in a church service that have little connection to what is happening in the worshiper's personal life. Such words, spoken within a closed spiritual environment, are made even more meaningless with pointless repetition.

The less we appropriate God's power in our daily decisions, the more inclined we are to distill our beliefs down to the status of clichés. I once sat in church next to a man who attended Sunday services religiously. That Sunday the church was observing Communion. Rather than bringing the elements to the people, the worshipers went forward and received the elements from the pastor. This man got up to take his portion of unleavened bread that symbolized Christ's body, broken for him on the cross, and the cup that represented His shed blood.

Just before he slid out of his pew, he leaned over to me and said, "It's time for me to go get my weekly birth-control pill." In the process, he showed me an extreme example of how something serious and sacred can be turned into a cynical cliché. This was a man who was brought up in the church and came from a family tree that was crowded with preachers and Christian workers. He'd heard it all. He knew it all. But the disconnection between what he heard and how he lived caused him to trivialize that which is precious and profound.

How jaded a believer's heart can become toward the things of the Spirit! And there is another even more subtle way to turn our children's faith into a cliché. Most would never think that what I'm about to suggest could play such a significant role in relegating our children's faith to a meaningless exercise. It not only can, but it does—far more often than most people would like to admit.

I'm speaking of the problems that occur when we place the spiritual training of our children within the context (and curriculum) of their education. Without meaning to, Bible and theology can end up being viewed on par with history, social studies, and Spanish. The other problem inherent within this configuration is that it can move our children's academic pursuits into a higher and more significant position than the role the local church plays in their lives. God's truth becomes part of a schoolhouse routine. Spiritual passion is standardized and measured against a checklist from a textbook. Without intention, Christian education can turn our children's faith into a long series of clichés.

All knowledge and truth has its roots in God. As the Creator of knowledge and the source of all truth, God and His Word can become a fitting backdrop against which we study the broader disciplines of academia (math, science, English, etc.). A young person's spiritual and biblical knowledge can enhance her relationship with her Savior. But this knowledge can also cause God's profound truth to slip into the background of children's lives like the wallpaper in their kitchen at home; always there, but they'd be hard-pressed to tell you what is distinctive about it.

It's difficult to keep Jesus as a priority in our kids' lives when their relationship to Him is, among other things, based on answers to a test. There's a fine line between knowing God and knowing *about* God, especially when our Christian experience can be distilled into a comfortable catechism. Once our children know all the predigested answers, their faith has a tendency to lose the vital edge it needs to stay vibrant. And when we can live our Christian life with relative ease, when we can experience God's truth without much inconvenience, there's a good chance our kids will see Christianity as little more than a canned faith. It loses its authenticity.

TRUTH THAT WORKS

There are two inherent drawbacks with distilling faith down to an academic exercise. These drawbacks can cause faith to become trite, overused, and underapplied. One problem is that children are given answers to questions they've never had to wrestle with in the real world. It's way too easy for truth to become a "what" in their life, rather than a "why."

The second problem is that the Christian academic environment does not always lend itself to processing their spiritual doubts. No matter what they may be feeling inside, the answers they give to the questions posed *have to* be the ones they were given in the first place. Questioning or weighing something as profound as personal faith has a way of intimidating a lot of the people in the pipeline—especially parents. It also might involve taking some huge risks. Out of fear of losing our children spiritually, we can slip into the trap of assuming that answers poured into their heads automatically transform into life-changing truths. Not so!

A lot of Christian schools (and, therefore, homes) are hotbeds for rebellion because of a shift that has taken place in how contemporary kids come to the conclusion that something is true. Josh McDowell has done some excellent work at outlining a clear shift in how kids think today compared to how most of their parents thought when they were the same age. Because we assume our children draw conclusions the same way we did, we easily make the mistake of thinking they've embraced something deep inside when in reality they haven't done any such thing. And the more we pound away on them with all the answers, the more inclined they are to doubt those answers and to go looking for the truth themselves.

Josh explains that most parents grew up in an era that drew conclusions about truth something like this: *If it's true, then it works*.[1]

For instance: In the 1960s and 1970s, you could pull out a *Four Spiritual Laws* (evangelism) booklet, walk a person through it, and find many of them ready to receive at face value the information you've just shared with them. They'd read that God loves them and has a wonderful plan for their lives, that man is sinful and separated from God, that Jesus is God's only provision for man's sin, and that we must individually receive Christ into our hearts as Savior and Lord. The Scriptures that supported each point were seldom questioned. For most people, it was not whether they believed the points the booklet made, but what they were going to do about what they'd just learned. During that time, millions of people gave their hearts to Christ through that simple booklet.

But times have radically changed. People don't accept things of the Spirit at face value the way they did thirty years ago. We've moved from holding certain truths to be self-evident, to believig truth, like beauty, is in the eye of the beholder. Instead of truth being absolute, it is seen as fluid, relative, and subject to interpretation. Although the *Four Spiritual Laws* booklet still has an impact on some people, for a growing percentage, it simply doesn't compute.

For one thing, this generation isn't partial to the idea of laws and absolutes. For them, you can't refer to "God" and assume they are thinking of the same being you are. In fact, it's not uncommon when you are sharing the gospel to hear questions like "Whose God?" (as if there were more than one), or "I don't believe the Bible is some final authority, so Scripture doesn't mean a lot to me."

We could summarize the shift in thinking to a new matrix for this generation: *If it works, then it's true.*

If anything, today's culture is more like the culture of the first century, when Christianity was introduced to the world. Just about everything within our children's society is working off this new matrix. As a result, everything is in question. Even the rule of the law is becoming more challenged, and the U.S. Constitution is not being embraced at face value—as saying what it is literally saying. For example, people read the First Amendment, which says, "Congress shall make no law respecting an establishment of religion; or prohibiting the free exercise thereof." Their response is, "Well, that could mean a lot of things." Before the dialogue is over, the First Amendment is going to mean whatever the reader's personal preferences want it to mean. Truth is up for grabs in the average person's eyes. We are raising our children in a culture where "everyone does what is right in his own eyes."

When it comes to spiritual truth, they want to see those who believe it back it up with action. This generation's tag line could be the old adage, "Actions speak louder than words." Kids today are more inclined to believe God's truth and embrace it when they have seen it embodied in a *changed life*. They especially give truth weight when they see it lived out *under stress*. They see truth as most authentic when the typical human response would be to reject it under the given circumstances. And it's hard to make a changed life look real within the safe confines of a controlled spiritual environment. The environment, for instance, of a Christian school.

GOOD NEWS AND BAD NEWS

The good news is, children brought up in homes that believe in absolute truth are more inclined to respond to truth as absolute. This stands in contrast with those who are brought up in a relative truth environment. But here's the bad news: those same children are still inclined toward the "seeing is believing" mind-set. Actually, that's built into human nature (think: the disciple Thomas). All the disciples of Jesus had this same inclination. It was the effect Jesus had on them that they could see—the power to heal, to save, and to transform—that made them willing to die for Him. The disciple John said, "That which was from the beginning, which we have heard, which we have seen with our eyes, which we have looked at and our hands have touched—this we proclaim concerning the Word of life."[2] John had seen the love of Jesus work in people's lives. Jesus' love *worked*; therefore, it was *true*.

A safe Christian home doesn't necessarily offer the spiritual dilemmas that confirm God's truth through observation. A child may have been taught all the right principles, but those principles may never have been put under severe stress tests to prove they are true. That makes it easy for kids to start seeing the things we teach them about God as clichés, like nice little promises hanging on a refrigerator door by a magnet. This is especially true if parents aren't living the truth in their everyday lives.

For the record, truth is supposed to transform us. Jesus said, "You will know the truth, and the truth will set you free."[3] Jesus meant that an understanding of His truth has a liberating effect on people. It frees them from the tyranny of doubt, confusion, insecurity, and temptation (just to name a few). Bear in mind that Jesus made that statement in the context of living His own life as an example to the disciples of how truth, indeed, sets you free. It would have made no difference what Jesus said to His disciples if His example wasn't backing it up.

Furthermore, there were ongoing *dilemmas*, both while Jesus was with His disciples and after He ascended to heaven, that gave the disciples reason to put His principles to good use. In other words, truth isn't transferred in a vacuum. It cannot be embraced academically. You can quiz a person about what she knows intellectually, but it isn't a bona fide principle in her life until it moves from principle to practice.

The word *truth* is used in the Bible as a synonym for God's Word. Using the words interchangeably, David said, "Thy word [truth] have I hid in mine heart, that I might not sin against thee."[4] Besides setting us free, truth helps us overcome sin in our lives. Obviously, if God's Word were being transferred into our children the right way, they would be less inclined toward rebellion. So how can we explain the tons of kids in Christian schools, for example, who rebel against God either through outright disobedience or through the more subtle but self-destructive attitude of indifference?

You may be wondering where I'm getting my information on these "tons of kids in Christian schools." It comes from several sources.

KIDS WHO "SPREAD THE FUNGUS"

My concerns about the disconnection between what many children with an "exclusively Christian" education *know*, as compared with what they *do*, can be quantified in many ways. My number one source is firsthand observation. I spent four years in a Christian school and will speak more about that later on. Over the years I've worked with lots of rebellious kids in Christian schools, and for many of them, their rebellious attitude grew directly out of their Christian school experience.

Second, I've talked to a lot of Christian schoolteachers and administrators over the course of my adult career. They tell of the unique challenges they have in getting kids in their schools to live what they are learning. They've told me several reasons why this difficulty happens (which I'm outlining in this chapter). I've also talked with tons of kids in Christian schools. Some of them are rebelling against the environment they are in. Others are not necessarily rebelling, but are frustrated by the tension they feel in trying to develop an authentic and original relationship with God within the context of their Christian school. Many of these kids think their parents put them there with good intentions, but now they are facing some serious challenges in trying to live a vibrant Christian life.

It might surprise you to know that when youth pastors get together to talk about their ministries, one of the standard problems they discuss is the negative influence that kids from their local Christian schools have on their youth group. Often these students are the ones who are less inclined to participate in worship or take an aggressive role in outreaches to the unsaved world. And when it comes to studying the Bible, it's standard to hear that the kids from the Christian schools are the most disruptive.

Sometimes these students display indifference rather than belligerence. It's as though they've heard it all so much, they aren't really interested anymore. This becomes evident in their body language and the blank expressions on their faces—expressions that communicate they'd rather be anywhere but at church. Other times it's demonstrated in clear antagonism to what the teacher or leader is trying to do.

In youth ministry, this attitude is called "spreading the fungus." It's obvious that a boy or girl is disinterested in the lesson, and that attitude has a way of permeating the attitude of the larger group. If you ask these kids a biblical or theological question, they almost always know the answer. In fact, they are probably the most *knowledgeable* of all the kids in the youth group. Sometimes they are even convinced they know more than their Sunday school teacher (an attitude often proudly shared by many of their parents).

Spiritual arrogance in parents, by the way, almost guarantees that those parents are going to have serious problems with their equally arrogant child. These are children who have knowledge about God, but lack the passionate heart the Bible says is evidence of the Holy Spirit's presence. The Bible says, "Knowledge puffs up, but love builds up."[5]

We need to keep in mind that the Pharisees were the most biblically knowledgeable people in Jesus' day. But Jesus wasn't impressed. The New Testament writer James spoke to this phenomenon when he said, "Do not merely listen to the word, and so deceive yourselves. Do what it says."[6]

One of the ways you know kids have the Bible hidden in their hearts and not just in their heads is in the way they want to turn what they know about God into loving actions. They try to encourage and build up the people around them. Ideally, kids who come out of a Christian school should be a positive addition to what is happening in church rather than a subtraction. But that's not always the case.

Youth ministers have an expression for kids who are brought up from day one in Christian homes and are saturated with a lot of Christian information through a Christian education. They call them "lifers." These kids have had Christianity transferred to them in an environment that oozes Christian behavior and information. But that doesn't mean it has changed their life. Many lack a sense of awe about the things of God. That's the standard product of a system that assumes

God's truth can be transferred academically. It's also the standard attitude of people who are brought up in a system that does not legitimately put faith to the test.

Obviously, there are exceptions—lots of them. And these exceptions are wonderful treasures. Some kids from Christian schools go into church youth groups ready to serve as an asset to the youth pastor, whatever he is doing. They are excited about their faith, passionate about Christ, and in love with the idea of being a light for God. Their love for God and their sophisticated biblical knowledge is a Christian school's dream and a youth pastor's blessing. Unfortunately, these types of children don't represent the norm.

And it's not the Christian schools' fault.

Part of the problem lies with human nature. When you are in an environment five days a week that starts each class with prayer, where you have assigned reading in the Bible, where you take regular tests on Bible knowledge, where your other classes (like math, science, and history) drop biblical insights into the curriculum, and on top of this, where just about every kid you go to school with claims to be a Christian, it's real easy to overdose on all the "Christianity stuff." There's no "heavy lifting" as far as appropriating what is being learned. The environment is tailor-made to make you look, act, and talk like a Christian.

Unfortunately, by the time these kids get to Sunday school, they're on biblical overload. Sunday school or youth group is just a rerun of what they've been getting all week long. Many are simply tired of hearing about it.

Some parents defend their children's attitude, saying, "My kids have already learned all of this at their Christian school (or through home-schooling). You can't expect them to be enthusiastic about something that is already so much a part of their educational life." When I hear this, I always think the same thing to myself: *Get ready, Mom (or Dad). There are some pretty rough years waiting ahead of you with this kid.*

I even heard a headmaster and a couple of Christian school teachers excuse kids' boredom and negative influence as the result of being "so much beyond where the other kids from the public schools are." Once again, my mind says, *They may be beyond those kids in biblical knowledge. But they don't come close to them when it comes to love and passion for Christ.*

HONORING THE CHURCH AS CHRIST'S BRIDE

There is a tension among Christian school educators when it comes to the spiritual role they should play in their students' lives. Although they may not want to be a substitute for the role the students' local churches play, many schools unwittingly are. Some do it with unabashed deliberateness. Regardless of the reasons, the question should be asked: Is Christian education supposed to take the place of or undermine the work of local churches—either deliberately or passively?

Not if they want God's blessing.

I want to make sure I clearly state this very important point. It's something every parent and Christian schoolteacher or administrator must get centered in their minds if they ever want God to bless their efforts. *Christian schools and Christian education should* never *do anything that undermines what God is trying to do through His church.*

Here's why. The church is Jesus' bride. Christian schools aren't the bride of Christ. They may be considered a parachurch ministry, but we must never forget that parachurch ministries are not the bride of Christ. These institutions are not now and never will be the Church. The Church is the body of Christ and the family of God. It is a "cradle-to-grave" organization that places no conditions on who can participate. When it comes to the Church, "Whosoever will may come."

Parachurch ministries work in specific areas that align with their spiritual assignment and often work with people only during a season of their lives. Christian schools have the luxury of being able to set some standards on whom they allow in. They can kick people out if they don't perform to a certain standard, and they are primarily in existence to *educate* kids in various academic disciplines. Since Christian schools are not a church (and never will be), neither should they do anything to *substitute* for the church in a child's life or to *supplant* the church's work. Ever.

Last time I checked, if you really wanted to get on the wrong side of a man, all you had to do was speak disparagingly about his wife. Just try telling a man you appreciate him but think very little of his bride— which he loves with all his heart. See what happens. Or worse, just try wrecking his marriage. See how he responds to your trying to build a wedge between him and his wife. The Church is Jesus' bride. God will judge any and all organizations that work to undermine or substitute for His relationship with His precious bride.

When a parent or a Christian school has no problem wedging a child's education between his or her relationship with God through their local church, they're asking for consequences from God. And one of the saddest consequences of this attitude is the spiritual indifference or blatant rebellion of their kids.

We are not only supposed to enthusiastically participate in our local churches; we are supposed to go there ready to serve. Passionate Christian parents send their kids to church with a commitment to give even more than they receive. I realize that some parents wonder if their children are capable of offering that kind of spiritual leadership. They would be encouraged to see how many parents in churches across America have kids who are engaged and involved in worthwhile ministry week after week.

But if kids show up for church burned out and disinterested in helping the adults who serve them succeed, those kids have become spiritual liabilities. It would be one thing if they were coming out of an unbelieving home with little spiritual background. But when they are fresh from their classes at a Christian school, there's a clear problem. When they have the attitude of "I've been there and done that many times over in school, and I'm bored with it," you can't be surprised if that child ends up rebelling against God *and* his family. In fact, with that attitude, he already has. Christ has been presented to him in such a way that He is no big deal. It may even be that the things of the Spirit actually annoy this child.

NOUNS AND ADJECTIVES

Some of the attitudes children develop toward the church during their youth harden into habits as they mature. I'm old enough to have observed a generation of kids educated in Christian schools who were not encouraged to embrace Sunday school and service to the body of Christ while they were young. As adults, far too many have put their kids in Christian schools, don't attend much more than Sunday morning church, and seldom serve their church in sacrificial ways. Their educational environment, which was designed to do them so much good, may have instead conditioned them for detached and disinterested behavior when it comes to Jesus' precious bride. Let's look at another reason this can happen.

One of the surest ways to turn something into a cliché is to switch it from a noun to an adjective. For instance, if I say, "I'm a Christian," obviously I'm using *Christian* as a noun. It refers to a person who has put his or her faith and confidence in Christ. The word *Christian* defines someone who is a follower of Jesus.

If I shift the word *Christian* from a noun to an adjective, as in "Christian school," I am no longer using the word to refer to a person or a relationship. Instead, the word has now become descriptive of a thing, a qualifier, in this case of a school. The word *Christian* could have lots of meanings when used as an adjective. By using "Christian" as a description of a school, I, by default, disconnect it from a person and attach it to the priorities and methodologies of the school. I'm using it to mean (among other things) that this is a school operating according to Christian principles (whatever that means). It might indicate that it's a school that teaches Christian doctrine, uses the Bible in its curriculum, and infuses principles about Christ into the curriculum. A person might assume that all the teachers and administrators are Christians.

The adjective *Christian* could also refer to a standard that is set for the school by others. This last point is a two-edged sword. Because the school has used "Christian" as its clarifying description, it's impossible for the school to live up to the unrealistic expectations that parents and students will inevitably put on it. Because the school is made up of humans, they will make human mistakes. Yet the parents and students are likely to measure teachers and administrators by a much higher and stricter standard. This can cause a lot of disillusion in kids when they see a large gap between what the teachers teach and how those same teachers sometimes behave.

Added to this same dynamic is the fact that because the expectations and rules for the students in Christian schools can be arbitrary and even superficial (like clothing and hairstyles), a child can unwittingly confuse these arbitrary and superficial rules as somehow representing God's moral absolutes. When rules of convenience (which Christian schools have every right to create) are used to measure spiritual commitment, it is not at all uncommon for a kid to have a knee-jerk reaction toward rebellion.

It would probably be more descriptive if we referred to these schools as "a school run and taught by Christians." There's more slack available for people who say they are Christians compared to the slack cut for an institution that says it operates according to Christian principles. Regardless, using the word *Christian* as an adjective has the power of turning the school into more a caricature of Christianity than a true reflection of Christ, thus reinforcing the cliché mentality.

Also, parents sometimes choose to send their kids to a Christian school even if they aren't Christians themselves. In fact, that happens quite often. Although some Christian schools require one or more of the parents to profess to be followers of Christ, most do not set that standard. And no school can realistically verify that parents are committed Christians. Parents might want their children at the Christian school not so much for the Christian teaching but for the quality of the education and the personal attention available for their child. They may have also run out of other options because of a past history or failure or expulsion from other schools.

And of course, every child in a Christian school is not necessarily a Christian, either. I realize that many Christian schools require students to be believers in Jesus, but many do not. And, as with the parents, you can't always be certain. Also, when the children are in the early grades, a school puts itself on extremely shaky ground theologically in requiring personal salvation for enrollment. Such a requirement would be putting God the Holy Spirit on a strict timetable to get His saving work done. Most school leaders are savvy enough to know that you can't tell God He has to save someone before you'll teach them anything about Him.

All this illustrates my point: by shifting the focus from being a Christian (noun) to studying about Christianity or doing things in a "Christian" (adjective) manner, Christ moves from being my life to being a subject I take. Obviously, if a person is a committed follower of Jesus, the things they learn about Him could enhance their relationship with Him. But if she is an unbeliever, or an immature believer, it would be easy to decide that whatever the school has to offer spiritually is disconnected from any personal relationship she may have with Him.

Anytime we learn about Christ in a way that has little or no impact on our spirits, emotions, or lifestyles, we're in danger of turning our faith into a cliché. It's not that hard for me to get a passing grade on a quiz or to know all the right answers about God without any of it affecting me in a personal way. Once a belief system is distilled into a series of answers on a page or actions on a checklist, it becomes superficial to the people studying it. It's a paint-by-numbers imitation of the real thing—a cliché.

SCHOOLS THAT GET THE JOB DONE

I'm so grateful for the myriad Christian schools that clearly understand their role. They see themselves as responsible for educating students in an environment of Christ's love, support, and grace. It's clear to them that God has not called them to do the parents' job or the church's job. They don't get in the way of either of these important influences in the child's life. Rather, they simply equip boys and girls to be intricately involved in what God is doing through their families, their churches in general, their youth groups in particular, and through other outlets of service to the body of Christ.

The savviest Christian schools out there work overtime to show their students how to relate to kids from public schools in significant and substantive ways. They want their students to love and respect their youth pastors and workers, to develop a deep affection for the kids in their youth groups, and to experience a passionate desire to be used by

God as witnesses for Him to the unbelieving kids they encounter both inside and outside their schools. Christian schools that do this are doing their job.

Human nature is one reason kids get burned out on Christian activities. But there's a bigger problem, and it is the reason why many of the administrators and teachers in Christian schools feel trapped. They know they are on biblical thin ice on some of the things they are doing, but they don't feel they have much choice. That's because of the unrealistic view and expectations parents have toward the Christian school.

There are many good reasons to put a child in a Christian school. Sometimes the local school system is in disrepair and is having trouble delivering a basic education to its students. There are some children who simply thrive better in a Christian school. Maybe they need more individual help, or they do better in small classes, or perhaps the hostility they encountered in the public school was distracting and discouraging. Often these kids blossom in a Christian school. I've seen children who were discipline problems in public school become exemplary students in a Christian school. The firm structure, the committed and loving teachers, and the individual challenges were all they needed to get back on target. These are just a few of the reasons why Christian schooling can be just what your children need.

Christian schools work best, however, when they are extensions of a passionate love for Christ at *home*. Kids whose mothers and fathers are actively living out their faith in a grace-based environment may find that a Christian education is a wonderful complement to their home lives. This mutual cooperation enables the school to truly come alongside the parents and bolster what they are already doing.

But this beneficial partnership can be undermined by parents who approach the school with misguided assumptions about the role or effectiveness of Christian education. Many families turn to Christian schools with the idea that the school will be responsible for their children's relationship with God. No, it will not. It is responsible for educating students in math, science, English, social studies, and other academic pursuits. The *parents* are responsible for the child's relationship with God.

GETTING FROM THE HEAD TO THE HEART

To make matters worse, many parents think that putting God's truth into children's heads through their Christian school curriculum somehow translates it into their hearts. In actuality, it often does absolutely nothing for their relationship with God. It's just information about God. David said he had put God's Word in his *heart*, not his *head*. In fact, he said he "hid" God's Word in his heart. In other words, he engaged so much in a passionate study and application of God's truth in his life that it actually ended up imbedded safely in the inner recesses of his being. It was down deep where it couldn't be stolen by the powers of darkness.

Unfortunately, too many parents think that by simply putting their children in a Christian school and by the school, in turn, putting biblical knowledge and theological understanding into their children's brains, that God's truth just naturally becomes part of the students' spiritual DNA. It doesn't work that way. All they have is information in their heads. They may know the theological answers and make good grades on their Bible tests, but it's just theological and biblical information they are giving back. Knowing it and personally embracing it are two completely different things.

Obviously, children can move biblical and theological information from their heads to their hearts, but a Christian school can't *make* them do it. Nor is there anything within the system that assumes they will. That transformation requires facing personal struggle and learning to rely on Christ for help. Turning spiritual information from answers on a test to convictions of their hearts has to be done outside the academic environment.

The second factor in turning the biblical/theological information into part of students' spiritual mainframe is based on how deliberately the child is trying to let her light shine in an unbelieving culture. Is she engaged in trying to be a light to the world and salt of the earth in her contacts outside the school? Unfortunately, many kids in this kind of environment are discouraged from having unbelieving friends. Too many are encouraged to stay in a spiritually sterilized environment. It's an environment that lends itself to fearing and condemning those who don't run in their same circles. As we'll see in chapter 8, that is actually an excellent way to create rebellious kids.

The biggest determining factor as to whether a child's Christian education will be stuck in his head or hidden in his heart has to do with the home he comes from and how passionate his parents are about Jesus Christ. If students come from homes where their parents have traded their passion for Christ for the glory of the Christian life (as we discussed in chapter 4), or Jesus is more of a hobby and tradition than a personal Savior (as discussed in chapter 5), these kids are going to struggle at making their biblical studies personal.

Jesus said, "From the one who has been entrusted with much, much more will be asked" (Luke 12:48). If anything, kids who are receiving an exclusive Christian education should be leading the charge for Christ in their church and in the world. They should be the outspoken, passionate, joyful followers of Christ they've been learning about at school. Having kids from local Christian schools in a church youth group should raise the spiritual stock value of that group. Based on what Jesus said in Luke 12:48, these kids should make the youth pastor's job more effective and they should make things better for the other kids. They should also be growing up into effective and passionate servants to the body of Christ in the future.

I think it's fair to simply do an inventory. Are the kids in your church who come from Christian schools making your Sunday school system and youth group better or worse? Are these kids who have been taught the truth seeking out those who don't know it and sharing it with them? Are the kids who come from Christian schools stepping up to sacrificially serve in various capacities in your church? Are the kids from your Christian schools going on to make a huge impact in the cause of Christ when they grow up? If this isn't happening on a grand scale, the people in charge and the parents investing so much money ought to be asking themselves, "Why?"

FIRSTHAND EXPERIENCE

I went to a Christian college. I also have two graduate degrees from seminaries. All three schools were great experiences for me, but they were also a crash course in how easy it is to find oneself in a state of spiritual mediocrity. My college experience was especially eye-opening. My close friends and I unanimously agreed that it was one of the hardest environments we'd ever experienced in maintaining an intimate relationship with Christ. The problem lay in the fact that everything about the school was designed to prop up your ability to *appear* spiritual. With very little effort, you could act and talk "Christian." Simply obeying the rules listed in the Student Handbook, participating in class, and getting involved in the many other spiritual activities on campus would help you pass for the real thing.

But an intimate, passionate relationship with Jesus isn't about information and activity. It's about a personal, one-on-one discovery that is going on in your heart, regardless of what your Christian environment supplies. It was so easy in this setting to coast and let all the spiritual activities replace my own personal walk with God. Like a spiritual life-support system, the exclusively Christian environment made it easy for me to substitute it for the work of God's Holy Spirit in my heart. After a while, I realized that everything was just turning into a cliché. We talked about God in class and sang about God in chapel. We had required Bible studies on our dormitory floor and preheated devotions done for us by our early morning professors. All I had to do was move with the flow and keep with the rhythm, and I came off looking as spiritual as anybody.

But I was dying inside. I realized how much my faith was turning into a hollow shell. A chapel speaker would present a powerful spiritual truth, and it would have no emotional effect on me. I'd hear it and say to myself, *Yeah, I know that. I believe that.* But I wasn't necessarily moved to let it change my life. It was old news. I could have stood up and given the same points, but those very points were starting to have little meaning in my day-to-day life.

I was learning great stuff about God in my classes. I was studying New Testament books and making elaborate charts about them. But it was academic. Regardless of what we studied, it tended to just add up to be more stuff about Jesus. It carried little weight and really didn't mean much to me or play much of a role in my maturity as a believer.

It would be easy to dismiss this as a problem that had nothing to do with the environment. But keep in mind, this apathetic attitude wasn't what I showed up with on campus. I gave my heart to Christ in the middle of my junior year of high school. I was on a public-school campus at the time, and I immediately turned on my spiritual lights. There was an ongoing resistance to my faith from the environment that made me want to get stronger. The Bible was exciting. I couldn't get enough of church. I loved hanging out with my Christian friends, and we all collectively encouraged one another in the deliberate relationships we were cultivating with our unbelieving friends. I couldn't wait to tell people about the Lord.

But the biggest thing about that time in my life was the closeness and intimacy I felt with Jesus. We walked together and talked together every day. I would think about Him shortly after I woke up each day. And the last thought in my mind each night was usually either about Him or about my girlfriend, Darcy. But Darcy was equally passionate about Christ, so many of my thoughts about her were merely extensions of my thoughts about Jesus.

That all changed about six months into my Christian college career. Being at that college was like having a spiritual Thanksgiving dinner *every* meal. After a while, you just weren't impressed with the turkey, dressing, and pumpkin pie. I wasn't hungry. Another way of seeing it was as though I were involved in one long spiritual dress parade. The problem was that we were celebrating a victory to a battle that we weren't involved in. It just became too easy to take all of the spiritual environment and biblical information for granted.

You might think I was just an isolated case. I wish I had been. But the truth was that faith was becoming a cliché to me and to most of the people around me. And I'm not drawing this conclusion as a result of subjective observation. I'm drawing this conclusion from frequent conversations I had with guys and girls who were struggling with the same thing. We'd lost that lovin' feeling. We had developed a smug, know-it-all attitude of an indifferent, rebellious Christian. The Christian environment we were in made it easy for us to trade our passion for glory.

TWO LIFE-CHANGING QUESTIONS

I remember a pair of incidents that helped me pull out of the spiritual free fall I was in. The first was a conversation I had with a sold-out Christian girl who had transferred to my college from Moody Bible Institute. At the time, Moody was a two-year school. If you wanted to get a BA or BS degree, you had to complete it at a four-year college. We had several Moody transfers. I remember sitting on a bench out under a huge oak tree on the campus talking to this girl. She was filled with passion for Christ. She loved life. She cared for people. When she got in proximity to you, you automatically felt more valuable. That's because she was all about others. I never sensed her focusing in on herself. She wanted to live life making a difference.

Because she had something I felt I'd lost, I thought she might be a great sounding board for some of my internal frustrations. The main thing I wanted to talk to her about was how the Bible had become so academic to me. In fact, it seemed all the Christian activities on campus had become routine. I was grateful that when I outlined my frustrations, she knew exactly what I was talking about. She explained to me how environments that are exclusively Christian tend to have that effect on most people exposed to them. She said she'd struggled with similar attitudes herself early on in her Bible school career. That's when she let me in on a little secret that had made all the difference in the world to her.

"Let me give you two questions to ask yourself every time you are exposed to the Bible," she said. "Whether it's a Bible class, a testimony you hear, or a speaker you listen to in chapel. Regardless of what they are teaching, ask yourself this question: *So what?* If you can't figure out what difference that lesson or Scripture or testimony makes in your life, then it amounts to nothing more than information—biblical or spiritual knowledge that stacks up in the back room of your head collecting dust. So the first thing you want to do with everything you're learning is answer the question, 'So what?'

"The second question you want to ask yourself is, *What now?* It's not enough to define what difference a biblical or spiritual principle makes; you've got to turn it into action. It's got to convict you of sin or change your attitude or get you treating people differently or motivate you to do something God wants you to do."

So what?

What now?

If those aren't a standard part of the way a pastor delivers his sermon, a youth worker teaches his lesson, or Christian schoolteachers work through their curriculum, then it's extremely easy for the people listening to turn their Christian lives into a cliché. I was a college student. I was old enough to take responsibility for asking those questions every time I was exposed to God's truth. And I did. It revolutionized my attitude toward what I was learning. But we can't assume that children are sophisticated or savvy enough to do that on their own. Between the things we teach them at home and what they are taught at church or at their Christian school, we need to challenge them to personalize it with a "So what? What now?"

One of the best ways to get them to do this is by modeling it in our own lives. When our children know we are in the habit of personalizing God's Word and moving it into specific action in our lives, it can become second nature to them, too. If they are in a Christian school, it can become a way of thinking that makes all the difference in the world to them. This also works when your kids are in public school and they are wrestling with some moral or spiritual issue. These two questions force them to turn God's Word from abstract information to concrete principles in their lives. They also move His truth from a life lesson to a lifestyle. God doesn't want to be part of our minds. He wants to be alive in our hearts and moving our feet.

LOSING OUR SPIRITUAL EXCITEMENT

I said there were two great incidents that had a profound effect on me. The first was this casual conversation with a spiritually passionate student. The second happened in a chapel service that was part of a series of lectures put on at the beginning of my second semester. Charles Stanley was the recently installed pastor of the First Baptist Church of Atlanta. He had been invited to address us for something dubbed "Spiritual Emphasis Week."

I remember bristling at the title because I felt it implied that on other weeks we didn't have to emphasize the spiritual. Actually, as it turned out, it was well named. My college was savvy enough to know that the things God did during this week could have a long-term effect on students who paid attention. In my case, it had a lifetime effect. The school leaders were also savvy enough to know the inherent drawbacks of being educated in a spiritual environment, and they were doing deliberate things to help us overcome these drawbacks.

Charles Stanley taught from the passage in John 15 that talks about Jesus being the vine and we Christians being the branches. In his patented Tommy-gun style of preaching, Dr. Stanley kept firing away from the power and authority of the Scriptures directly at my heart. And then, as though he had hired a private detective to follow me around, he started talking about how easy it is to fall away from a close and intimate relationship with Christ in a Christian school.

He talked about all the things I talked about earlier in this chapter. He even mentioned how naive many parents are when they pay their kids' tuition bill and say good-bye after they've installed them in a dorm room. They assumed that because we were in some idyllic spiritual environment, that it would somehow create spiritual hunger and develop spiritual maturity in us. And then he said, "If you haven't found out by now, you will. This is an easy place to take God for granted. This is an easy place to lose your excitement about God." I wondered to myself, *How did he know that?* And as though he could read my mind, he went on to explain how it's the nature of the beast.

But fortunately, he had a cure for spiritual mediocrity. He told us that if we spent our college career on this campus just taking it all in and not doing anything with it, we'd be much like the Dead Sea . . . dead. As you may already know, the Dead Sea got its name because it is a large body of water, fed by the Jordan River. But it has no outlet; nothing flows out. It's rich in mineral deposits, but it stinks if you're standing nearby. Fish can't survive in it. It is a lovely blue color at a distance, but you don't want to live very close to it.

With this analogy, he challenged us to put some things in our lives to force our faith to grow and our relationship with Jesus to thrive. First he said that we shouldn't let our academic study of the Bible be a *substitute* for our personal study of it. I had made that mistake. So had many of the people around me. Studying the Bible for a quiz or a test is a lot different from studying it to draw closer to Christ.

The second thing he said was that we should be doing more than just attending a local church. We should be serving in one. Until then, I had been taking up a space in the pew. I was there only because I was required to be.

The third thing he said was that we should be developing relationships with people outside the safe confines of our Christian peer group. If we couldn't connect with anyone locally, we should be maintaining contact with high-school friends back home. But this was where he got specific. He said we should be developing these relationships with people *who don't know Christ*. He was careful to say this wasn't for the purpose of ambushing them with the gospel or trying to jam Jesus down their throats. He encouraged us to remain close to them so we could demonstrate genuine love and loyalty to them. From that, he assured us, there would be natural and comfortable ways for us to show them what the light of the world looks like and what the salt of the earth tastes like.

The last thing he said was that God had placed a passion in each of our hearts. There was something that stirred us and made us want to do something about it. It might be a moral or social issue. It might be attached to a particular gift or talent we had. Regardless, we needed to act on that passion and turn it into a ministry.

Here's what happened. I started using the two questions every time I studied the Bible formally in school, informally in my personal devotions, or heard it expounded on in chapel or church. God's Word came alive to me again. I didn't have to go to town to develop friends with unbelievers or become a pen pal with anybody back home. It turned out there were plenty of people right there on campus who didn't know

Christ but still needed a good friend. They are still close friends of mine today.

I taught Sunday school the next year in a poor Appalachian church. And the last two years of college, I pastored a little church about forty miles from my campus. I've always had a passion for the disenfranchised. I started teaching a moral lesson at the local elementary school once a week, and I became a big brother to two extremely poor boys in a town up the highway from the college. One of the greatest joys I had was bringing them to campus on Saturday afternoons and letting them eat in the cafeteria with me. Often it was the best and most complete meal they'd get that particular week.

And you can guess what happened to my educational experience. It went into the ionosphere. It turned out that the people running my school were very aware of the inherent spiritual dangers of studying and learning within the confines of a spiritual greenhouse. That's why they brought in guys like Charles Stanley, and why they assigned me patient and encouraging professors who could coach me about how to shift all the things I was learning from my head to my heart.

Education is very important, but it isn't sovereign. Parents that see their child's education as a higher priority than their child's relationship with God are just asking for rebellion to raise its ugly head in their home. Parents who assume that a Christian education is the equivalent of a relationship with God are deluding themselves. Education isn't meant or designed to serve as a child's spiritual anchor. That's who *Jesus* is supposed to be. Expecting your child's Christian school to be your child's primary spiritual support system is a good way to undermine both the school's spiritual influence and its academic effectiveness.

TURNING CLICHÉS INTO CONVICTIONS

I've spent the bulk of this chapter on how learning about God abstractly or trying to memorize Jesus by rote can turn a child's Christian experience into a cliché. Since so many Christian parents sacrifice to put their kids through a Christian school, and so many precious people sacrifice to work or teach in these schools, it behooves us all to make sure we are doing all we can to turn the Christian educational experience into something life-changing. I've also been speaking to a lot of you who have been disappointed in the effect of a Christian education on your child. But there's hope. Your child may be exactly where God wants him to be. He (or she) just needs to be squeezed!

We've got to squeeze them every day. We have to help them find ways to serve others, to test their faith, to move from Christian clichés to heartfelt convictions. We can't afford to let them take everything in and not give anything out. That's the Dead Sea syndrome. It stinks. And it leads to rebellion almost every time. It puts scar tissue on their hearts and can harden them against the tugging of the Holy Spirit. If your kids are given more, expect more out of them. And you need to lead the way.

When kids see parents who aren't resting on their laurels or coasting on their knowledge but are actively living a life committed to making an eternal difference every day, they are much more inclined toward a passionate relationship with Christ themselves. It will turn all they've learned from academics to action, from knowledge to wisdom, and from lessons to love. We need to show them how to serve and to encourage them to cultivate relationships with people who need a burst of light and a dash of salt. We need to help them pursue their spiritual passions. *We need to help them see that Christ is to be pursued personally, not just academically.*

Speaking of clichés, there are a lot of people that view their time at church as part of a weekly habit that doesn't have a lot of bearing on what they are doing the rest of the week. Kids walk into the youth group and people walk into the church service expecting predictability. We might want to call what we're doing over and over again "our traditions." But sometimes our traditions are really boring ruts. People come to church and hear the same songs, the same phrases, and the same lessons done in the same ways. And then they leave, with little or no difference having been made in their lives. Talk about a cliché. And frankly, that's the way some people would like it to stay. But we can't let that happen, especially not with our young people. Living with clichés sets them up for a life of rebellion against God.

We need to break any of the patterns that turn our faith into worn-out, overused platitudes. When I was a kid growing up in a little Baptist church, the pastor would do the sermon, have an invitation, and then while some other person was closing in prayer, he'd slip out to the lobby so people could shake hands with him as they went out. Same old, same old.

"Good sermon, Pastor."

"You really hit the nail on the head."

"Boy, that was a good one today, Pastor."

And then they'd light their cigarettes, get in their cars, drive home, and pick up where they left off before they slipped into their little parentheses with God.

Just once, I wanted the pastor to respond to one of these Christian clichés with a mini-salvo of questions.

Parishioner: "Nice sermon, Pastor. You really delivered a good one."

Pastor: "Really, what part of the message affected you the most? What did God say to you personally through it? What difference will what I said make in the grand scheme of your life? In fact, what specifically are you going to do or change in your life as a result of it?"

Obviously, cornering some unsuspecting clichéd Christian like that could cause more trouble than it's worth. But it's a reminder of how easy it is to turn spiritual events into spiritually meaningless exercises. It's a problem that many kids in our Christian schools deal with day in and day out. Spiritual clichés are toxic. As we've seen, they can lead to rebellion among the very boys and girls who have been given the best opportunity for a healthy spiritual life.

MAKING THE MOST OF A CHRISTIAN SCHOOL EDUCATION

Parents who ponder the ills of our public educational system often turn to Christian schools as the ultimate antidote. But when you choose to put your children within this system, it's easy to develop a false sense of security about your child's spiritual well-being—as though none of those ills exist in a Christian school environment. Without realizing it, there is a natural tendency to assume that your job will be a lot easier with your children safe within the bunker of the Christian school.

If you allow yourself to embrace such a false assumption, you'll let down your guard. Like the commanding officer at a military base built safe within the borders of a peaceful nation, you might figure that since the threat is so distant, day-to-day vigilance isn't as necessary. It's a phony sense of safety that causes a lot of the ongoing drilling and training to fall by the wayside. Parents stop the dinner table discussions on moral issues, the fervent prayers, the monitoring of friends, the passing down of values, and the deliberate teaching by example.

One of the biggest mistakes is that they stop utilizing the church as their greatest ally. It would be like our country telling our allies, "We've got everything under control. The enemy is at bay. We don't need you guys anymore." Meanwhile, our weapons get dirty, our uniforms get sloppy, and we stop posting guards on the wall and at the gates. That's when the enemy slips in. Not only does the enemy go unchallenged, he often goes unrecognized . . . until it's too late.

The purpose of a Christian school is to provide your child with a comprehensive education against the backdrop of a Christian world-view. You cannot subcontract your role as a parent, nor should it take the place of your local church. To have such expectations is irresponsible Christian parenting and leaves the door open for rebellion.

Maybe that's why so many of the conscientious Christian kids in the public schools aren't inclined to rebel or feel the need to rebel. They can't afford to let their guard down. For them, it's either spiritual vigilance or spiritual annihilation. Parents who feel they can let their guards down simply because their children are in Christian schools set their children up for a toxic spiritual apathy that can only lead to their defeat. It's a naiveté that Satan loves to use against them. Never forget that Satan "prowls around like a roaring lion looking for someone to devour."[7] He loves it even more if they are wearing plaid, pleated skirts and blue button-down shirts.

If you want to help the people be more effective who serve your child at his or her Christian school, if you want to help keep your child from developing a bored, indifferent, and rebellious attitude toward what he is learning; here are some guidelines to keep in mind:

- Make sure the school never takes the place of the church in your child's life.
- Expect your children to be active contributing members of their church youth group.
- Teach your kids to serve others, giving out of the abundance of their excellent education.
- Don't make it easy for kids to harbor a judgmental or critical spirit against other believers or the people who serve them at their church.
- Expect your children to be leaders and contributors to their school, their sports, their friends, and their youth group.
- Keep them on the front lines in the battle for the kingdom of God. Help your kids develop outlets where they can be the light of the world and the salt of the earth (neighbors, unbelieving friends, sports, music groups, etc.).
- Expect the school to cover the academics while taking your proper role as the person primarily responsible for your children's spiritual and social training.

DISCUSSION QUESTIONS

1. Have you seen any of the things that were vital parts of your early faith become a cliché in your life? What things? How do you think this affects your children's view of God?
2. Although Tim has a high regard for the people toiling in our Christian schools, he's concerned that the very nature of the environment of Christian education can turn much of what a child believes into a cliché. Have you observed this phenomenon? In what ways?
3. Does it surprise you that kids from Christian schools often become negative influences in their churches' Sunday schools and youth ministries? Do you think it is fair to expect a higher level of Christian passion from kids who have been given more?

4. What role do the parents of kids who go to Christian schools play in those children's attitudes toward Christ? What role do they play in a child's attitude toward their local church? What are some specific things parents should do (or not do) to improve their children's attitudes toward God and the church?

5. Do you think we create an environment that is more conducive to rebellion when we use *Christian* as an adjective, as in the term "Christian school"? Why or why not? Do you think unrealistically high standards are placed on schools that claim to be "Christian" in nature? How would this lend itself to kids in these schools rebelling?

6. Because parents pay so much to send their kids to a Christian school, many feel that the school should carry much of the burden for developing the child's spiritual character and passion. Is this a reasonable expectation? How do you think this plays into the kids in this environment rebelling?

7. Tim wrote, "The biggest determining factor as to whether a child's Christian education will be stuck in his head or hidden in his heart has to do with the home he comes from and how passionate his parents are about Jesus Christ." Do you really think parents play that big of a role? How does that make you feel when it comes to the issue of one of your kids rebelling?

8. Do you think the moral challenges that Christian kids face in public schools (or non-Christian private schools) can have a positive effect on them? What would be the biggest factors in whether kids in public schools rose to the challenge rather than succumbed to it?

9. How much do your personal fears about the wicked culture surrounding your kids and your kids' vulnerable nature play into your choice of how your kids are educated? Does your attitude communicate a confidence in God or does it give your children reason to question His power?

10. What is one thing God has taught you through this chapter?

CHAPTER 7

Comfortable Christianity

When my cell phone started ringing, I had just finished making a cut with my Skil saw. It was 9:30 on Monday evening, the first week in December. I was at our church working with three other men to build the set for the Christmas musical. One of the men was my son-in-law, Michael, who was the project boss. Michael had been recruited by the music department at our church to create the perfect context for the series of events that were to occur throughout the Advent season. Everything was going to lead up to an elaborate musical that would be seen and heard by thousands of visitors from our community. My son-in-law doesn't believe in shortchanging God's message, and he had designed a two-and-a-half-story set, centering on a Georgian mansion complete with big picture windows, a charming front porch, and a second-story balcony. We were building far more than a backdrop for this wonderful story of God in a manger—we were building a house.

Woodworking is my hobby. That's one of the reasons I was on his work crew. The other reason is that the music department at our church has never invited me to sing with them. This seemed the better way to do my part in helping to get out the Christmas message. The problem was that we had to get the entire set built, painted, and wired with lights before the next Sunday. The second problem was that different choirs were rehearsing every night. That meant we couldn't get to work until around 9:00 P.M. every evening. And since we all worked elsewhere during the day, we knew we were going to have to do the bulk of the building every night from 9:00 P.M. to 1:00 A.M. until it was completely done.

We were just picking up a head of steam when a phone call came in from my wife, Darcy. She had just received a call from our son Cody, saying our van had just been stolen. Cody had called from the headquarters of an inner-city ministry in downtown Phoenix. He and his sister Shiloh had been going down there every Monday night since the beginning of the semester to put on a program for inner-city kids.

This was the second year they had been working with this ministry, and they had really grown to love the kids they worked with. They not only enjoyed the chance to work hand in hand with these kids, but they loved practicing their Spanish while they told them about Jesus. That particular evening, Cody had also taken our youngest son, Colt, with him to play the drums for the worship time. Another friend of Cody's had stopped by our house in a pickup truck to take Colt and his drum set.

Cody had, as usual, driven our well-used Dodge Caravan down there that night to transport himself, Shiloh, and four other high-school kids that served with them. Once they finished their work for the evening, they went out to pack up the van and realized it was missing. Cody called the Phoenix police, and they were there with him taking down all the information.

I had my small car with me, so that meant I would have to go home and get Darcy's bigger SUV before I could run downtown and pick up all the kids. As I drove to our house, Darcy called me again on my cell phone. She had a real sense of urgency in her voice. "Tim, Cody's journal was in the van."

Our son Cody is, among many other things, a musician. Over the years he has written several dozen songs, and he always recorded them in his journal. There were no copies. Other than the handful of songs he had recorded, the only way he could reference his songs was from that journal. The car meant nothing to me. It was just a piece of equipment. We could get another one. That journal, however, meant everything to me—because Cody meant everything to me.

A PRAYER FOR HELP

I had to drive about twenty miles to reach the kids. On the way down, I prayed something like this: "Lord Jesus, thank You that everyone is okay. That van is Your van, and if You choose for us to lose it tonight, so be it. But, Lord, You know how precious Cody's journal is to him. Please help us recover it." What I didn't realize until later was that Cody and all the kids with him had joined hands, also praying that God would see fit to get his journal back to him.

My cell phone rang again. Darcy. It seemed a Phoenix policewoman had just rung our doorbell. She wanted to know if we were missing a vehicle. Cody was still talking to the policeman who was taking down information at the site of the theft and had not yet put the report in the central police computer. At the same time, two Phoenix police officers had been patrolling about five miles from where the theft had taken place and saw two boys driving recklessly in a van. They pulled them over. They were ages twelve and thirteen.

When the officers checked their names against the Phoenix police data bank, it turned out this was the second time one of the boys had stolen a car, and the fourth time for the other. What was really interesting was, they were not the first ones to steal our van that night. They had come upon it just as the guy who had originally stolen it was getting out of it and riffling through all its contents. When he abandoned it in their neighborhood, they decided to take it for its second drive as a stolen vehicle.

When I arrived at the inner-city headquarters, one of the first things I noticed about Cody, Shiloh, Colt, and all their friends was how calm they were. They were sitting on the curb waiting for me to pick them up. No one had panicked. Once Cody realized his car had been stolen, he contacted the cops, called for other transportation, and mentioned to the other kids that they might get home a little late that evening. He suggested they call their parents and let them know his father was on the way down to get them.

I picked up all the kids and then proceeded to where the police were waiting for us . . . with the van . . . and with the two boys they had caught driving it. Colt and Cody's friend followed us in the pickup with the drum set.

The person who had originally stolen the van had used a hammer and screwdriver to poke a hole just above the lock on the driver's-side door. After he was in, he popped the end off the ignition and used a screwdriver to start it. Before he abandoned the car, he had gone through and taken all the valuable things. He had some CDs, several of our kid's schoolbooks, one of their backpacks, and a coat. He had been kind enough to leave the screwdriver he'd used to start the van.

We turned on the interior light to assess the situation. Immediately Cody and Shiloh started to list the things missing. As they bent down to look under the seats and benches, it was obvious that the car had been cleaned out. Cody went to the back of the van, put his key in the tailgate, and lifted it up. Behind the last bench was a huge bag of candy the kids had bought, planning on giving it to the people in charge of the ministry to distribute to the children over the following week. The car thief had missed this. In my opinion, it would have been the one thing in the car I would have wanted, were I him.

Cody picked up the bag, and underneath it—safe from the thief's view—was his journal.

It was one of the most wonderful nights of ministry the kids had ever had. They got to work with the children, they got their car stolen, they prayed that God would get Cody's journal back, they got the car back, and, ultimately, they saw God answer their prayers.

Before we took off, the kids huddled in a circle and did two things. They thanked God for giving back the van and the journal. And then they prayed for the two boys in the backseat of the police car. There was no malice in their voices, no condemnation in their words. Just, "Help them, Lord. Use this incident, and the consequences of it, for good in their lives. Reach them, Lord, before it's too late."

We split the kids up between the two cars, with Colt and Cody's friend following in the pickup. Cody got in the van and realized his key wouldn't work because of the missing ignition. We all laughed out loud when the Phoenix policeman came up to his window, handed him the screwdriver, and said, "Son, you forgot your keys."

On the way home we stopped at a Wendy's. The kids had built up quite an appetite after everything they'd been through. It was such an honor to pick up the tab for those eight young men and women, and to sit back and watch them chattering away about all the things God was doing in them and through them. I returned to the work site at about 11:30 and had the pleasure of telling the story to the guys there. The entire experience reminded me just how rich my life is.

LIVING A GREAT SPIRITUAL ADVENTURE

I've noticed over the years that kids who are encouraged to live life as a great spiritual adventure don't have much time for rebellion. However, a great spiritual adventure is not something you can just encourage them into or assign to them. The parents need to lead the way, realizing that the benefits and rewards of living adventurously far outweigh the risks and inconveniences.

Families that live passionate, front-line lives for Jesus Christ can still have kids who rebel. But that's unusual. Rebels are rare in those homes because the Christianity the kids are exposed to isn't canned, academic, or the outgrowth of worn-out traditions. Instead, the living, breathing, moving presence of God permeates all ideas, all plans, and all priorities.

There is a kind of Christian life, however, that's easy to slide into without even trying—a Christian life that is *convenient*. There are two brands of comfortable Christianity. On the one hand there's *static* Christianity, which involves nice people, people who love God, love their church, love the Bible, and genuinely love people. They get emotional when they hear that someone has come to know Christ. They sense an intimacy with God when they take Communion. These are also people who serve God in some way.

The drawback to their static, comfortable Christianity is that there is no real risk attached to anything they do, and they aren't willing to do anything that would change that. They can point to everything on the list that outlines what a conscientious Christian does and say, "Yes. That's me. I do that." But it's all *convenient.* It's a predictable, manageable Christian life that fits them like a nice relaxed pair of blue jeans. It's a faith that looks good on them and a faith that makes them look good.

This kind of Christian life is enjoyed for its *ease.* And those who enjoy it might be mature Christians if you were to compare them to the average believer. But their primary spiritual growth already happened. It's not in the present. What they do for God they do well, but because it doesn't press them hard or demand much from them, they can function in commendable ways without having to take any real risks. They can be Sunday school teachers, elders, and even pastors. They can be doing very good things, but if the truth were told, they're on *spiritual cruise control.* Most of the victories they've experienced are in the past— mostly *way* in the past. Their relationship with God isn't "new every morning,"[1] it's old, tired, and a bit sedentary.

Comfortable Christians' prayers tend to fall into two categories. They are either "personal success" prayers, where they are entreating God to make their good lives better (prayers that appeal for promotions, money, great health, wonderful vacations, nicer amenities to their life, etc.), or they are "deliver us from discomfort" prayers that ask God to make bad things go away (risks, unknowns, an uncomfortable supervisor, a negative influence on one of their children, a bad health report). To a certain extent, discomfort is looked on as something evil. That's why comfortable Christians are often critical of preachers who challenge them to a higher holiness and a more sacrificial service. A life that pushes them out of their spiritual comfort zone may even be looked on with spiritual suspicion.

GOOD REASONS FOR LIVING UNCOMFORTABLY

There is another brand of comfortable Christianity that is the rational next step from the static brand. It's what happens if a static Christian doesn't break out of their spiritual sleepwalking. For lack of a better term, let's refer to it as *deteriorating* Christianity. This process slowly destroys the relevancy of the particular Christian who has embraced it.

This person's spiritual atrophy ultimately has a diminishing effect on them and those around them.

This brand of comfortable Christianity adapts to our fears, accommodates our wants, and subordinates to our shortcomings. This would all be okay if Christ merely wanted to be our Savior. But He actually has something bigger and sweeter in mind—He wants to be our Lord. And when we let Him do that, He becomes our life.

One of the great by-products of letting Christ have all of you is that it communicates to your children that your beliefs are more than theory. Your faith is not just a collection of religious platitudes. You demonstrate to your children by your actions that what you believe is not only the *truth*, but it's also *truth that works*. A comfortable brand of Christianity blocks that message from getting through to our kids' hearts.

It might be helpful at this point to review the things that the Bible says put a smile on God's face. These things should be natural outgrowths in those who have handed their hearts over to Jesus. Paul calls this our "spiritual act of worship."[2] Another way of saying it is, "This is the least we can do based on what He did for us."

God has given believers good reason to *love* Him with all of their hearts. Hosea 6:6 says, "I don't want your sacrifices—I want your love; I don't want your offerings—I want you to know me" (TLB).

God has given believers good reason to *trust* Him for everything in their lives. Psalm 147:11 says, "He takes pleasure in those who honor him, in those who trust in his constant love" (GNT).

God has given believers good reason to *obey* Him in every nuance of their being. Psalm 119:33–34 says, "Just tell me what to do and I will do it, Lord. As long as I live I'll wholeheartedly obey" (TLB).

God has given believers good reason to *thank* Him and *praise* Him continually. Psalm 68:3 says, "The righteous are glad and rejoice in his presence; they are happy and shout for joy" (GNT).

God has given believers good reason to *use their various talents and abilities* for His glory. "Whatever you do, whether in word or deed, do it all in the name of the Lord Jesus, giving thanks to God the Father through him" (Colossians 3:17).[3]

TALLYING UP THE COSTS

There is one problem when you look over this list. If you're going to make it your aim to love God, trust Him, obey Him, thank Him, praise Him, and use your various talents for His glory, it's going to cost you. Let me point to a few of the items on the ledger.

Giving Your Life Completely to Christ Is Going to Cost You Time—Lots of It

People committed to God don't set aside a parenthesis in their schedule to slip Him into their lineup. He *is* their schedule. He *is* their lineup. Whether it's their work or their play, whether it's the time in their normal day that is spoken for or the time in their normal day that is up for grabs, every moment of every day represents an unbroken commitment to Him.

I've often heard people outline their priorities. It's not uncommon to hear them say something like, "First, there's God. Then my spouse. Then my kids. Then my work. Then my church. Then my leisure." I always think the same thing: *You're close, but you've got to format it differently if you want your life to work spiritually and have the best influence on the people around you.*

God isn't supposed to be a stratum in our priorities—even if we put Him at the top. God *is* our priority. He's everything. It makes more sense when you say something like this: "First, there's God. Then there's God and my spouse. Then there's God and my kids. Then there's God and my work. Then there's God and my church. Then there's God and my leisure." When we arrange our priorities this way, however, we've got to know going in that God may have it in His mind to reestablish our family time, reenergize our work time, rearrange our free time, reclaim our quiet time, and reformat our downtime.

Giving Your Life Completely to Christ Is Going to Cost You Energy

Serving God with all your heart tends to trifle with your sleep patterns. It can exact quite a toll even in the middle of the day. There are certain areas of service in your local church that take unusual amounts of effort to complete. Being a genuine friend can wear you down, too. It takes energy to be there for a person who is discouraged. Christians that are paying attention often find that the next tug on their heart by the Holy Spirit might wring them out to a point of exhaustion. I remember when our son Cody went to India to serve during the Christmas break of his junior year of high school. He got very little sleep on the way over and a lot less once he was there. He came back almost beyond the point of exhaustion but absolutely overwhelmed by what he saw God do in people's lives.

I had a similar experience in an exhausting trip to Papua New Guinea. Another time, my wife and I came home half dead from two weeks of service in Africa. In both cases, we couldn't have felt more contented than we did. Even those headaches you get when you're so tired are *worth* it. Mission trips are not only a wonderful opportunity to see God work, but also a phenomenal time of personal growth. Still, there was clearly a temptation to hit the snooze button when these opportunities were first presented to us.

Giving Your Life Completely to Christ Is Going to Cost You Money

This isn't really a problem when you start with the reality that all your money is really His anyway. As God says in His Word, "The silver is mine and the gold is mine."[4] The neat thing about God is, He really knows how to handle our money better than we do. And when we let Him have control of our entire budgets, He does wonders with them. Not only does He show us how to be generous and sacrificial in our investment in things that are eternal, but He also makes it possible to have plenty left over.

Unfortunately, comfortable Christians have a problem with this concept because it forces them to put their entire trust in God instead of in their portfolios. Christians that wholeheartedly love God, trust Him, obey Him, thank Him, praise Him, and use their various talents for His glory realize that you've got to hold everything you have in an open palm. You can't really do these things if you clutch God's money in a tight fist and leave a tip behind for Him in the offering plate. Living a spiritual adventure means He might ask for your budget to reflect His value system. He might want to borrow your car, or even keep it. You even might have to pick up the tab at Wendy's for kids who aren't yours, again and again, for the rest of your life.

Giving Your Life Completely to Christ
Is Going to Cost You Your Pride

He might ask you to serve behind the scenes, do some thankless jobs, and not get your name mentioned in the program. He might expect you to approach the person who has hurt you to initiate the process of restoration. You might have to do all that you do in submission to someone who is younger and less experienced than you (like your son-in-law). Living a passionate spiritual adventure forces you to put your fears and doubts on notice and let them know they can no longer run your life. And you'll probably have to say good-bye to that idea of maintaining a selfish personal agenda--permanently.

THE TYRANNY OF COMFORTABLE FAITH

There is a major problem in many Christian homes, and it feeds a child's inclination toward spiritual rebellion. It's the presence of a faith that doesn't cost much. It's a belief system that fits comfortably into our personal agendas. It doesn't demand much time or sweat or cash. And it seldom puts our egos at risk. Comfortable Christianity hears only what it wants to hear. It believes only what it wants to believe. And it serves only when it feels like it.

A comfortable faith believes it's okay to edit the Bible, as in "I know what the Bible says about divorce, but I just need to be happy." It allows for the harboring of grudges and an occasional evening of the score. The neat thing about a comfortable faith is that it adjusts to the whims of your heart. In fact, I'd have to say that as you look at it in comparison to, say, a passionate sold-out Christian life, there is no comparison. At least not when it comes to the personal demands of the two. Comfortable faith is clearly easier and cheaper, at least on the surface. When you stack the two options next to each other, it's obvious that living sold out for Christ is both demanding and inconvenient. But that is only if you are looking at it in the context of the here and now—the immediate. When you look out beyond, however, the price tag flips upside down—radically upside down.

I could make a long list of the shortfalls Christians experience when they choose to take the course of least resistance in their relationship with Christ, but we don't have the time here. I'll just mention a few areas to give you a taste of the consequences, and then camp on one in particular.

Comfortable Christianity Keeps People Shallow and Immature

Since comfortable Christians only want to accept from the Bible what fits with their personal agendas, the Bible—technically—is removed from the big picture of their lives. Therefore, God's Word cannot be used as a guide for getting them down life's dark alleys. And without it, they really never get to turn all the experiences they're going through into wisdom. That's because the fear of God is the beginning of wisdom.

A person who places little priority on the authority of God's Word obviously missed the memo about fearing Him. So these comfort-lovers move into their forties, fifties, sixties, and older still behaving like spiritual babies. They still pout, whine, bark orders, and throw tantrums. And when things don't go right with their fellow Christians, they assume they are justified in rejecting them. When things don't go their way at church, they either throw rocks or leave.

There are many churches where comfortable Christianity is so much in control that it doesn't permit the pastor to address "uncomfortable" issues such as the roles of men and women, homosexuality, sin, abortion, or the blood of Jesus. These churches are like comfortable Christianity to a power of ten, and it's where any individual who chooses this path is likely to end up and, sadly, fit right in.

Comfortable Christians Seldom Get to See God Work in Supernatural Ways

These believers attend church, Sunday school, and the occasional retreat. It's not uncommon for comfortable Christians to go to a lot of

Bible studies. In fact, comfortable Christians *love* Bible studies—so long as they don't have to teach them or change much to participate in them.

It is interesting how jaded comfortable Christians can get about the Holy Spirit. They can hear God's truth taught with clarity and conviction, but they're so safe in their comfortable Christian world that it doesn't move them to make any of the radical changes that truth might be calling for. They serve, but it's usually something that fits easily into their schedules, stokes their egos, or looks good on their résumés. They put their kids in the local Christian school. They drop money that can easily be spared in the offering plate.

So what are they missing? They don't get to see God's hand moving in obvious and powerful ways. They don't get to experience that breathless wonder of seeing God take our feeble efforts and undeveloped skills and use them to change people's lives for eternity. They don't get to watch God turn the substance of their wealth into dividends that compound for eternity. They are simply glad to pay an occasional light bill for the church, and then they wonder why, with all the money they have left, they feel so deeply unsatisfied.

Comfortable Christians Are Extremely Susceptible to Spiritual Disease and Moral Decline

If Christ isn't our passion, if His Word isn't our guide, if His church isn't an extension of our lives, and if His Spirit isn't our constant conscience, we become easy targets for every kind of false doctrine that comes along. Comfortable Christians can easily get sucked into fringe beliefs— those occasional theological anomalies that are fun to talk about but have nothing to do with the core of the gospel. They are also prone to becoming preoccupied with singular doctrinal studies that consume them at the expense of their greater calling as a Christian—things like end-times prophecy, arguments about Bible translations, and speaking in tongues. Even worse is how easy it is for Satan to stick a hook in them. Because Christ isn't the central focus of their every breath, it's easy for the powers of darkness to gain control of their inner inclination toward greed, lust, jealousy, envy, and pride.

ONE OF THE BIGGEST COSTS OF COMFORTABLE FAITH

But all this hits home the hardest in how the next generation views the faith they've been fed by their parents. Kids want to see more in the Christian faith than mediocrity and convenience. They want a God that is more than a family pet. When they observe that our faith doesn't really require very much from of us, it causes them to lose respect for us and deters their own relationship with God. When you add to this mix some of the standard statements that parents make when their children are rebelling, it only widens the chasm between a child and their parent's faith.

"You know, you ought to go up into your room right now and read your Bible!" The child is thinking, *Why? You read the Bible, and it hasn't had any life-changing effect on you!* If kids don't see an ongoing transformation happening in their parents' lives, it's hard for them to see why they should submit to the confinements that seem to come along with their Christian beliefs.

Frankly, sometimes our children's rebellion can be a statement about their loss of respect for our faith. Our beliefs come across as cheap, and our kids want something valuable. They behave like the prodigal son that ran away to Party Central because they live in a family that has a lot in common with the passionless older brother.

Until kids find something worth dying for, they don't have anything worth living for. When they see parents who aren't willing to be inconvenienced, let alone to die for their faith, it's no wonder they rebel. It's their knee-jerk reaction to wanting more out of their Christian lives.

One of the good things that can come out of kids' rebellion is that it has a way of shifting convenient Christian homes out of neutral. Suddenly parents are studying God's Word with a deep hunger for more. Suddenly Mom and Dad get rid of the airbrushed prayers about themselves and truly plead a case before God on behalf of someone they actually love more than themselves. God moves from a plush toy to a sovereign Creator who has His arms around us all. But why does it have to get to this before we let Him have all of our lives?

KING DAVID'S TRADE OF PASSION FOR GLORY

When most people think of the biblical character David, they think of the giant-killer, the great warrior, the king of Israel, "the man after God's own heart." True, he shot himself in the foot a couple of times, but for the most part, David is more revered than reviled. When I think of King David, I see him as a great example of someone in the Bible who "traded his passion for glory." And although I've learned many good lessons from his greatness, I've learned my best lessons from his failures.

Let me give you a quick crash course in the life of David. My goal is to encourage anyone who may have slipped into a comfortable pattern of Christianity to get out of it as quickly as possible.

After he burst on the scene with that fatal shot to the head of Goliath, David took Israel by storm. He had height, moral stature, and knockdown good looks. There was a tone of courage in his voice and poetry in his words. He was all man, but he had an eye for the aesthetic. Even the lowliest Israelite could figure out that he was everything King Saul wasn't. As a result, King Saul decided David's head would look better in a jar on the mantel than on his shoulders. That's why David found himself running for his life, hiding in the hills, and ultimately living in caves.

For many years, there wasn't one comfortable thing about David's life. And it was during this time that David's passion for God was the hottest. Even though he waded through the muck of discouragement for a long period of time, his faith only grew. His confidence in God was pushed to the brink, but he ended up trusting Him more. He wrote many psalms during this time, poems of praise that not only attest to his emotional struggles but also validate his ultimate confidence in God.

It was during this time that God decided to bring David some nice people to provide him with company. "David left Gath and escaped to the cave of Adullam. When his brothers and his father's household heard about it, they went down to him there. All those who were in distress or in debt or discontented gathered around him, and he became their leader. About four hundred men were with him" (1 Samuel 22:1–2).

So let's make sure we're getting this straight. David is Israel's hero. He saves their rears from the Philistines, becomes Saul's right-hand man only to become the target of his insecurities. And in the midst of David's near clinical depression, God sends him the dregs and rejects of society to cheer him up? Most people would think this would be all he needed to slip over the edge and fall headlong into rebellion against God. Actually, it was just the opposite. One of life's greatest lessons is that most believers don't realize how much they really have in their relationship with God until God's all they've got.

David learned the same lesson in the cave of Adullam that the apostle Paul learned about fifteen hundred years later from his "thorn in the flesh," namely, that God's grace is sufficient for him . . . that God's power is perfected in his weaknesses.[5] For the next few years David lived on the lam, surrounded by this whiny, bickering, unkempt collection of Israeli riffraff. These were people who were down in the dumps, poor money managers, and angry at the world.

Twice during this time, David had a chance to kill King Saul. But he didn't. Even though David had already been anointed as the next king of Israel by the prophet Samuel, and regardless of what King Saul had done to him, David refused to give in to the pleadings of the men around him to get revenge and seize the throne. King Saul, though a nightmare, was also God's anointed. And as long as he was, David wasn't going to lay a finger on him. He figured when Saul's time was up, God would get David on his throne.

David's passion for God was at his all-time high. His love for these men who had come to cast their lot with him was earnest. He trained them, encouraged them, and ultimately built them into one of the most feared fighting forces of his day. They were called his "mighty men of valor." It was during this worst chapter in his life that he actually enjoyed his best years with God. And then . . .

David got comfortable.

King Saul met his end in battle with the Philistines. David took his rightful place as king of Judah. After seven years and a mild tug of war with one of Saul's predecessors, David became king of the entire nation of Israel. Some of those same men who lived with him in the cave became his cabinet, key advisers, and military leaders. He brought the ark of the covenant to Jerusalem and established the sacrifice once again in Israel. Everything got civilized real fast. And so did David. He traded his running sandals for a chariot, his cave for a palace, and his passion for glory.

In the seven years he was enjoying the comforts and securities that came with being the king of Judah, his priorities started to change. By the time he was sleeping in the king's bed in Jerusalem, his priorities had started to go into a free fall. Speaking of beds, David came to the throne as the husband of two wives. But after he got to Jerusalem, he thought there was room in his bed for more.

"After he left Hebron, David took more concubines and wives in Jerusalem, and more sons and daughters were born to him."[6] The king's libido became an active member of his royal cabinet and, in the process, a major part of his downfall. The truth is that there are all kinds of "traps for fools" lying around for believers in God to step into. When you are enjoying a comfortable relationship with God and your guard is down, you seem to step into these traps more often.

You can just imagine how quickly the number of people in the annual family portrait started to multiply. David's wives and concubines were popping out sons and daughters as fast as he could sire them. Unfortunately, David didn't have much time for his kids. After a while, he didn't have time for his kingly duties, either. It says in 2 Samuel 11:1, "In the spring, at the time when kings go off to war, David sent Joab out with the king's men and the whole Israelite army. They destroyed the Ammonites and besieged Rabbah. But David remained in Jerusalem."

There are two things about being a king that are important to mention here. In those days, kings consistently led their armies into battle. The Bible is filled with accounts of conflicts where Israel defeated a foreign army and captured their king in the process. David's not going out to battle with his army was a serious breach of standard royal protocol. The second thing we need to understand is that when you went out to battle, you obviously put yourself at great risk of being injured or killed. Even if your army ultimately won the battle, you could still find yourself seriously embalmed. By staying back in Jerusalem, David was communicating that he was choosing safety over courage.

LUST, ADULTERY, AND MURDER

In those days, springtime was when the armies of all the surrounding countries gathered on battlefields to hold the annual territorial Olympics. It was a nice way to figure out who would be in charge for the next year. David may have had great confidence in General Joab's ability to return a victory for him, but he should have been out there himself, leading the way.

With little to do, he decided to take his coffee up on the roof of the royal palace. It's doubtful there were any buildings taller than the one he was on, which gave him a great vantage point for looking down on the porches and into the apartments of his loyal subjects. That's when he saw Bathsheba taking a bath. Keep in mind, few people had anything that looked similar to a modern-day bathtub. Using a basin of water, this particular bather probably gave herself a sponge bath. The process gave David plenty of time to take in this beautiful woman.

When he inquired later about who she was, he was told that she was Bathsheba, the wife of Uriah the Hittite. Uriah was out of town—in fact he was on the battlefield with Joab where David was supposed to be. He is listed in 2 Samuel 23:39 and 1 Chronicles 11:41 as one of David's "mighty men of valor." There is an excellent chance that he was one of the four hundred men who had joined David in the cave of Adullam. He had been fighting with and for David many years. No doubt, because of his status and rank in David's army, he was able to attract this gorgeous woman as his wife after they established themselves in Jerusalem. David knew Uriah very well. He just hadn't met his wife before. Not until now.

Most people know the rest of the story. David invited Bathsheba to join him for a romp in the royal hay. By the way, although she could have refused him, it was not as easy as you think. When you take into account how many women in modern times have found themselves in lose-lose situations at the hands of powerful men, you see how all this could happen.

After their little tryst, she went home. A couple of weeks later, when things weren't as they should be, she did a home pregnancy test and discovered that she was carrying the king's baby. When she sent David a note regarding this little detail, his response demonstrates one of the standard reactions comfortable believers have when confronted with their sin—he thought, *How do I get out of this?*

Every time we try to minimize or escape the consequences of our sins, we've got to remember that we are being watched. Our children don't miss a thing, and our behavior during these stressful situations has a powerful influence on their own beliefs. David's children were watching . . . and taking notes.

David came up with an idea that he felt could adequately cover his tracks: send for Uriah, bring him home from the battlefield, schmooze him, and send him home to sleep with his wife. He figured, *When Bathsheba finally starts to show, everyone will assume the baby is Uriah's.*

He didn't count on Uriah having more integrity in his pinkie than David had in his whole body. As planned, David made Uriah feel important and then sent him home. But he was surprised to find that instead of going home, Uriah slept at the threshold of the king's door. When David asked why, Uriah explained that as a soldier of the king, he was supposed to protect the king. Plus, he felt it wouldn't be right to be home enjoying the sexual delights of his wife when his fellow soldiers were out on the battlefield.

Even after David tried a second time to get Uriah to go home and sleep with Bathsheba, this time getting him drunk first, Uriah remained true to his allegiance as a soldier. This noble attitude, by the way, ultimately cost Uriah his life. David figured, *If I can't frame him into appearing to be this child's father, I'll just have him whacked.* And just like Tony Soprano, who can have veal parmesan with you at lunch and have you turned into fish food by evening, David sent a sealed message to Joab, instructing him to make sure Uriah was killed in battle. His courier for this message, by the way, was Uriah.

Joab complied.

David had a wonderful heart for God. He of all people knew what it was like to sense God's presence and to be in tune with God's voice. But he allowed himself to get comfortable in his relationship with Him, and compromise slipped into his life in the process. Satan can figure out if we have an Achilles heel, and, if so, what it is. In David's life it was pornography and sex. And before it was over, all the king's horses and all the king's men couldn't put David together again.

LIKE FATHER, LIKE SONS

In the process of this tragic interlude, not only did David's kids become rebellious, but they followed in their father's footsteps in the kind of rebellion they chose. They just took David's sin to new and sicker heights. Amnon, one of David's many sons, developed a burning lust for one of his stepsisters, Tamar. He feigned sickness and requested that Tamar come to his room to fix him some food. In the process he raped her. And then, like a light switch that can be turned from on to off in a second, his attitude toward her did a complete reverse. Once he was finished using her, he spurned her. He had his servant remove her from his quarters like a dead rat in a trap.

Tamar ultimately confided in her brother Absalom. Absalom was a lot like his father, David. Among other things, he was not a man to be messed with. At the opportune time, he had Amnon murdered. The logic worked from the value system his father had modeled. It went something like this: *If my father can have one of his loyal officers put to death, even when he was innocent, surely there shouldn't be a problem with my having my brother killed when he is guilty.*

This was just the beginning of the fall of the house of David. Absalom attempted a coup d'état. It failed. Usually when a coup fails, the person who attempted it ends up dead. Following is one of very few verses in the Bible that capture the utter sadness of a father lamenting over the consequences of a rebellious son's actions: "O my son Absalom! My son, my son Absalom! If only I had died instead of you—O Absalom, my son, my son!"[7]

I could give you other examples of how David's years of comfortable faith drove his own children to rebel against God—the same God their father wrote such beautiful poems about. I'll just mention one more. David ultimately handed his throne over to his son Solomon. Although Solomon enjoyed forty years of the most peaceful, prosperous, and *comfortable* years in Israel's history, he followed in his father's footsteps in one tragic area of his life. Solomon had a penchant for beautiful women. But instead of having a couple of wives, he married women a dozen at a time. He had seven hundred wives, and those were just the ones of royal birth from all the princes, governors, and kings of the surrounding countries. He also had three hundred concubines.

David's problems started when he allowed his faith to get too comfortable. He in turn incited his own children to lives of rebellion toward God. I believe the Bible shows it was David's example that inspired such a huge sense of unbridled sexual irresponsibility in his son Solomon. And I think it's easy to demonstrate that the turmoil over many generations of David's royal descendants had its roots in those years when he traded his passion for God for the glory and comfort of his kingdom.

It would take the ultimate heir to the throne of David, Jesus the Messiah, to finally bring hope back to the equation.

It was David's son Solomon who said, "There is nothing new under the sun."[8] He was right. Just as David's slide into spiritual mediocrity took its toll on his children and grandchildren, so also does our comfortable faith incite our offspring to rebellion. The decision to allow yourself to entertain a comfortable level of faith can have repercussions through your family tree for many generations to come.

But just the opposite is true when you decide to give your heart over completely to God. When you determine to love God, trust Him, obey Him, thank Him, praise Him, and use your various talents for His glory, God will make your family the recipient of His many promises in the Bible. Deuteronomy 7:9 says, "Know therefore that the LORD your God is God; he is the faithful God, keeping his covenant of love to a thousand generations of those who love him and keep his commands."

The great thing about God is that He allows any generation to change the direction of the generation before them. If you have been following the pattern of your parents with a powerless, traditional, or risk-free faith, why don't you consider turning things around once and for all in your life? It is true that your decision to give your whole heart to God may not change your rebelling children's behavior, but it would be the best first step to modeling a better way for them to live. Stop telling them God is worth your life; show them.

George Bernard Shaw was a cynical critic of Christianity. But even someone with a spiritual chip on his shoulder can occasionally make a valid point. He once said, "The problem with Christianity is that it's never been tried." His point is well taken. Some of our rebellious kids have never seen our faith putting us out. They want a God who is worth risking everything for. They want parents with a faith so bold, so confident in their love for God that they'll hand Him their bodies, their emotions, their intellect, their checkbooks, and the deeds to their entire lives and let Him use them in whatever way He sees fit. Every person would prefer that their life be significant. Show your children that a life lived for God makes a difference here on earth, as well as for eternity.

OLD DOG, SAME OLD TRICKS

We'll spend more time with David in later chapters. But for now, I'd like to point out one more lesson from his life. In one sense, it shows that even later in life, he still hadn't dealt with some of his blind spots. But it also demonstrates that it's never too late to figure things out.

Most people would say the darkest blot on David's life was his sin with Bathsheba. Although it is a formidable stain on his record, it actually isn't the worst thing he did—at least it isn't if you are measuring in terms of loss of innocent life.

David actually came up with a harebrained scheme in his latter years that topped anything he'd done up to that point. And what he did demonstrates how much he was vacillating between his confidence in God and his confidence in himself.

David decided he wanted to take a census to count all the men who were old enough to serve in his army. Maybe you're thinking, *What's so bad about that?* The problem is that God had made it clear before the nation of Israel even came into the Promised Land that their victories over their enemies were going to be because the Lord, Jehovah, was fighting on their side. And the historical record up to this point was clear: It was God who had always gone before Israel into battle, and it was God who had always given them the string of successes they had enjoyed. It had nothing to do with their own strength or numbers.

What makes David's census so tragic is that it is clearly the opposite of what he believed as a young man with a slingshot facing a giant. Just before he buried that deadly stone from his slingshot between Goliath's eyes he said, "You come against me with sword and spear and javelin, but I come against you in the name of the LORD Almighty, the God of the armies of Israel, whom you have defied. This day the LORD will hand you over to me, and I'll strike you down and cut off your head."[9] It was obvious, at that point, David knew where the real strength of Israel came from. When he walked out to meet that giant, he knew—personally—he was no match for Goliath. But he also knew Goliath was no match for God. And since God was with David, he was confident that Goliath's days of intimidating the armies of Israel were about to come to a conclusion.

He also knew the impact God's victory would have. He said, "The whole world will know that there is a God in Israel. All those gathered here will know that it is not by sword or spear that the LORD saves; for the battle is the LORD's, and he will give all of you into our hands."[10]

When David told General Joab about his plan to take a census, even Joab knew it was a foolish idea. He tried, but to no avail, to talk the king out of it. There's a good chance David was starting to see the mistakes he had made with his children. He was about to transfer his crown over to his son Solomon. Maybe since he'd failed to imprint upon Solomon a faith that could follow God into battle, he figured he needed an assessment of how well his son's armies were going to stack up against his enemies when he went out to battle in his own power. In any case, the census exacted a huge toll on the people of Jerusalem.

It took Joab nine months to complete the count (800,000 fighting men in Israel and 500,000 in Judah). It took David only a few minutes after he heard the numbers to realize what a mistake he had made. It occurred to him that regardless of the numbers, it was God and only God they needed when they went into battle. Numbers were irrelevant. But by taking the census, he had said just the opposite to God. David was conscience-stricken and said, "I have sinned greatly in what I have done. Now, O LORD, I beg you, take away the guilt of your servant. I have done a very foolish thing."[11]

Indeed he had. God sent word to David (through His prophet) that as a result of his actions, He was giving him three options for punishment. Basically He said, "Pick your poison: three years of famine, three months of fleeing from your enemies, or three days of a national plague."

A nation starving to death didn't sound like a good idea. And David had already done that second option when he was on the lam, running from King Saul. He chose the last one.

God sent a plague throughout Israel. In three days' time, seventy thousand people died.

What a shame. All because one man, who knew better, decided to let the comfort and ease of his life neutralize the convictions of his beliefs. This is an action that would have made more sense back when he was living under such incredible personal stress in the cave of Adullam. Instead, his cave experience stretched him and forced him to put his entire trust in God, inspiring him to write so many beautiful psalms. In those younger years, when his faith was inconvenient, David knew he had all he *needed* in God alone. But once he got to that point where he could have all he *wanted* through his cushioned royal lifestyle, he lost his way.

But all was not completely lost, because in the aftermath of this horrible tragedy for Israel, David was able once again to gain his focus. In the process he left all of us with a great rule to follow when it comes to living our lives for God.

The angel of the Lord was sent out to destroy innocent people in the wake of David's sin. Just as he approached the threshing floor of a citizen of Jerusalem named Araunah, God told him to stop. Apparently, God had allowed David to actually see this angel as he moved with deathly certainty from one poor soul to the next. When he finally stopped at this threshing floor, David headed over there to build an altar and offer a sacrifice of repentance to the Lord.

Araunah apparently had not been privy to the metaphysical eyesight David had been given. Nor, it seems, was he aware of how close he had come to being the death angel's next victim. He and his staff were working at this threshing floor when they saw David and his royal entourage approaching them. He came up to David and said, "Why has my lord the king come to his servant?"[12] David explained that he had come there to *purchase* Araunah's threshing floor. He wanted to build an altar and offer a sacrifice to God so the plague on the people would stop.

Araunah said something like, "You came here to *buy* my land? You can *have* it. In fact, take these oxen here and use them for the sacrifice. And use these threshing sledges and the yokes from the oxen for the wood. All that I have, O King, I give to you, and I hope as a result the Lord will hear your plea." Araunah actually understood what a passionate attitude toward God looks like. You hold all you have in an open palm and you let the Lord use it, and you, in whatever way He wants.

Fortunately, David had figured out the same thing. And the next words out of his mouth were not only rich in truth, but tempered from many years of being such a bad example. David said, "No, I insist on paying you for it. I will not sacrifice to the LORD my God burnt offerings *that cost me nothing.*"[13]

PROVEN FAITH, PASSIONATE CHRISTIAN KIDS

David's words are wise words to live by. A spiritual free ride and sacrifices that we make on the cheap are no example for the kids living in our homes. For them, a comfortable Christian life begs the question "Why bother to embrace this faith—especially in the areas of my life where it is at odds with my selfish will? It hasn't cost my parents much. I don't see a lot of our friends putting out for it. It must not be worth the bother."

If you've recognized characteristics of your family in this story, I've got good news. You can change the pattern in your home. The first step is on your knees. The next step is into the battle for the cross. Let God use you in whatever way He wants, and let Him take whatever He wants. In the long run you will see that you are far more the beneficiary than God is. It all starts with you. As you begin to change, your rebellious children will finally get a good look at a faith that is worth living and dying for.

You might have to sit upright in the coach section of a crowded jet halfway around the world, or work into the wee hours of the morning building a Christmas musical set. You might have to get your car stolen, and pray your son's music journal back from the dead. I don't know what God will ask of you or your family. But in the end, you will be far richer than you ever thought you could be. You'll discover that living an inconvenient Christian life will become the kind of family affair that pays positive dividends for generations to come.

DISCUSSION QUESTIONS

1. Tim implies that spiritual risk and adventure play a big role in building an authentic and personal faith within your child's heart. But to do this, you really have to trust in the Holy Spirit to lead and protect them. Does this come easy to you? How does the absence of spiritual risk undermine a child's passionate relationship with Christ?

2. Do you think it's very wise to let your high-school kids venture into dangerous parts of town on a school night to do ministry? Is this something you'd expect a rebellious Christian kid to be doing? What is the cause and effect between spiritual adventure and an attitude that does not need to rebel?

3. What effect do you think the comfortable spiritual life a parent lives has on a child's view of God? How does living our lives on "spiritual cruise control" push our kids toward rebellion?

4. In the Bible, we are called to love God, trust Him, obey Him, thank Him, and use our various talents and abilities for His glory. How would our doing these things discourage our children from wanting to rebel? How would they help a child who is in the middle of rebelling?

5. Tim said that giving your life completely to Christ is going to cost you time, energy, money, and your pride. Do you think our unwillingness to pay any or all of these prices has any effect in pushing our kids into rebellion against God? How?

6. Our human nature wants our Christian lives to be safe and comfortable. The Holy Spirit tends to lead us more into a wild and risky Christian life. Which message do you think your child is getting as a result of living in your home? Going to church? How does this affect his/her faith?

7. What are some specific ways you could demonstrate to your children that your faith is worth living for—even when it is inconvenient?

8. What is one thing God has taught you through this chapter?

CHAPTER 8

Cocoon Christianity

It's time to move headlong into the most fragile but critical part of our discussion on why kids in Christian homes rebel. It's critical because this chapter is going to address the most prevailing reasons why kids in *conscientious* Christian homes rebel. By "conscientious," I am describing parents who take their job of raising Christian children very seriously and want to do everything in their power to make sure their sons and daughters have the best possible chance to embrace Jesus Christ as Lord and His ways as a lifestyle.

A CRITICAL LOOK AT SAFE CHRISTIAN PARENTING

There is a traditional philosophy of Christian parenting that encourages moms and dads to create a safe cocoon in which to raise their kids. This philosophy not only includes the type of church and youth group they attend, but also the kind of friends they have, the level to which they are exposed to the world around them, and how they are educated. We're going to look at four compelling reasons parents choose a path of high protection. As you'll see, this type of configuration is often the very reason why so many kids in this environment end up rebelling against God and their parents.

To set up the first reason, I want to visit a bizarre story I ran across in the autumn of 1999. It's a story that had its origin on a bleak day back in 1942. It took place in Poland, not far from the Russian border.[1]

Stephen was a teenager in a small Polish village. He had grown up living with the ongoing threat of invasion by Russia, an ancient enemy that had always looked on that part of Poland with lustful eyes. The people in Stephen's village figured it was simply a matter of time before they'd see Russian troops storming across the border to claim them as a prize. All the Russians needed was the right excuse.

But on this particular day, the troops arrived from the opposite direction. The shifting gears and grinding metal of Hitler's tanks shook cans off the shelves in Stephen's family's kitchen as they moved through the defenseless town, and the crisp crack of jackbooted troops could be heard running through the back streets of his neighborhood. He knew that soon one of those soldiers would kick in the door of their home. Because he was a young male, the family knew if the Germans found him, his fate was dismal—he'd either be shipped off to Germany to fill voids in the factories or pressed into service in the German army or shot. Regardless, his options looked grim.

Stephen's parents did the only thing that made sense at the time; they raced him up the narrow stairs to their attic and created a hiding place for him where he could hole up indefinitely. Both his parents and his sister committed themselves to doing everything within their power to shelter Stephen from discovery by the Germans. They were willing to do this as long as the circumstances demanded it. So they kept Stephen hidden in the attic for the duration of the German occupation of their village. In their view, it was the least they could do to protect his young life from what they assumed was certain doom.

Then, as quickly as the Germans had arrived, they left, rushed into retreat by the oncoming Soviet army. But there was no celebration in this liberation. Stephen's village was now occupied by their ancient nemesis. And when the armistice was finally inked between the Allied superpowers, it became a sad reality that the Russian army was there to stay. The section of Stephen's beloved homeland where his village was situated would be absorbed into the Ukraine. On top of that, the Russians were conscripting every able-bodied young man they could find. Those who were uncooperative were shot. Stephen stayed put, huddled in his hiding place in the shadows of the attic.

It was a desperate ruse that worked and worked well. No one ever discovered him: not the Nazis, not the Russians, not even any of his fellow villagers. He was never conscripted, never had to defend his homeland, was never forced into hard labor, never had to lay his life on the line. However, in the process, Stephen managed to morph his specific fear of the Nazis and Russians into a general fear of *fear*! So much so that he maintained his position of hiding long after any of these enemies posed a threat to him.

Eventually, Stephen was finally motivated to slip out of his hiding place and join the world he'd so successfully avoided. But the Stephen that slowly moved down those attic steps was quite different from the young man who had bounded up them that first time in 1942. There was no spring in his step, no passion in his eyes, no determination in his grip. Just the tired and ambling shuffle of an old man who had let his fears define him.

The month Stephen emerged from hiding was October; the year was 1999—*fifty-seven years* after he had first taken up his hiding place in the attic. For almost six decades his family had accommodated his fears. And even after his parents died, his sister had continued to bring him food. Just ten days before, she, too, had died—the last surviving enabler of his pathetically useless life. Now, forced out of hiding by his hunger, he faced the world he had missed—a world he'd done nothing to make, a world he'd done nothing to improve. He was a miserable old coward who had retreated from real threats only to be taken over by phantom fears.

Stephen reminds me of someone. He reminds me of the element of the Christian community that, out of concern for legitimate threats to their children's safety, creates a safe hideaway in the midst of the spiritual war raging around them. They construct a handy and holy haven designed to accommodate their children's vulnerabilities *indefinitely*. It's a strategy that formats their childhood so deeply that it often becomes the defining attitude of their adulthood.

These parents retreat at a time when the Christian village around them could sure use their help in standing against the threats from evil. Many families seclude themselves from real threats only to end up living their lives hiding from fears that no longer exist—maybe even *never* existed. Their fears grip them, define them, and force them into being the antithesis of everything Christ called them to be.

The first reason, therefore, that many Christian parents raise their children in controlled, spiritually isolated environments is because . . .

They Are Convinced It Makes Their Children Safer

The concept of a need for safety is driven by real fears of the apparent threats surrounding their children.

Christian parents fear the corrupt world system that they're certain wants to churn up their kids and pollute their lives. They are convinced that if the world system can get to their children, it would certainly get ahold of their hearts. It would either conscript them into its army of sin, force them to work in its factories of shame, or simply *destroy* them. So parents hide their children in safe evangelical enclaves.

Within these enclaves, they have everything they need. That's because, over the last forty years, evangelical Christians have produced knockoffs of everything the world had to offer—except that they have been spiritually sterilized. Name it: books, television, movies, radio programming, fellowship, schooling, music—even our own amateur sports leagues. All that makes the evangelical enclave a safe place to hide a child. But it's also a tempting environment to hole up in for the rest of your life. Once a person is in, it can get so comfortable that he never wants to come out. Yet if he does (which many rebellious kids do), he is not prepared to handle what's waiting for him.

This isolation is justified by reports of the wicked and depraved generation just outside the attic walls. So the children hide in their safe and controlled Christian environment with its nice Bible studies, worship, and fellowship. Meanwhile, a desperate world slips deeper into its darkness while the kids in the spiritual attic memorize verses such as: "Let your light so shine before men, that they may see your good works and glorify your Father in heaven,"[2] or "Take courage; I have overcome the world."[3]

***Christian parents fear the powers of darkness*,** even though the Bible says, "Greater is He who is in you than he who is in the world,"[4] and, "Resist the devil and he will flee from you."[5]

***Christian parents fear their own inadequacies*,** even though God has given them His Holy Spirit to not only indwell them, but to give them insight, strength, and courage to lead their children across the battlefield.

Christian parents fear their children's vulnerable nature. This is, of course, a genuine concern. Children are extremely impressionable and naive, especially when they are young. The problem with all this is that basing your style of parenting on your children's fragile and impressionable nature is guaranteed to keep that child fragile, impressionable, and vulnerable. Why? Among other things, it's difficult to know at what point our children are ready to stand on their own two feet. If our focus is on them, they almost always appear like they aren't ready.

Guess what? They aren't. And they'll never be ready *by themselves*. Reality teaches us that all Christians are vulnerable to the influences of the corrupted world system for their entire lives. The issue isn't—nor should it ever be—how weak our child is, but rather how strong our God is. But since the focus is on our children's vulnerable state and the corrupted world system surrounding them, it's easy to let our concerns rule the day, and the year, and the rest of their lives.

All of this concern confuses many well-intended parents. We feel pretty sure about when to hide the child in the attic; we're just not sure when we should bring him back down to street level. That's because our enemy is always there, vicious, heartless, and foreboding.

Who can blame you for wanting to protect your children from serious threats to their faith? My wife and I felt the same way as we raised our kids. It's natural to want to slip them up the attic stairs when we hear the grinding armor of the enemy, but it's also easy—very easy—to encourage them to make their home there. It's easier for us to accommodate their needs in their hideaways than do the work of preparing them to face the risks that wait for them out in the open.

It's too bad. We miss the perfect opportunity to watch God overcome our threats, and so also do our children. And in the process, we hand over the burden of the cross, which Christ has called us all to take up and carry, to a weary handful of faithful warriors. In the face of serious threats, nice Christian parents often make decisions that end up causing their children to grow indifferent, weak, old, and defenseless to spiritual threats.

WE'VE SEEN THIS PHILOSOPHY BEFORE

These times we live in are tough times for Christian families. But they are not even close to the worst of times for families in history. In fact, American families, on average, face far less threat to their children's spiritual safety than most other Christian families in the world. And our conditions, compared to so many generations that have raised their kids before us, are mild. The families that came to know Christ in towns like Corinth, Philippi, and Ephesus were surrounded by hedonistic and philosophical threats *every day*. But there is nothing in Paul's advice that suggested they isolate from these threats.

Archaeological discoveries of the ancient region of Galatia show a culture that was far more violent, depraved, and sexually driven than anything we face in contemporary America. Yet, when Paul learned of their condition, he couldn't wait to make his way there and bring them the good news of salvation in Christ. He didn't establish churches in this region to lead them into a safe and secluded spiritual Shangri-la. He established them so families within those cities could demonstrate the overwhelming power of God to change lives, while at the same time sustaining them in the midst of a hostile spiritual environment.

There are two basic reasons why so many American Christian families are quick to create attic scenarios for their children. First, we have been living in a prolonged era of spiritual comfort and biblical co-dependency in America. Unfortunately, comfort and codependency tend to take priority over convictions and commitment—especially when it comes to our children. We've been spoon-fed for many decades now and have grown accustomed to subcontracting much of our spiritual responsibilities to evangelical professionals.

But there's a second major reason why many American families are quick to create long-term environments that preoccupy and protect our children in the face of spiritual threats. We can *afford* to. The material abundance of the average American home (even the poorer ones) has made necessities out of spiritual programs that most Christian families in the world would consider luxuries.

TAKE ANOTHER LAP AROUND SINAI

Even the Promised Land that God called Israel to enter and occupy was filled with serious threats to the people's physical and spiritual lives. But God assured His people that He would go before them and deliver their enemies into their hands. He referenced the amazing way He had already delivered them from the Egyptians, brought them through the Red Sea on dry land, gushed sweet and soothing water for them from solid rock, and brought them room service of manna and quail every morning and evening. They had also received the Law on Mount Sinai. It was the first installment of God's written Word. It, alone, put them light-years ahead of their forefathers.

But when they finally were positioned to go in and take the land (shortly after receiving the Ten Commandments), the Lord asked Moses to select a representative from each of the tribal families of Israel to go in ahead of them to *explore* the land. When I hear this story taught, I often hear these men referred to as spies. But they were not selected to *spy* out the land, but rather to *explore* it. *Explore* is the word God used when He asked Moses to put together this team of men.[6] What's the difference? Well, actually, it's huge. Spies go out to *evaluate a threat*. Explorers go out to *catalog an opportunity.*

A dozen men were sent out as explorers. During their trip, however, ten of them took it upon themselves to turn into spies. Instead of reporting on all the opportunities that were there for the taking, these ten "explorers" couldn't get the enemies they had observed out of their minds. As a result, they spread a bad report among the people. It's interesting that when Moses recorded this incident, he used the expression "spread" a bad report instead of "gave" a bad report. He was making the point that these ten spies reported their findings in such a way as to incite panic and fear. I guess even back then it was still true that bad news travels fast and misery loves company.

The cowards' report gripped the entire camp with fear (over a million-plus people). They said, "We can't attack those people; they *are stronger than we are* . . . The land we explored *devours those living in it*. All the people we saw there are of great size . . . We seemed like grasshoppers in our own eyes, and we looked the same to them."[7]

Ten of these explorers made the same mistake I see so many Christian parents making today. First, they played the "comparison" game. It's a game you can never win. They compared the size of their enemy to the size of themselves. There was no comparison (and there never will be). The enemy was far bigger, more powerful, and better funded than they were. God knew that when He sent them in to check out the land, but, to Him, it was an irrelevant point. God had not only proved He was capable of helping them to overcome the worst challenges they would ever face (think Pharaoh, too much water, too little water, the Ten Commandments, etc.), but He had also assured them that they would have nothing to worry about when they finally faced their enemies.

Comparison wasn't the only mistake they made. These explorers also made the mistake of thinking their enemies would view them as easy prey and simply devour them. They said, "We seemed like grass-hoppers in our own eyes, and *we looked the same to them*." The first part of their statement might have been an accurate comparison if you were looking at the situation strictly from a physical perspective (minus the Lord Almighty factored into the equation), but the second part was a stretch. How did they know the enemies figured they were grasshoppers by comparison?

There's no indication the explorers ever sat down with any of these "giants" to discuss Israel's pending attack to get their take on the whole situation. So how could they speak for the giants? They couldn't. They *assumed* their enemies viewed them that way, just like so many intimi-dated Christian parents do today. They compare themselves and their kids to the gigantic enemies that surround them in the entertainment world, the public school system, and the typical bedroom community, and then they draw a conclusion out of thin air that the enemy is planning on having their entire family for dinner.

In fact, in the biblical account it was the other way around. Forty years later, while the next generation of Israelites camped on the east side of the Jordan River, Joshua sent out "spies" (real spies this time) to assess the enemy threat that awaited them in Jericho. These spies hid in Rahab's apartment (Rahab was a *prostitute*) until it was safe for them to sneak back out of the walled city.

Listen to what Rahab told them before they went back to make their report to Joshua: "I know that the LORD has given this land to you and that a great fear of you has fallen on us, so that all who live in this country are melting in fear because of you . . . Everyone's courage failed because of you, for the LORD your God is God in heaven above and on the earth below."[8]

This could happen now in our country. In fact it should be happening. If the Christian community feared God the way they should, they wouldn't fear man or the powers of evil at all. And the world system would have an intimidated and healthy fear of what righteous believers can do if they stand in unison in the power of the God they serve. Instead, it seems the church's overconcern about the power of the wicked culture has rendered God lame, framed the Christian community as a large group of irrelevant, whiny cowards, and in the process given all the high ground to the enemy.

While I'm on this subject, I should mention that there is a third mistake some Christian parents make. They may not compare themselves to their enemies or assume their enemies already view them as vanquished, but they listen too much to fellow Christians that do. There are a lot of loud voices out there, pleading for parents to get their children into the attic and keep them there as long as they can. They must be fairly convincing, because there is a wholesale following of them heading up the narrow stairs into spiritual hideaways.

If you take a peek at Leviticus 26, you realize that the ten explorers should have known better. Listen to what God had already told the entire nation of Israel:

If you follow my decrees and are careful to obey my commands,
. . . I will grant peace in the land, and you will lie down and no
one will make you afraid. I will remove savage beasts from the
land, and the sword will not pass through your country. You will
pursue your enemies, and they will fall by the sword before you.
Five of you will chase a hundred, and a hundred of you will
chase ten thousand, and your enemies will fall by the sword
before you.[9]

Just an aside here: The sword for today's warrior is the Word of
God.[10] It's amazing how confident young Christian soldiers can become
in their faith when God's Word is embedded in their hearts.[11] God's Word
is able to overwhelm the clear and present dangers they face every day
they live in the midst of the hostile world system.

In this Leviticus passage, God goes on to say, "I will walk among
you and be your God, and you will be my people. I am the LORD your
God, who brought you out of Egypt so that you would no longer be
slaves to the Egyptians; I broke the bars of your yoke and enabled you
to walk with heads held high."[12]

God had already told them their size was irrelevant; it didn't matter
how small they were or how big their enemies were. The only *fact*
(read: *truth*) they needed to remember was that if they put their confidence in the power of God, He was going to go out ahead of them. They
and God were not only going to be a majority, they were going to be a
victorious majority.

Nothing has changed. The odds are still the same when you assess
the danger your family faces next to whatever or whomever you are
depending on to protect you. Any Christian parents that put their confidence solely in the finished work of Christ on the cross can enjoy a victorious life without fear of the enemy. They can also go into the world
knowing that God will honor their faith. They don't have to adopt a posture of ducking or always living in fear of the enemy's salvos, but can
hold their heads high because of their position and power in Christ. On
the other hand, those who are counting on the thickness of the walls of

their evangelical compound to protect their children are simply deluding themselves. The enemy will eventually find them and attack.

It's interesting how God follows this promise of His provision in the book of Leviticus. He goes on to say,

> If you will not listen to me and carry out all these commands, and if you reject my decrees and abhor my laws and fail to carry out all my commands and so violate my covenant, then I will do this to you: I will bring upon you sudden terror, wasting diseases and fever that will destroy your sight and drain away your life. You will plant seed in vain, because your enemies will eat it. I will set my face against you so that you will be defeated by your enemies; those who hate you will rule over you, and *you will flee even when no one is pursuing you.*[13]

I see a lot of parallels between what God told the children of Israel and the problems plaguing many Christian families today. We have been given many mandates: Go. Stand firm. Resist the devil. Be a light unto a dark world. Be salt to a bland culture. God did not put age limits on these commands (as Joseph, Samuel, David, Daniel, and a brave young man in Acts 23:16–22 attest to). But we cannot follow God's mandates as families if we are holed up inside some evangelical bunker. We can only give lip service to them.

The historical record shows that the evangelical movement has pulled away from the world's lost culture as families and sometimes as entire churches. We have created all we need inside our safe systems and no longer require any real prolonged and intimate contact with the corrupted world around us. But unfortunately, this actually changes the odds against us in favor of our enemies. Instead of being the occupying and stabilizing force in culture, we have handed that honor and privilege over to the enemies of God. Instead of our being the primary influence in our culture, the enemies of God are. We're not occupying anything. We're too cloistered in our attics.

That's why it looks like the enemy is winning. And that's why so many of our kids are inclined to reject our faith. Many families who have placed their kids in safe and sterilized Christian educational systems through their entire childhood are shocked when the enemy steals the spiritual seed away with ease once they get out on their own. The enemies of the cross have the high ground in our culture, and they seem to be ruling the agenda. And this has happened, in large part, because we have surrendered the high ground to them. We've handed the entertainment world, the educational system, and even the broader community over to the Prince of Darkness. We didn't need to engage any of these points of influence in our culture because we had replaced them with evangelical knockoffs that accommodated our personal needs.

Safe and protected spiritual environments become substitutes for the Holy Spirit and the application of God's Word. Kids may learn a lot of Bible in these environments, but they don't learn to depend on the Bible to thrive because they don't need to. Eventually apathy and indifference move to the surface. The god that has been modeled for them is not a god who can protect them. Kids' rebellion is often a reaction to an environment that makes God appear weak, anemic, and helpless.

The most telling parallel in the passage above is the statement "You will flee even when no one is pursuing you." That's wholesale *paranoia*. Like Stephen in the attic for fifty-seven years, many Christian families hide from threats that don't even exist. Keep this in mind: When your focus is on the power of Jesus Christ through His work on behalf of you on the cross, these threats *don't* exist!

You say, "Listen, there's nothing phantom about the things I'm worried about." The Bible disagrees. It says they are real only if you are putting your trust in your own ability to overcome them. If everything depends on you or some evangelical life support system to protect your kid from the evils of their culture, then I'd suggest you hide your children even deeper in the attic you have created for them because, ultimately, the forces of evil will find you and they will get your child. That is the case if you are trusting in your own abilities or your evangelical life-support system. If, on the other hand, your focus is on the Lord Jesus Christ, you have *nothing* to be afraid of.

The sad result of Israel's fear was that God told them to take another lap around Sinai. And for forty years that generation of fear-based followers kept walking and walking in the safe surroundings of a desolate desert until one by one they died off. As a side note, the Christian movement made a wholesale escape to the attic around the early 1970s. Although there have been many wonderful and bold freedom fighters standing tall and taking ground against the enemy in the meantime, a significant number within the body of Christ have chosen to take the safe way out.

We're coming to the end of another forty years. I find it so fascinating that the buzz among a significant percentage of the newest generation of parents is that they want nothing to do with hiding from culture. It may well be that God has finally allowed the generation that chose safety over strength four decades ago to slip out of the way so He can finally do what He intended to do all along. But He will do it through their more courageous offspring. And by the way, many of these courageous offspring are the very children that rebelled against their parents' substitute Christian life-support system. As I look around and see some of the great victories for Christ being won, I am absolutely encouraged.

THE TOXIC NATURE OF FEAR

The reason fear-based parenting is a breeding ground for rebellion should be obvious to most, but apparently it isn't. It bears repeating: when parents allow their culture or the powers of darkness to intimidate them enough to raise their children in a cloistered environment, it sends the wrong message to the child. This is especially true when the parents subtly move their confidence in their child's spiritual well-being from the Lord to whatever system they've built for protecting that child (Christian school, homeschool, and spiritually sterilized relationships).

It says to the child, "Our God can't protect us. The enemies are too big. We're grasshoppers next to them." The problem is not in taking precautions or in protecting children from the evils of their culture (especially when they are young). That's actually part of wise parenting. The problem is when we do this *based on our fears*. Take Christian schooling or homeschooling, for instance. When done for the right reasons, these can be excellent outlets for educating our kids. But when done for the wrong reasons, these same outlets can transform within the child's mind into an attic hideaway. This keeps them from having to learn how to thrive through the Holy Spirit's power at street level. These kids figure out that their parents have signed them up with a feeble God.

And there is something very important we need to understand here. When using educational options as spiritual hideaways, it is irrelevant what we teach our children about how mighty our God is. They are going to draw their conclusions about Him from the fear-based example we set as parents and spiritual leaders. Talk has always been cheap. It's only when we line up our words with our actions that our words have any true impact. It's like a drill sergeant thinking he has prepared the men and women of his platoon for combat simply by having them watch *Saving Private Ryan* and *We Were Soldiers*, but never taking them through the dangerous rigors of basic training lest they get injured.

Many rebellious kids are simply tired of life in the attic. They are tired of hiding. They are tired of the lethargy in their souls and the atrophy in their spiritual muscles. They are bored with a faith that takes no risks. They want to know either that their God is big enough and powerful enough to provide them safety among their enemies, or that He isn't. They especially want to see parents who claim to believe this living their lives in the face of their spiritual enemies.

I've been guilty of what I am talking about. There have been times when I've given the enemy far too much credit and not given God enough. There's a chance you and your kids have been hiding, too. Please reconsider. Get those kids out of their attic before it's too late—before you or your kids are too old and too scared to make a difference. Don't let a childhood of opportunity pass your kids by. Attic air is stagnant and musty, the view is lousy, and because of what Christ did for us on a cross, the threat we imagined no longer exists.

Let me close this part of the discussion on fear with one of my favorite quotes from one of my favorite presidents, Teddy Roosevelt: "Far better it is to dare mighty things, to win glorious triumphs, even though checkered by failure, than to take rank with those poor spirits who neither enjoy much nor suffer much, because they live in the gray twilight that knows neither victory nor defeat."

THE POWER OF RESISTANCE

The second reason that many Christian parents raise their children in controlled, spiritually isolated environments is because . . .

They Are Convinced It Makes Their Children Stronger

This is probably the biggest deception of cloistered Christian parenting. It actually sets kids up for rebellion by making them vulnerable to the whims of evil. Let me tell you another story that illustrates the problem of raising your kids in an environment that is tailored to keep out the bad elements of the world system.

Ladies and gentlemen, let me introduce you to *Biosphere 2.* It was one of those extravagant experiments that only a Texas billionaire would fund. The purpose was to see if we could sustain a livable existence in other parts of the universe. With space exploration moving to new levels, it just seemed a matter of time before we would be tempted to colonize the moon or some nearby planet.

To successfully maintain human life for an indefinite period of time in a completely hostile environment, we'd have to somehow re-create all the ecological necessities of earth in a closed system that could sustain both itself and the human life living within it. It would have to be able to produce oxygen and water as well as the other elements necessary for the ongoing demands of plant and human life. A "dry run" was staged in a pocket of the Arizona desert just a little northeast of Tucson. It was called "the Biosphere."

The jury is still out as to whether they proved their point. Some design flaws and early setbacks skewed the findings. I'll let the scientists argue whether the investor got his money's worth from the whole process, but there is one thing they did discover that offers a rich insight for parents trying to raise great kids in a hostile world.

The lesson came from the trees.

For humans to flourish in the vacuum of space, a sealed environment with multiple ecosystems had to be created. The systems had to work in harmony for the arid, temperate, and tropical systems to produce the vital pieces of the earth's life cycle. The trees were essential. In fact, they were the most vital link to sustaining life. They would not only produce fruit for the food chain but oxygen for the life chain. They would be the essential players in the production of moisture and rain. Nothing but the best trees were selected. They were put in place well in advance of the actual experiment so they would be firmly established when it was time for them to play their strategic role.

But once the scientists were sealed inside the dome for their two-year-long experiment, it was obvious that something was seriously wrong with the trees. They didn't flourish. They drooped, sagged, and struggled to stand upright. They got top-heavy and fell over. Their lack of strength diminished the amount of oxygen they were creating. This put in motion a string of life-threatening problems with the experiment. If it had gone on indefinitely, the oxygen levels would have dropped well below the minimums for sustaining human life. As it was, they had to pump in oxygen before the experiment was over to keep the internal atmosphere from falling below life-supporting levels.

There was one key factor to raising strong trees that the scientists had failed to include: wind. There was no wind in the Biosphere. The trees were never forced to contend with the contrary winds that trees in the forest would normally face. Contrary winds and occasional fierce gales have the effect of developing healthy bark, deep roots, and strong, nimble cores. Without wind, trees are anemic, brittle, and vulnerable. A tree that doesn't have to fight the wind as a sapling can be felled by a mild storm as an adult.

Do you see how this applies to what we're talking about? It's easy to conclude that a spiritual greenhouse would be a better place to raise kids. The word I hear thrown around the most is *safe*. We want an environment for our child that is physically safe, intellectually safe, emotionally safe, sexually safe, and spiritually safe. We assume that without it, he or she can't possibly survive. And we mistakenly conclude that with these safe environments, kids are automatically made strong.

That type of thinking is as flawed as the kind the scientists used when planting their trees in the Biosphere. When it comes to spiritual growth, contrary winds force kids' true character to the surface. A contrary environment drives their spiritual root system deeper into both the Word of God and the heart of God. Exposure to the fierce and stormy winds of culture demands that our children completely rely on Christ. Our children need to deal with reality—far more than the *canned* resistance of a parent or a Christian schoolteacher playing the devil's advocate.

Too often, Christian families pull their children as far away from everything contrary as possible. Whether it's in the area of education, the media, entertainment, or relationships, we unwittingly assume safe is better. It might seem that way at the moment, but in the long run, *strong* is better. Spiritual strength is not created in a sealed environment. It requires substantial resistance.

Some of the standard responses I hear from parents at this point are "But she's not ready," "He can't handle that!" "I just feel that they'll be overwhelmed." So we put them in environments where they aren't forced to *get* ready, *handle* it, or *rise above* it. Then we seem surprised that they have struggles getting their act together as adults. All those points about our children's weaknesses may be true. But there are a few other points that are equally true, and when we ignore them, we may be setting our children up for a life of mediocrity, spiritual irrelevance, and perhaps even spiritual annihilation.

Points like this one: "My grace is sufficient for you, for my power is made perfect in weakness."[14]

Or this one: "No temptation has seized you except what is common to man. And God is faithful; he will not let you be tempted beyond what you can bear. But when you are tempted, he will also provide a way out so that you can stand up under it."[15]

Again, I need to remind you that there is no age limit for when these truths kick in for a believer.

Jesus *intentionally* led His disciples into a fierce storm on the Sea of Galilee. He proceeded to take a nap while they fought for their lives against the angry seas. When they finally awakened Him to inquire why He seemed to have such little regard for their personal safety, "He got up, rebuked the wind and said to the waves, 'Quiet! Be still!' Then the wind died down and it was completely calm. He said to his disciples, 'Why are you so afraid? Do you still have no faith?'" (Mark 4:39–40).

It was watching Jesus *order around* the weather that got the disciples finally thinking that perhaps He was more than just an enlightened rabbi. Seeing Christ work on their behalf in the midst of the storm validated His deity in their minds.

I'm certainly not suggesting we maintain no standards. And when our children are youngest, they need the most protection from us. That's when they need to grow safely as saplings within the shadow of their parents—the mature trees. In those early years, we can and should shelter them from the fiercest challenges of the corrupted world system that surrounds them.

But as they grow in our grace-based families, we need to move our role from *protecting* them to *preparing* them. It's not just because we have to equip them to survive in a hostile world. It's because we have to equip them to *flourish*—to *love the people* in that world, to *reach out to them*, to be *an agent of God's mercy and grace*. If we do it right, there's something in it for everyone. In the end, our children will be able not only to grow their roots deeper in their love for God, but also to be used by Him to breathe life into a desperate people in a hostile world. They will become strong trees creating abundant spiritual oxygen for the suffocating people around them.

The Bible illustrates a lot of truth from trees: "The ax is already at the root of the trees, and every tree that does not produce good fruit will be cut down and thrown into the fire."[16]

"He is like a tree planted by streams of water, which yields its fruit in season and whose leaf does not wither. Whatever he does prospers."[17]

This last verse is interesting, since it is from a passage that many fear-based Christians use to justify growing their families in isolation from the world around them. Psalm 1:1–3 says,

> Blessed is the man
> who does not walk in the counsel of the wicked

or stand in the way of sinners
  or sit in the seat of mockers.
But his delight is in the law of the LORD,
  and on his law he meditates day and night.
He is like a tree planted by streams of water,
  which yields its fruit in season
and whose leaf does not wither.
  Whatever he does prospers.

In the first part of this psalm, David refers to a man who is giving authority in his life to three types of people: the wicked, the sinners, and the mockers. This man *walks* with them, *stands* with them, and *sits* with them. The overriding point of this verse is that this man is putting himself in a subordinate position of being influenced by these negative elements. David is saying, "That's foolish." I couldn't agree more. Parents who expose their children to the world system at large without placing a careful system of filters around them are simply reckless parents. The world, and the evil forces behind it, will crush their children like bugs.

But there's nothing in this psalm suggesting we have no contact with the world. It's just saying we need to be firmly grounded in an environment that is conducive to a deep spiritual root system and the production of the kind of fruit that nourishes the world around us. This environment is found in grace-based homes where parents are paying attention to what their children have to contend with. These parents coach their children with the living Word of God and model a passionate faith that validates the presence of God in their lives. This is how children learn for themselves how to appropriate the power of the Holy Spirit to stand strong.

I've often heard 1 Corinthians 15:33 as a justification for keeping our children from exposure to the dangerous elements of the world system. It says, "Do not be deceived: 'Bad company corrupts good morals'" (NASB). This is actually a quote of a quote that was floating around in Paul's day (notice the punctuation). There's no hidden meaning here. It's a great piece of advice to naive kids. "Don't be irresponsible with your heart or your mind. If you hand either of these over to bad elements in society, they can corrupt your moral core."

But this statement does not say, "Don't allow yourself to be exposed to the world." It's just saying, "Don't be stupid!" Paul is not saying Christians should have no contact with the world system. Such a statement would contradict all of his other writings that teach believers how to flourish in the midst of the corrupt world system. I so often hear parents applying this verse to children. Paul isn't directing it to children in particular but people in general. It's not age-specific, but is simply good advice for believers of all ages.

With all the Christians raised in cloistered and safe Christian environments that boast of producing "uniquely Christian" assets for the kingdom of God, you'd think once those kids are adults, we'd have a lot more of them signing up for service on the front lines of the cause of Christ. The sad fact is, for the most part, they simply take their "hiding" mind-set to more sophisticated and comfortable levels. Meanwhile, the kids who were raised on the front lines move into adulthood ready to continue what they've been doing from the beginning.

SAFE VERSUS STRONG

I went out of my way in my book *Grace-Based Parenting* to make this point. Parents whose goal is to raise a spiritually safe kid usually get a spiritually safe kid in the process. But they also often get a spiritually *weak* kid. The child is weak when it comes to standing up against the harsh pressures of a lost world. Once they are exposed to the full gale, down they go. On the other hand, parents who want to raise strong children realize it cannot happen without the children having to work their spiritual muscles. They realize that no cultural pain results in no spiritual gain.

Just as God enables our bodies to get strong and stay healthy, He does the same for our spirits. I read an article that said doctors had located the healthiest kids on the planet. They were the street urchins of São Paulo, Brazil. These were children who had been exposed to horrendous amounts of germs and diseases, which forced their internal antibody systems to kick into high gear. These children didn't have the luxury of synthetic drugs or antibiotics. This actually turned out to be better for them. The fact is, modern medicine is learning that overprescribing antibiotics has only left people weaker and more susceptible to every new germ that comes along. Antibiotics not only destroy the bad things in us, they destroy the good things in us, too. The Brazilian children's bodies had been forced to rise to the challenge. In the process, they had developed phenomenal health.

In the same way, God has designed our spirits to work at their maximum when the strength and protection come *from the inside out* in resistance to external challenges. Love for Jesus, His death and resurrection, the Holy Spirit, and the Word of God all come alive in the hearts of those who depend on them to overcome outside threats to their beliefs.

A cloistered, safe environment is an *outside-in* configuration. When we're putting our confidence in an external evangelical system, our children are only as safe as our ability to keep that external system in place. The systems are easily penetrated, and the penetration is all it takes to finish many kids off. Much like the outer protective shell of a crustacean, if it is breached, the crustacean doesn't get uncomfortable or sick. It dies.

Probably the number one justification I hear from parents of why we should not allow our children to be exposed to the world system is the old white glove versus the mud analogy. The father says to me, "Listen, Tim, if you put a white glove on your hand and stick it in the mud, what happens?" Answer: "You get mud on the glove." And then he goes on to say, "See, Tim, there is no excuse for letting your kids be exposed to the world. It will get all over them!"

I always think the same thing: *You're giving all the power to the mud. You haven't given any power to the* blood. What did Christ's death on the cross do? Did it give the believer any power to stand up against the evils of the world? Of course it did! And He doesn't reserve its power only for grown, mature Christians. It's available to everyone. My wife and I have never worried about how much of the world gets *on* our kids. Our concern has been how much of the world gets *in* our kids.

Lest you think I've totally lost my mind, let me bring Rick Warren into this discussion. In his powerful book *The Purpose-Driven Life* he writes, "God develops the fruit of the Spirit in your life by allowing you to experience circumstances in which you're tempted to express the exact opposite quality! Character development always involves a choice, and temptation provides that opportunity."[18]

But forget about my opinion or Rick Warren's. Look at what *God* says about this issue. As we've seen, cowardly explorers brought back a bad report when they were sent in to explore the Promised Land. As a result of their fearful account and the people's fearful response to it, the entire wilderness group had to wander around the Sinai desert until every member of that unfaithful generation had died (except for the faithful Joshua and his friend Caleb).

Forty years later, that generation's children went into the Promised Land under the leadership of Joshua and took it over. It was the offspring of *this* group (i.e., the *grandchildren* of the original unfaithful generation who died in the wilderness) we're introduced to in the beginning of the book of Judges. These are the kids of the parents who had looked down the barrel of their enemy's gun. This experience taught their parents there was no need to be intimidated by their enemies. Jehovah God was destroying their enemies in front of them as quickly as they could confront them.

Their enemies were real and were imposing. But God still expected them to strap on their armor, don their weapons, and go out onto the battlefield and face them. Even with God on their side, there were still personal risks. The Israelites lost some of their noble soldiers. But that believing generation learned just how mighty their God truly was (and is).

The children of this generation who took over the land did not face combat. Their parents had done all the hard work for them. They were getting the benefit of a wonderful land for which they didn't have to pay any personal price. Sound familiar? Does it sound like they enjoyed the glory of the land while their parents had to passionately pay for it (à la *Rocky III*)? Does it sound like having someone else pay for your sacrifice (à la King David)? That's exactly how it came across to God, too. He knows that a life without risks, and a paycheck without a workweek, doesn't make people strong. Look, therefore, at what the Bible says in Judges 3:1–2: "These are the nations the LORD *left to test* all those Israelites who had not experienced any of the wars in Canaan (he did this only to teach warfare to the descendants of the Israelites who had not had previous battle experience)," (emphasis added).

Then you read the names of the nations God left remnants of for them to contend with—Philistines, Canaanites, Sidonians, and Hivites—and you realize God left extremely dangerous influences for them to face. These were people who would feel right at home on Bourbon Street or in a *Nightmare on Elm Street* movie. God knew there is no safety in safety. Safety comes only from being strong—from being pushed into conflicts that force you to appropriate His power.

I hear so much whining among the evangelical Christian population about how corrupt and evil our culture is. How do we know God didn't want some of this corruption facing us so we would have an excellent opportunity to raise strong and mighty warriors for His kingdom in the midst of it?

When Our Anger Gets the Best of Us

The third reason that many Christian parents raise their children in environments that don't expose them to the world is because . . .

The Parents Can't Stand the Worldly Culture

I certainly understand this attitude because there are many things about a world system without boundaries that can turn a believer's stomach. The hedonism, the debauchery, and the way the world system flaunts their condescension toward the things of God, well, it's enough to make a preacher cuss (if that wasn't already unacceptable). Put these reasons together with about fifty others, and you can understand Christian parents who want neither themselves nor their kids to have anything to do with our fallen culture. Every inclination is to stay as far from it as possible.

Here's the problem: disdain for the things of the world can slip across a thin line and become a disdain for the *people* in the world. Children that grow up in homes where parents are quick to speak critically about people caught up in the world's way of thinking are going to have a tough time personally appropriating God's grace. If grace is not shown toward the people who need it most, how are kids going to learn to show it in their day-to-day involvement with others, including their own parents?

Disdain for the people of the world also makes these people appear bigger and more sinister than they actually are. It also gives the culture itself greater power than God gives it in the Bible. Children exposed to their Christian parents' disdain for the world system—including its people—can grow up with a paranoid attitude that causes them to live in lifelong isolation.

Another problem with speaking so harshly against "voices of evil" is that we are demonstrating that Christians can't stand them. This may not be true, but it's hard for people caught up in the traps of the world system to know that. It is equally hard for young, impressionable Christian kids within our homes to sort this all out. Any child in a family that habitually berates the lost world is destined for problems and likely to become a candidate for rebellion. That's because, as we've said before, the message communicated by the frustrated or angry parent contradicts the message of the gospel.

Let's take the famous verse John 3:16, for example: "For God so loved the world that He gave His only begotten Son, that whoever believes in Him should not perish but have everlasting life" (NKJV). When John wrote these words, he did what would take hundreds of committed Christians months to come up with if they were forced to write a purpose statement for Jesus Christ. Just about everybody in America—saved or unsaved—has heard this verse or at least seen it printed somewhere.

Christians love this verse because it is about us. We were born as members of the world God loved enough to die for. And when we decided to hand over the deed of our lives to Jesus, we became the immediate recipients of all the hope that is contained in the words "should not perish but have everlasting life." It's easy, however, to get wrapped up in all the pomp and pageantry that goes with this statement. Sometimes we forget that we started out as hopelessly lost members of the same world we now shun. Instead of remembering our own pasts, we fall into the trap of accumulating a pile of rocks for the next attack on our enemies. We plink away with our verbal condemnations at the problems and the people who frustrate us.

We get angry when a fatherless family moves in next door to us. The kids are out of control and sometimes the mom is out of ideas. I've known Christian moms in these situations who have prayed that God would move these kinds of families out of their neighborhoods. When you ask them what they'd like in their place, it's always the same: "a nice Christian family with kids that my kids could play with." They want the opportunity for evangelism and spiritual growth to move away, so they can enjoy a little touch of heaven. Maybe we all need to be reminded that heaven was never intended to be experienced on earth. It's what God has waiting for us when our work *here on earth* is done.

Here's another scenario I recently ran across. A nice Christian family woke up to the news that a gay couple had bought the house a few doors down. Standard operating procedure for this mother was to put together a welcome basket and go to the new family's house, with her children in tow, to welcome them to the neighborhood. This was always followed with an invitation to her home for a barbecue.

But when Mom heard that it was two men—and sexual partners to boot—who moved in, she made it clear there was no way her family was going to roll out the welcome wagon. And it was out of the question that the two men would ever be invited to their backyard for a welcome party. In the process, her kids learned how to fear and loathe people caught up in the world system.

There are many problems in this kind of thinking, but the biggest is that it embodies complete rejections of John 3:16. Anger and loathing toward people in the world system is like coughing up a large mouthful of spit and firing it right on John 3:16 in your Bible.

You say, "That's a bit harsh, Tim. Just because I have serious problems with people who flaunt their sin and would rather keep some distance between them and my family, doesn't mean I have anything but love for God's message in John 3:16."

Actually, yes, it does. You see, John 3:16 is part of a longer statement. It's almost always quoted as a stand-alone verse, but John connected it to the verse immediately following it. He used a word that indicates a continuation of his thought. He said, "*For* God did not send his Son into the world to condemn the world, but to save the world through him" (verse 17, emphasis added).

One day God pulled me up by the collar with this verse. I was extremely "offended" by the debauched behavior of a particular group of people and had become outspoken against them to some friends. Fortunately (or unfortunately), I was in the company of Christians who shared my misguided disdain for these people. Shortly afterward I was alone with God, reading John 3:17. Although I've never heard God's voice audibly, I clearly sensed Him putting thoughts in my mind. It went something like this: *Who do you think you are? How dare you speak this way of these people! How dare you even* think *these thoughts! These are lost people. I* love *them. I came to die for them. Let Me decide who stands or who falls. In the meantime, you extend to them all the love, grace, and mercy I extended to you.*

In homes where fear reigns, where isolation prevails, and where criticism of the lost is commonplace, kids are going to rebel. They *should* rebel against it. It's antithetical to the heart of God. Unfortunately, when they do, they often find themselves running headlong into the very arms of the system their family was so outspokenly against.

Completing the Foursome

I said there were four reasons why Christian parents prefer to raise their children in highly controlled spiritual environments. They are convinced it makes their children safer, they are under the delusion it makes them stronger, and it's the logical conclusion of an internal attitude that loathes the worldly culture around them. The fourth reason that many Christian parents raise their children in environments that don't expose them to the world is because . . .

It's Easier
I'm not suggesting that conscientious Christian parents don't work hard at raising their kids. They certainly do. Nor am I saying it is necessarily

easy to raise a kid in a tightly controlled environment. It's just easier than raising them in the middle of the world system.

Parents who raise their children in controlled environments study the Bible, but they can afford to have comfortable Bible studies. These parents pray, but they can afford to pray comfortable prayers. They can spend their time thanking God for the protection and safety their children enjoy in their spiritual attics and biospheres. And I can see why this is so attractive.

The alternative is clearly nasty. If you choose to raise your children on the front lines, there is no such thing as a *comfortable* Bible study. You are forced into the Bible out of desperation, and there's no way you get to settle for superficial answers. When it comes to prayer, you seldom get to share any conversation with God that doesn't include a discussion about some imminent threat that is staring down at you or your children. Prayers don't get to be short or sweet, either. Usually they're a running conversation you slip out of when you drift off to sleep at night and pick up with abandon as soon as your eyes open in the morning. In fact, I'd have to say that raising your kids in the world *guarantees* that you'll *never* be comfortable with how much of the Bible you know, and you'll *never* be satisfied with how much time you've spent in prayer. You'll just become more comfortable with God. You'll be satisfied with Him, too.

In the process, your kids will see something that is hard to detect inside the safe confines of a controlled Christian environment: Walking headlong with Jesus into the challenges of the harsh world is the safest place we can ever be. Having Him working from inside us through the power of His grace is the strongest we can ever be. His presence dramatically diminishes the size of the world's threats and eclipses its allures.

It's much easier to choose a path that doesn't require us to pay close attention to what is happening in our kids' lives. It's also nice because it accommodates our lack of biblical knowledge and limited spiritual experience. It's a plan that actually works . . . as long as Satan doesn't challenge it. The problem is what to do when something goes haywire and the kids start seeing their spiritual lives for what they really are—

inadequate for the challenge. This, of course, catches parents off guard. A sudden change in kids' behavior that is contradictory to everything they have been taught sends Mom and Dad into a tailspin.

This sharply contrasts with what happens to parents who chose to raise their kids in the world from the beginning. These parents have been helping the kids process their innate, low-grade rebellion from the get-go. They know how to use life's circumstances to raise a child's spiritual temperature from lukewarm to white-hot.

Meanwhile, parents inside the attic are suddenly confronted with a kid they assumed was on fire for God but who has gradually grown cold. Since they were more preoccupied with avoiding the culture rather than engaging it, these parents don't know what to do once they're confronted with the totality of its ugliness. They don't know what to do with the music, the philosophies, the entertainment, the clothing, or the hairstyles. Mostly, they don't know what to do with the rage. Usually they panic. Sadly, this only communicates to their children that their parents are in over their heads and haven't a clue what they're doing. These children lose even more confidence in the beliefs they've been taught.

The painful truth is that we often choose a greenhouse environment for our kids because in the end, it requires less from us. We don't have to pray as hard, study God's Word as much, lean on His Spirit as often, or trust in His promises as consistently. In the end, we all lose.

What happens to many of the kids who have been raised in an attic/biosphere configuration? Too many of them grow up with an unrealistic view of the world system. They tend to take sides at one extreme end of a continuum or the other, either of which creates shallow faith.

These kids may turn out to be *overly critical* of the world system, wanting nothing to do with its lost and corrupted people. The problem with this attitude is that the Bible doesn't support it. In fact, this attitude comes straight from *Satan's* playbook. They marry people similar to them, maintain nice Christian lives inside a relatively safe environment, raise nice kids, do some workshop-type evangelism and service. In the end, however, they don't even come close to making the kind of impact for Christ they could have. They really do have a nice life, though. But sadly, it's a life that doesn't make much of a difference in the long run—certainly not the difference God meant for it to make.

On the other extreme, there are the children who come out of these *safe* Christian environments *naive* about the world system. All this does is make them putty in Satan's hands. Their lack of firsthand training on how caustic the world system is and how utterly evil Satan is sets them up for the kill. Satan usually uses a recipe that includes the base ingredient of lust of the flesh, throws in a double portion of lust of the eyes, and then gradually stirs in boastful pride of life. Cook it all in an environment of sex, drugs, and rock-'n'-roll until it comes to a boil and then, voilà: "Sautéed Christian Kid."

I don't think Satan could script some of the philosophies of Christian parenting better than many Christians already have. Lest you take certain personal umbrage at that, remember, he is the master deceiver. His primary targets are not those who have already lost their way. He focuses most of his attention on those who are card-carrying members of the Way, the Truth, and the Life. And he needs only to get us a couple of degrees off to get us to miss the target entirely.

LEGALISM

The safe route is the easiest route. Unfortunately, taking the easy route is also the fast track to a legalistic mind-set. Nobody likes to think that their system of child rearing is legalistic. When I suggest it in person, I'm usually looking for something to hide behind to protect myself from the angry salvos that almost inevitably follow the suggestion. Jesus ran into the same reaction when He made a similar point to the Pharisees. But the Bible teaches us that any time we distill our relationship with God down to a system that substitutes for a complete and total dependence on Him and Him alone, we have slipped into the trap of legalism. I've observed over the years that when someone gets hostile over the suggestion that their dependence on man-made systems might put them in the legalist camp, it's a dead giveaway that they've already paid their campground fee, pitched their tent, and have a nice campfire crackling.

But there's a logical reason why so many parents won't acknowl-edge that the system they've set up is nothing more than state-of-the-art legalism. It's because it isn't legalism when they evaluate it from the per-spective of what they are experiencing personally. Let me explain . . .

Mom and Dad may have a living, breathing relationship with Christ. For them He truly is new every morning. But the way they transfer that relationship to their children becomes legalism. Let's do some comparisons to make the point. You may automatically read your Bible every day without prompting, but the only way you can get your child to do it is by *making* them read it. You may automatically mem-orize Scripture in order to enrich your relationship with God; but if your children memorize Scripture, it tends to be because you've asked them to, or it's part of their home-school or Christian school homework assignment.

You may get up on Sunday morning anxious to go to church, and you go there whether you feel like it or not. It's an activity that is part of your spiritual second nature. It's the logical extension of your inti-mate relationship with God. Some of your kids may feel the same way. But there are others that would just as soon stay home. They go to church because they have no choice. You serve God out of the good-ness of your heart. Your children, however, may serve Him out of guilt or to complete a requirement of their Christian educational curriculum. You don't swear, cuss, or use the Lord's name in vain because you don't want to. However, your children don't swear, cuss, or use the Lord's name in vain because if they did, they'd get into trouble. They are doing the same things as you, but not for the same reasons. You're doing it out of a wonderful heart for God. They're doing it because—at least while they're young—they don't have much of an alternative.

That's the way children develop a legalistic relationship with God. Am I saying you shouldn't have your child read the Bible or memorize Scripture or go to church or serve or watch their language? Of course I'm not. And of course you should. But realize that just because your children are doing these things doesn't mean they're doing them with enthusiasm. These actions are good for them, but they don't represent a true measure of faith—at least not as long as they are done under compulsion. What moves these noble actions from compulsion to passion is the environment in which they are done.

In the meantime, however, parents who are raising their children on the front lines of their culture turn those same actions into avenues that lead directly to a wholehearted relationship with God. On the other hand, if the kids live in a highly protected environment for a long period of time, these actions lose much of their significance. They do them because they have to, not because they need to. For some kids, they lose any and all of their meaning.

RAISING YOUR CHILDREN IN THE WORLD

I want to suggest to you that there might be more wisdom in raising your kids on the front lines of their culture than you think. It's true that down at street level, Satan has pulled out all the stops. He's playing dirty, and he's playing for keeps. But this is also where God's power demonstrates itself most forcefully. God is not interested in holing up with us in our evangelical attics. He's in the business of seeking and saving lost people, and empowering those who are saved to live a victorious life in the midst of a lost and dying world. He's in a deliberate and determined battle for the hearts of the people caught in our culture's web of sin and deceit. He loves the lost and wants to reach them. And He loves to work through people who walk with Him by faith. His power is infinite, and He's ready to bestow that power on any and all who ask for it—young or old, novice or seasoned veteran.

As parents, you have the choice of raising your kids in an environment that either pushes them toward God or draws them to Him. Raising your kids close to the action for the cross gives them a ringside seat when they're small and a place on the fight card when they're older. All the while the God of creation has them right where He wants them, sheltered under His wing, rather than huddled in the corner of a man-made hideaway.

Raising your kids in the world brings them up to speed gradually. But there's something you absolutely must understand: It's a responsi-

bility that cannot be delegated. You cannot subcontract the job of raising passionate Christian warriors to your youth pastor or to all those nice
people trying to educate your child over at their Christian school. You
must *show* your kids the way; you must raise the banner for them; you
must lead the charge.

Let me show you how you can do this carefully and shrewdly. The
secret of raising children in a hostile culture is found in knowing the balance between *protecting* them and *preparing* them. To illustrate this,
please study the chart below. Once you've taken a good look at it, pick
up the discourse with me and I'll show you how to make the gradual
transition of a child who is totally dependent on you to a child who is
totally dependent on Jesus Christ.

Preparing Your Children to Flourish for God in a Hostile Environment

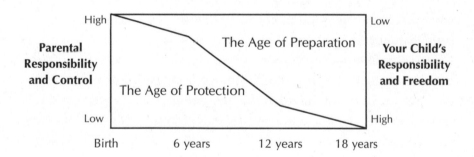

The simple idea behind this diagram is using your child's eighteen
years under your roof as an opportunity to gradually introduce him or
her to the world they must flourish in. It's a balancing act between protection and preparation as well as between parental control and a child's
individual freedom. Before we speak specifically to this process, let me
mention the two mistakes I see many Christian parents making—both of
which can lead to full-scale war with their children.

The first mistake is the one we've been addressing in this chapter.
This is when the age of protection starts at birth and goes all the way to

eighteen years old or beyond. There is no gradual decline. There is no "age of preparation." There is no string of years where children practice individual responsibility and freedom under their parents' roof. And even though parents who do this would never admit it, it is quite common among very conscientious Christian parents. Sure, they'll let them make choices, but they aren't the choices that force the children to learn to walk by faith with God. Often in these homes, the children aren't allowed to wrestle with the issues of popular music, movies, clothing, or hairstyles. Many of these kids aren't allowed to spend much time with nonbelieving kids their age, either. And some families don't allow their children to date when they are teenagers.

There is another parenting mistake that is not uncommon to Christian homes. If you were drawing it as a chart, it would look almost identical to the one above, with one exception. The age of protection and the age of preparation would switch sides. These are homes where the parents are much more lax. They let the kids have the run of the store from the outset. The children control the schedule, the agenda on that schedule, and the tone of any given moment. Basically, it's a great example of the patients running the asylum.

Parents do this for two reasons. One, they have no idea what they're doing when they first bring the kids home from the hospital. Two, when the kids are little, a lot of what they do comes across as cute and relatively harmless. But when they get older and their wills get stronger and their actions more dangerous, these same parents freak out. They realize their children are out of control, unusually selfish, and have no sense of boundaries. So to get things back under control, the parents start to put the brakes on their kids. This doesn't work. In fact, it only makes the kids step up their out-of-control game.

You don't give kids large amounts of freedom on the front side of their childhood and then take it away from them when they become teenagers. You want to do it the other way around. Control should be high on the front side of their childhood and low on the backside. Individual freedom should be low in early childhood, gradually increasing as they move through adolescence.

Which brings us back to our diagram. The rectangular box not only represents the duration of childhood, it also represents the *entire time* that you have parental authority. From birth to the time your child is grown, you're in authority. You're the parent. You're in charge. God is holding you accountable for what happens during this time. I make this point earnestly because I'm amazed how some parents balk at a plan to transfer responsibility and freedom, as though this somehow cuts off their role as leaders of the home. It does no such thing.

All that said, your job is to gradually introduce freedom and responsibility to your children. In the first six years of their lives, a very fragile and vulnerable time, you call almost all the shots. Small children are both defenseless and clueless when it comes to processing the world around them. They need to be operating on a daily schedule that is created by loving and careful parents.

This is when you want to pour the foundational cement in place when it comes to their inner needs for security, significance, and strength. Your goal for each day is to build more and more into these three inner needs by providing them with secure *love*, a significant *purpose*, and a strong *hope*. If you want to look at an expanded and in-depth plan on how to do this, please refer to my book *Grace-Based Parenting*. During this first six years, you also want to give them a ton of "lap time." This is where you read the Bible to them, pray with them, spend individual time with them, and sign up to be a part of their Sunday school experience. It is ideal if both parents do these things.

Once the kids enter the educational time line, you want to start gradually moving them from a position where you make their day-to-day decisions to a position where they are making most of them themselves. This takes place in an approximate corridor of time between six to twelve years old, a period of phenomenal physical growth as well as emotional, intellectual, and spiritual development. They are moving ahead quickly, and it is essential to make sure the trade from total dependence on you to a position of freedom with responsibility moves at the same pace.

This is where you let them start to pick their outfits for school, and give them more choices when it comes to friends and acceptable leisure activities they may want to do. You help them start experimenting with sports, musical instruments, and hobbies. This is a good time to start allowing them to make their own choices from restaurant menus. During this transition, it's also a good idea to have them read the Bible to you and pray aloud while you listen.

This middle shift into freedom with responsibility is when they need to start learning how to develop and keep good friends. You want to protect them less and intervene less in struggles they have with other children. Talk with them about their problems and pray with them, but make them work through problems on their own as much as possible. Usually, school or community gives them ample opportunity to practice this. Because they are still quite young, however, you'll need to control some of the types of friends they have. At this point they are probably not ready to cope with friends who are diametrically opposed to your family's belief system.

Around twelve years old, start introducing them to a daily life of personal responsibility. By this time they should have an alarm clock and be expected to use it. They can participate in sleepovers occasionally. Let them choose more rugged and dangerous sports and hobbies (such as paint ball, horses, diving, mountain climbing, or hunting).

Friends become very important to kids during this time. Let them take risks with friends even though they'll probably make mistakes. They might choose a bad influence or two and make some dumb choices. Let them feel the full force of the consequences of these choices, and don't rescue them from the messes they get themselves into. They will quickly learn invaluable principles about healthy relationships.

Thirteen years old is a great line of demarcation. This is when you communicate to them that, as quickly as possible, you want to help get them to a position of total independence from you. Your goal is to give them complete freedom to call their own shots in life. How long this transition takes is based on one primary factor: how quickly they show personal responsibility.

My wife and I have used this birthday as a time to codify this process. We have a "rite of passage" trip with them. We have two boys and two girls. The girls go with Mom and the boys with me. Our oldest daughter, Karis, chose a cruise. She and Darcy spent several wonderful days marking the beginning of her transition to greater independence on a beautiful ship on the Pacific Ocean.

Our son Cody chose to tour Civil War battlefields with me. During those days we went from Antietam, to Harpers Ferry, to Bull Run, to Fredericksburg, to Chancellorsville, and to Appomattox. We enjoyed many wonderful hours talking about all the great things waiting for him in adulthood. We finished off our time visiting the Officers Candidate School of the Marine Corps in Quantico, Virginia. A friend who was a Navy SEAL and serving as a chaplain at OCS showed us around.

Our daughter Shiloh chose to go to a hands-on aquarium in Florida with her mother. She had a wonderful time swimming with the minnows, dolphins, and everything in between.

While writing this manuscript, I took our youngest son, Colt, on his "rite of passage" trip. He chose an Xtreme Mexico trip. What is that? That's when we spend several days doing just about anything you can think of that requires a helmet or kneepads. We rode motorcycles, Jet Skis, parasailed, fished, and set off quite a cache of fireworks.

Adapting these kinds of activities to your family's interests will mark the beginning of your child's transition into adulthood. This transition also changes you, the parent, from being a *resource* in their life to being more of a *reference* point. You'll have many, many one-on-one conversations with your son or daughter during the next five to six years. In fact, one of the key priorities during this process is personal discussions. The best way to initiate these conversations is by asking a lot of questions and listening to a lot of answers.

Sixteen is not only that age when most states allow children to legally drive, but it's also a good age to allow them to start individual dating. Parents that allow their children to date before this are really asking for a lot of problems with sexuality. Each year your children wait represents a huge amount of maturity, which will be put to good use in making wise dating decisions. To show you just how much *chronological maturity* makes a difference, look at this information Josh McDowell put together for his "Why Wait?" campaign:[19]

Age Dating Begins	Percent Who Have Sex before Graduation
12	91%
13	56%
14	53%
15	40%
16	20%

Because you've told your children that your goal is to give them what they most want—freedom—they're less likely to demand it ahead of time. Investing more of yourself in one-on-one scenarios makes you less the person running their life and more the person grooming them for greatness.

It is during this time that you should encourage them to make their faith their own. Send them off to good camps. Encourage them to read books that might be contrary to your Christian world-view, read them yourself, and then discuss them. Allow your kids to develop more of their own taste in music. Listen to their music with them (without criticism) and then discuss it. Encourage them to branch out and develop friends with the friendless, the confused, and possibly even a person who may have an ax to grind with Christianity. Don't discourage them from signing on to outreaches and ministries that might be out of the main flow of Christian activity. Encourage them to go on mission outreaches—the riskier, the better (obviously, calculate these risks). This is the time when kids should be encouraged to give back more than they take. You might have to lead the way on this, which means you, too, may end up traveling with them to third-world countries, denying yourself the creature comforts of home, and putting yourself in situations where you aren't working from strengths. When they see you having to lean on God, not only do you become more human to them, but God becomes more real.

WHAT ABOUT THEIR EDUCATION?

In chapter 6, as well as this chapter, we've talked about some of the built-in problems inherent in a spiritually controlled educational system.

I've said several times that every educational option has some great advantages (including public school), and each one has its shortcomings (including homeschooling and Christian schooling). You'll have to choose the one that is the best match for your child and the one that will most empower (read: *force*) her to make her faith her own.

In some families, it has worked very well to homeschool children from kindergarten to third or fourth grade. The kids are enrolled in Christian school up to the seventh or eighth grade, then transferred into public high school to put the final touches on them so they can flourish in a hostile culture. My wife and I have seen many families throughout the United States use this transitional plan with great success.

We've also seen people who have very effectively homeschooled their children all the way through to college. Others have had similar success with Christian schools. Good results really have little to do with the method of schooling and more to do with how parents properly apply that method in the child's life. Wise parents never use educational institutions as a substitute for doing their own God-given job. More important, they never use educational methods as a substitute for an authentic relationship with Jesus.

My wife and I put our children in public school from day one. I have often been questioned about whether we used good judgment in this decision. A couple of times I have been publicly scorned for it. It has worked out extremely well for our children. We have two that have gone through the system. We have a third that is almost out and ready for college. Our last child will soon take his place on our local high-school campus. Each child has his or her own faith, each has a strong sense of purpose, and all of them have a driving desire to allow God to use them to make a difference.

People challenge me on this because of the many things our kids were either taught or exposed to that ran contrary to our faith. Take the theory of evolution, for example. They say, "How could your kids handle the consistent barrage of evolutionary teaching?" Actually, it was quite easy. We've found that when you're trusting in the power of the Holy Spirit to instruct and convict a heart about the things that are true, it doesn't actually require twelve years of indoctrination for someone to become convinced that evolution isn't how they got here. Between what they learned in church, Sunday school, and a few lively dinner discussions with us, we took care of that threat. They went in knowing what they'd be taught, knowing what God's Word teaches, but more important, they went in with an inner confidence that regardless of what their curriculum dictated about how they got here, they knew from their own relationship with God that they were not some chance happening on a purposeless planet. It was also a great opportunity for them to have respectful dialogue with adults that disagreed with not only their beliefs, but also their values.

I've been challenged about deceptive teaching regarding American history that often pops up in public-school curriculum. Once again, a few great dinner discussions, as well as the ongoing monitoring and mentoring from us, and we put that problem to bed. Plus, we found that it wasn't as one-sided as everyone warned us it was. In fact, many of the concerns we heard were straw men.

What about the teaching on abortion, safe sex, and promiscuity? Dinners, several one-on-one discussions, and they were clear on these dangerous threats. More important, their public-school education provided them with a forum to introduce a biblical world-view into the class discussions on these issues. It's amazing how respect, graciousness, and even humor allowed them to share very heartfelt convictions on all these moral issues. It was through these discussions that our children picked up some of their best public opportunities to outline alternatives to conventional thinking. These forums also gave them chances to develop great connections with fellow students who were looking for a better way.

What about all the unbelieving teachers? First of all, they weren't all unbelievers. Our children had some fabulous Christian teachers in the public-school system. And just because a teacher is an unbeliever doesn't necessarily mean he isn't capable of teaching effectively (and, by the way, just because a teacher is a Christian doesn't mean he or she is automatically good at what he or she does). Having nonbelieving teachers gave our children a wonderful opportunity to appropriate God's power to respond respectfully to them, even though they might be coming from a much different philosophical position. Our kids developed the ability to enjoy engaging conversations even with teachers they didn't always agree with, without being frightened, frustrated, or resentful—all the while protected within their hearts by the *infinite* power of the Holy Spirit.

What about all the lost and sinful students that surrounded them every day? Once again, we need to make sure the record is straight here. They weren't all lost and sinful. All the way through school, our children had many friends who were fellow Christians that were excited about the chance to be a light as well as salt on their campus. As far as the students who weren't Christians were concerned, our children had many opportunities to befriend boys and girls who could really use a good friend—one whose sense of security, significance, and strength wasn't so undeveloped or immature.

Interestingly, when my wife and I checked into putting our kids in our local Christian school at the beginning of their educational careers, the headmaster was kind enough to point out that there were a lot of nonbelieving kids in his school, masquerading as Christians. In any case, when it comes to all the lost and sinfully formatted kids surrounding our kids, wherever they are, the apostle Paul gave us a reason to be encouraged. He said, "Where sin abounded, grace did much more abound."[20]

Keep in mind that God enrolled Daniel, Shadrach, Meshach, and Abednego in the public schools of Babylon. You can read about it for yourself in Daniel chapter 1. These boys learned all about the philosophies and world-view of this pagan culture. There is no indication that God was the least bit concerned about this. Nor were they.

I might mention for the record that Moses went to the state-run schools of Egypt. Talk about a morally messed-up society! But he did just fine. His success had far more to do with the spiritual tutoring he got from his committed Jewish parents than the academic tutoring he got from all those goofy Egyptian professors. God knows, and so should we, that the real battle isn't won in the minds of our children. It is won in their hearts.

RISKING YOUR CHILDREN TO GOD'S CARE

There is no doubt that we live in a wicked and depraved culture. Only a fool would suggest it doesn't present very genuine risks to kids. But it doesn't present a risk to God. That's why parents need to carefully choose their plan of attack. We need to create an environment that allows our children to maximize the strengths they can appropriate within an authentic relationship with God. When they're young, they can discover this relationship by observing it in their parents. They need to see us cultivating genuine, "close-to-the-heart" relationships with people who may be our spiritual polar opposites, maybe even hostile to our faith. Our kids will watch us loving them, praying for them, and being available for them when they are in need, and will learn to do the same.

As for the wicked culture around us, kids need to see two things—our *concern* and our *engagement*. Our children will be watching when we express sincere concern and hurt over troubled people caught up in it and will notice when we ache enough to pray for God's help. They will be aware when we are studying God's Word for greater insight into how to respond.

They will also take note of our attitude toward our culture when we are *engaged* in it. They need to see us putting forth an effort that entails more than criticizing its corruption from a safe distance. When we are engaged in the culture, God's hope is spread to all whom we encounter. There is no end to how we can do this. But our engagement should be deliberate, sincere, and with the intent of making a positive difference for Christ.

ONE MORE THOUGHT

I've given a few suggestions about how to keep rebellion from raising its ugly head in our families. It's good to remember, however, that some of our children's rebellion is actually essential to their spiritual pilgrimage. If they did not have it, they'd never be sure whether or not their faith is something canned that they got from church or their Christian school or from us. They sometimes need to push the envelope to finalize their faith in a personal way.

The tighter we hold them within our evangelical bunkers, the more their need to break away increases. The more we hide them in the attic from the enemy out in the street, the more they wonder if their family's faith is really enough. I absolutely love how Dr. James Dobson summarized this truth. He said that there comes a time when teenagers ask themselves, "Do I really believe what I've been taught, or is it all phony?" If that question is never asked, then their faith belongs to their parents and has never been incorporated as their own. That's why we must permit our sons and daughters to struggle spiritually, remaining calm while their faith is on trial. That's a time for private prayer in our closets.

I know this: the more we trust our children to God, the more at risk they will *appear* to become. But it is an illusion. They couldn't be safer than they are with Him. God had the first word. He's going to have the last. Satan may be the prince of the power of the air, but God has the whole universe in His hands. Satan may be the Prince of Darkness, but God is the Light that can consistently pierce that darkness.

I recall a woman who spoke when I was a little kid in a program at our church we called "Junior Church." She had come from a long line of missionaries—both her parents and her grandparents had been missionaries to China. When the communists took over, they all had feared for their lives. Her grandfather was tortured and imprisoned. Ultimately, they were expelled from China. All this served to give them a new opportunity—focusing on bringing the gospel to Chinese-speaking people in other parts of Asia.

But in her little presentation, she threw out a tiny side comment that never left me. She said, "A long time ago, before there was airline travel, missionaries would have to pack up their belongings and put them on steamer ships to get them to their mission field. Often it would take weeks or months before they arrived. But what they packed their belongings *in* told the whole story about how they viewed what they were doing."

At that point she gave this young and impressionable boy a great peek at what a passionate love for Christ looks like up close and personal. She said, "They packed their belongings in *caskets*. That's because the places they were going often didn't have the kinds of materials necessary to construct a good casket. But the other reason they did it was because they weren't assuming they'd necessarily survive their mission work. They knew there was a good chance they might be killed. Regardless, they were going with the intent of staying until they died."

That kind of commitment was not forged hiding in the corner of an attic safe from an enemy at street level. It wasn't the by-product of a childhood lived in a hermetically sealed educational biosphere. It grew up in the real battle for the cross.

These are difficult times for raising kids. But I could turn back the clock just a few decades and put you in a place and time that would make what you're facing today look like a Sesame Street challenge. Let me take you to London. Christmas. 1939. King George of England was addressing the British Empire in his annual Christmas speech. He wanted to bring them cheer and give them words that would encourage them. But it was difficult. Across the channel and within the very heart of Europe, the poison of Nazi Germany was spilling through the lowlands, Poland, and across the Rhine. Hitler's goal was clear. He wanted to own Europe.

It was obvious to everyone that England presented his biggest challenge. There was no way he could meet his goals in greater Europe without first bringing the British Empire to its knees. Everyone knew it was just a matter of time before the German *Luftwaffe* would darken the skies over London and start raining its bombs down on British people. In fact, that reality was only a few months away.

In order to offer hope in the midst of despair and courage in the face of certain calamity, King George borrowed a quote from a lady named Mini Louise Haskin. Her words that he shared in his Christmas address were the most appropriate words anyone could offer at the threshold of war. Not only were they profound then, but they are even more profound now. They are also the best advice I know for conscientious Christian parents wanting to raise great kids in the midst of a harsh culture. I close this chapter with King George VI's words:

I said to the man who stood at the gate of the year, "Give me a light that I may tread safely into the unknown." And he replied, "Go into the darkness and put your hand into the hand of God. That shall be to you better than light and safer than the known way."[21]

DISCUSSION QUESTIONS

1. How much does the safety of your child control how you are raising them? Is it possible to be too careful when it comes to your child's emotional, moral, and spiritual safety? What does a highly protective spiritual environment say to our children about our God? Do you think it plays a big part in why some kids in Christian homes rebel? How?

2. Why do you think there has been such a shift in the Christian movement toward raising and educating kids in a safe environment? Do you think it has helped or harmed the impact of Christians on the lost world?

3. How different do you think our culture would be if Christian families were living vibrant Christian lives more among the lost community that surrounds them? What impact would that have on a Christian kid's tendency toward rebellion?

4. Do you see any paranoia in large degrees within the Christian culture your family is most exposed to? What effect do you think this has on your kids?

5. Like the trees in the Biosphere, things like our intellect, our memories, our muscles, and our personalities seem to develop better when they are forced to deal with resistance. Do you think deliberately minimizing the resistance of the world system and the wiles of the devil enhances our children's relationship with the Holy Spirit or handicaps it? How does it affect their relationship with the Bible?

6. How do you think the priority of raising a safe kid plays into a child's tendency toward rebellion? What are your biggest fears when it comes to raising a "strong" Christian kid?

7. How does a parent's disdain for the people caught up in the sins of the world system feed a Christian kid's tendency toward rebellion?

8. If you had your way, would you prefer nice Christian families

in your neighborhood over troubled, unbelieving families? What does this communicate to your kids about God?

9. Discuss the chart on page 195. How does this plan for parenting compare to how you were raised? How does it compare to how you are raising your kids? What are some specific things you need to do to help your kids move from dependence on you to dependence on God?

10. Tim gave a lot of suggestions on how to develop a sense of personal responsibility and freedom in your child. What are some things you've done or are doing to give your child independence? How would this strategy affect your child's inner bent toward rebellion?

11. If you've educated your kids in public school, what are some things you've done to help them flourish spiritually? What are some things you'd like to do a better job on? How could you get help in these areas of weakness?

12. What is one thing God has taught you through this chapter?

CHAPTER 9

Compromised Christianity

This won't take long.

At least it shouldn't. The title of this chapter should be all anyone needs to figure out the bigger point. It's called cause and effect. Another way the Bible puts it is that we reap what we sow. And as much as we hate to admit it, much of our children's rebellion is our own rebellion coming back to haunt us.

JERRY'S SMOKE AND MIRRORS

Jerry was a legalistic nightmare very cleverly masquerading as a pillar of his church. At least that's what his friends figured he was—the pillar part. For the unsuspecting Christians around him, he came across well because he knew all the right evangelical buttons to push. He also was able to put some serious heft into a Sunday morning offering.

Being a successful entrepreneur had its benefits and liabilities. On the one side, he brought his engaging personality to church on Sunday and used it to make everyone feel welcomed, warmed, and filled. Some would call what he did "glad-handing," but for me, he just came across as friendly and charming. He also knew his way around the Bible, which added a lot to the discussions in his adult Sunday school class.

The liability of a successful guy like Jerry is that it's easy to let certain things slide that don't add up. For a long time, that's what people in leadership did with him. They didn't hold him accountable to standards they set for themselves or for anyone else in a position of leadership.

When I first met Jerry, I was fairly young in ministry experience. I was the youth pastor, and I was more preoccupied with Jerry's kids than Jerry. He had three—two daughters and a son. As an outsider looking in, you'd think this family would end up on the front cover of a magazine featuring textbook Christian families. Besides being good-looking, they seemed to be checking off all the boxes on the menu for "Families Who Have Their Spiritual Act Together." They were in church, looking sharp, participating in worship, lugging their Bibles, and lighting up the conversations in the lobby afterward. The kids were all in the local Christian school, and their mom did her thing with the women's ministry department.

My wife, Darcy, has one of those internal alarms that goes off when she is around a person who is not what he or she appears to be. My gifts for detecting an individual's internal struggles aren't that sophisticated. It might be an IQ deficiency or that "fake me out first" look I tend to keep permanently fixed on my face. But the sad truth is, I can be easily snookered. I certainly was with Jerry. What I saw in Jerry was a successful businessman, a guy with a nice though somewhat quiet wife, a father who seemed to be proud of his kids, and a man who really wanted the best for his church. That wasn't at all what Darcy picked up. She sensed high-octane anger seething just below the surface of a painted-on evangelical smile.

The first clue I had that all was not well with Jerry's kids was a conversation I had with him in a restaurant. He was quizzing me about some college students who had volunteered to work with me on our high-school staff. They were chosen because of their passion for Jesus and their desire to serve.

Jerry's concern was about superficial things like their hair, their clothes, and their mannerisms. He was worried about the kind of influence they might be having on the kids they were supposed to be leading.

I explained to him how these college kids were great young men and women who had a deep faith in Christ. I assured him they were good examples to everyone, living exemplary Christian lives among their peer group.

And then I saw it. It was there for just a brief moment, but it flashed at me like the pilot light on a flamethrower flickering behind his eyes, about to flare out and scorch me. He brought his index finger up to a "wagging lecture" position in front of my face and started to shake it. His lips stretched tight over his teeth like he was going to spit out some words. Then, catching himself, he exhaled and said nothing.

Moments later, the conversation shifted gears and everything was fine. But as I left Jerry, I sensed this was a Christian man looking for a fight. And when I thought of what he was upset about, it gave me reason to think that with Jerry, what you see on Sunday morning is not remotely close to what you get. I began to wonder what that must be like for his children. I soon found out.

Summertime came and his oldest daughter, who was fifteen at the time, invited some friends to her house to swim for the afternoon. Because her mother wasn't able to be home, she required her daughter to also invite someone older to supervise and keep an eye on everyone. Her mom suggested she invite someone from the youth office of our church. As it turned out, some of those older college volunteers her dad had been concerned about went to serve as chaperones. Their main job on the youth team was to spend as much time with kids in the youth group as possible. It seemed like a great idea on a hot Arizona afternoon.

Let me tell you a little bit about this daughter. First of all, she was very pretty, like her mother. She had also recently gone through that transition girls go through where their bodies change from young girls' to young women's. In a brief few months, she had become a strikingly beautiful young lady. Unfortunately, when this happens, and without the girl doing anything, boys seem to suddenly appear on the family's horizon. This is a time when fathers understandably get nervous. If you're a spiritual legalist who measures everything by external, superficial, and arbitrary standards, a blossoming teenage girl in the family puts you in way over your head.

According to one of the college girls who went as a chaperone, the bathing suit this daughter was wearing was as modest as you could get, given the person wearing it. It was a one-piece with conservative lines. To a certain extent, it was irrelevant what she wore; she would have looked very attractive regardless. But in her defense, she had chosen her bathing suit with modesty in mind.

One of the older college guys was over on the side patio sitting in a lawn chair talking with one of the other kids when he heard someone yelling. A man's voice came booming from just inside the house. The kids had all been swimming and splashing in the pool when Jerry came charging outside.

His words to his daughter went something like, "You disgusting slut! What do you think you are doing?" The girl (who shall remain unnamed) said, "Daddy, we're all just swimming."

The next thing that happened was one of those memories that gets burned into everyone's "permanent" file. Jerry reached down to his daughter and grabbed her by her hair. The hairstyle for teenage girls back then was long and thick, and this girl had plenty of hair for him to grab. Before anyone could say anything or do anything, Jerry snatched his daughter out of the pool by her hair like she was a rag doll and dragged her sideways across their cool deck and patio and into their kitchen.

All the while she was screaming, "Daddy, what? Daddy, what?"

The college girl who related the story couldn't make out all that Jerry was yelling about, but the group said it had to do with her "dressing like a whore around boys."

Well, as you can imagine, the afternoon swim get-together came to an early and abrupt halt. The college guy from our church went into the kitchen to try to figure out what was going on. By that time, Jerry's humiliated daughter had run crying into her bedroom. I found out later that the side of her leg had bled from being scraped across the concrete.

Jerry was startled by the presence of the young man. "What are *you* doing here?" he demanded.

"Your wife asked us to come over and chaperone the kids. What on earth is going on?"

That's about as far as the back-and-forth conversation went. Jerry said something about his daughter needing to be more modest, and then yelled out to the pool area to the others that the party was over.

I tried to get together with Jerry to talk over the incident with him. He never made it possible. Looking back, I probably should have ambushed him at church and forced the confrontation, but we never discussed it. Some of the girls on the volunteer staff tried to work with his daughter, but she soon dropped off the youth department's radar screen. People called her, but she seemed less and less interested.

So what happened to her? What do you assume happened to her? If you think she got a boyfriend soon after that, you'd be right. If you figure they started sleeping together, you'd be right. They were sexually active through her last two years of high school and then married about a year after that. They had a couple of children. Then they divorced. She lived with a couple of guys. Last time I saw her, she was married again. "This time for money," she said to me, winking. All of the diamonds she had on her hands, ears, and around her neck made me think she'd hit the mother lode. I was glad to see her after all those years, but I was also saddened by what I saw. Her life had been a series of ugly vignettes at the hands of different guys who, like her father, had masqueraded as serious Christian men.

Her brother never married. He's spent his adult life falling off the wagon and then climbing back on. Her other sister married, had some kids, and then divorced. She's a real nice lady who's trying to raise her kids to love Jesus. But she's had it with men. I think she pretty much had it with men before she ever actually got to know one.

MAGNIFYING OUR MISTAKES

Two of the three kids—the daughter Jerry yanked out of the pool and her brother—moved out of the house and away from the area as soon as they could. During this time, they had minimal contact with their father. This was when the most damage was done to them. How so, you might ask?

It's a strange thing about our parental sins. When our kids move away and we haven't resolved our sins of commission and omission with them, these childhood disappointments grow larger and larger until they dominate our kids' focus and dictate many of their actions. In fact, our unwillingness to try to make peace with our kids before they leave home can set them up for a lifetime of bad decisions.

It might be the sin of letting our fears get the best of us and creating too tight of a system for them to live in (like we talked about in the last chapter). Or it could be our ongoing bad example and the specific sins against them that usually accompany a misguided life, as in Jerry's case. Somewhere through this process, they were hoping we'd come to our senses, own up, and lift the burden of our poor judgment off their shoulders.

Garrison Keillor has a lot of fun at Lutherans' expense. Over the years, millions of people have laughed at his weekly reports from the fictitious town of Lake Wobegon, Minnesota. And even though we all know he's exaggerating his characters and their lives inside this conservative little world, there is a sense of accuracy and truth to his reports, and we can see ourselves in the people he talks about.

I remember one story about his cousin Rose. She was a free spirit born into a family of strict Lutherans. Her parents couldn't figure her out or cut her much slack. Rose was a Technicolor personality in a black-and-white society. Because her parents couldn't see past their prejudices, there was no effort made to connect Rose's heart with the kind of grace that could help her find a balance in her life. Many of their rules were good, decent, and reasonable. But just as many were petty and arbitrary—harsh and unbearable for a young girl like Rose. She became inclined to rejecting all the rules and boundaries of her family, the good with the bad. Life between Rose and her parents was marred by unrealistic expectations and standards that were impossible to meet. Like Jerry's daughter in the pool, Rose was in trouble for things she simply could do little or nothing about.

Garrison Keillor told how Rose bolted from her house at the first opportunity and made her way as quickly as she could to Berkeley, California—the mecca of free spirits. Rose joined the Unitarian Church.

She won the Miss Nude Unitarian contest. She got married for a while, but found that the men in her life reminded her too much of her unreasonable father. Finally, she decided she was a lesbian and took up with a woman who managed to play the male role in her life without all the hassles.

After a couple of decades of living away and trying to figure out how to tie her free spirit down enough to bring some meaning to her life, she decided to go home for a visit. She took her partner with her, too. All the way there, she churned inside about finally seeing her parents and sister again after all the years.

It turned out they were very glad to see her. They were kind to Rose and gracious to her friend. But for Rose, it was like a trip to hell. She gritted her teeth through the entire ordeal and was glad when the day came that she could finally leave. Garrison Keillor summarized the story of Rose with a brief discourse that could describe any kid that leaves home angry with their parents:

> There are people who only feel themselves at full strength when they are in opposition to others. And that's what propels them. But when you rebel against your parents and make that your life, you never get over it, you see. You make your parents into these immense, powerful stone figures.
>
> The child who stays at home, for that child, the parents simply, gently dwindle and diminish over the years and become more human and weaker, and more worthy of sympathy and love. But for the child who runs away, they become a theme park, your parents.
>
> They're not that big. They're not that powerful. When you base your life on rebellion and opposition, it's a noble thing, in a way. But you so often find yourself in opposition to things that simply are true. And there are things we're taught . . . that simply are true. You *should* be cheerful. You *should* mind your manners. You *should* make yourself useful. And you should avoid self-pity at all costs . . .
>
> . . . Take small views of life and don't bother to solve the

past, because it will solve itself. It will gradually fade and all these figures will get smaller, and smaller, and smaller.[1]

Like Rose in fictitious Lake Wobegon, Jerry's daughter turned her father into an immense stone figure in her life. That figure dominated her, defined her, and drove her from one rebellious and self-destructive idea to the next.

WHEN CHICKENS COME HOME TO ROOST

A couple of years after this incident, I had a brief discussion with Jerry's quiet and subdued wife. She was concerned about the daughter who got dragged out of the pool by her hair. It seemed she was rebelling against the rules of their house and the rules of her Christian school—drinking, not coming in by curfew, and sneaking out late at night. She also knew her daughter was sleeping with her boyfriend and was trying to figure out why she had taken this sudden plunge into obstinate behavior. I thought, *Why don't you ask that guy you wake up next to every morning?*

It should come as no surprise that kids tend to emulate parents, but when that emulation happens to be rebellion, many parents simply don't get it. They can't see the connection to their own behavior. Actually, they should. It's one of the great rules of life. A long time ago, someone figured it was enough of a truth that they made up an aphorism to explain it: "Llike father, like son" (or daughter).

Kids in Christian homes may rebel against their parents based on something specific their parents have done to them or based on something the parents have modeled for them over a prolonged period of time. Jerry was this walking funnel cloud looking for a trailer park. His misguided attachment to legalistic standards, coupled with his readiness to fight about it every chance he got, not only terrorized his children, but set them up to reject all the good things he and his wife actually believed. I can't prove it, but I wouldn't be at all surprised to learn Jerry struggled with sexual sins, too.

We simply can't make huge mistakes, or make a series of small but consistently foolish decisions, and think they won't come back to live with us in the form of our kids. If we have a way of stretching the truth or misrepresenting the facts, we've taught our children that lying is acceptable under certain conditions. That's the thought that crosses my mind when I hear neighbors or friends lie around their children or encourage them to lie in order to get ahead. I think, *Well, get ready. You'll see that behavior again. Except it will be aimed at you instead.* When I mention this whole concept of "what goes around comes around" to some of these people, they often dismiss it or trivialize it. Then when their children turn their own behavior against them, they seem shocked.

Name it: Cheat on your taxes, and don't be surprised if your kids cheat in school. Dad, make cheap sexual comments about the professional sports cheerleaders that bounce across the TV screen, and don't be surprised when your daughter climbs in the backseat of her boyfriend's car. If she's heard comments like this throughout her childhood, she knows what is important to her father. When parents talk to me about how disrespectful their children are to each other, I ask about how they talk to each other as a couple, or how the single parent communicates with the ex-spouse.

And it's not just what we show them, but what we do to them that causes many of them to rebel. Probably the biggest hit to a child's heart is divorce. Any Christian couple that goes through a divorce should assume it will have a debilitating impact on their children. Regardless of the reasons and regardless of whether things appear better or worse after the divorce, the children will be wounded. And many children are going to process their pain in some rebellious way. Some will do it aggressively, some will do it passively, but all will have to work through the impact of the two people they love the most splitting up.

All children instinctively realize that divorce is still not the best option for their family. No matter what the culture says, the best option is for both parents to let God heal their love, heal their lives, and heal their marriage. Our current culture of divorce assumes that option is out of the question and even claims some children are better off after the divorce. It's no wonder that kids get hurt.

THE BIBLICAL LAWS OF THE HARVEST

The apostle Paul cuts to the chase on this subject in Galatians 6:7–8. This is where he summarizes in a handful of simple sentences a principle that, if we took it to heart, would save the average Christian family years of rebellion by one or more of their children. Paul qualifies what he's going to say with these words: "Do not be deceived." Even though people should know about the consequences of sin and selfishness, most people fail to grasp them. That's because sin in our lives dims our capacity to exercise common sense and causes us to be easily duped.

Many people who are blinded by their sins have a bad habit of thinking their actions (1) aren't that big of a problem, and (2) won't have long-term ramifications. Not only are sinful inclinations serious problems, but we may have to live with their ramifications long after the actions take place. That's how we are deceived in our sin. The powers of darkness say things like "What's the harm? It's no big deal." But in the aftermath a huge, heartbreaking toll is exacted on the people we love the most in ways we couldn't imagine possible.

Thus, Paul says, "Don't be deceived."

And then, after giving everyone this warning, he makes one of those statements that we all wish we had figured out a long time ago. He says: "God cannot be mocked. A man reaps what he sows. The one who sows to please his sinful nature, from that nature will reap destruction; the one who sows to please the Spirit, from the Spirit will reap eternal life."

Let me take a stab at paraphrasing the statement "God cannot be mocked." How about this: "Nobody is going to make a fool out of God." The psalmist gives the flip side of this coin when he says, "The fear of the LORD is the beginning of wisdom."[2] If we have that reverential respect for God, we would be less inclined to do things we think won't come back and bite us in the rear later on.

Sowing and reaping are another way of describing the principle of cause and effect. But it takes the principle to a greater and more sophisticated level. In fact, from this simple statement you can draw three practical laws of the harvest that explain a lot of the problems we see in our rebellious kids.

Law #1: What You Sow, You Consistently Reap

When a farmer throws wheat seeds in the ground, he doesn't find grapes hanging on vines at harvesttime. He gets wheat. If we lie, our kids lie. If we steal, our kids will steal. A great example of this is the sad story of David and his kids that we looked at back in chapter 7 during our discussion of the negative return on comfortable Christianity.

King David started out his free fall into sin by first exchanging his passion for God for the glory of being king. Next, he started accumulating wives. But not satisfied with the seven he had (that we know of), he allowed his pornographic urges to get the best of him, and you already know the rest of the story. So let me see if I get all the sins cataloged properly: first there was toxic polygamy, then pornography, then infidelity, then subterfuge, then murder, and then cover-up. David found out the laws of the harvest the hard way. And it's interesting that he got back exactly the same seeds he sowed:

- Solomon, one of David's sons, ultimately inherited his throne. His number one sin? Polygamy. But he wasn't satisfied with a little toxic polygamy; he went all the way to nuclear polygamy.

- Amnon, another of David's sons, became lustfully enchanted with his half sister Tamar. His problem started at a pornographic level as he kept feeding his incestuous lust with more and more thoughts about her. He fixated on her so much it made him sick.[3]

- Amnon used subterfuge and deception on both his father, David, and Tamar in order to get her into his bedroom under the ruse of feeding him while he was ill.[4]

- Amnon raped Tamar. And then, as quickly as his passions had burned for her, his mood shifted to its polar opposite, and he threw her out of his house like she was some dirty water in a basin.

- Absalom, Tamar's brother, heard about what Amnon did. He seethed with rage against Amnon for two years. Finally, he used deception against his father to try to get all his brothers to gather for a picnic where the sheepshearers were working. In the process, he got Amnon drunk (which was a trick he learned watching his father try to cover his sexual tracks with Bathsheba; David got Uriah drunk twice).

- When Amnon's guard was finally down, Absalom gave the word to his bodyguards, and they struck Amnon and killed him.

- Later on, when Absalom attempted a coup d'état against his father, he had a tent pitched on the roof of the king's palace. And with the citizens of Jerusalem watching from street level, he had several of his father's wives brought in to that tent where he had forced sex with them.

We reap exactly what we sow. David saw his sins come back on him through the rebellion of his children, almost as if they were his carbon copies. And look at the irony of that last crime—Absalom pitched a tent on the roof of the palace. Does that ring a bell? That's where David was when he saw Bathsheba taking her bath. Instead of him being off with his soldiers fighting wars, as a good king should be, he was home lounging on his roof. It was at this same site, where David let his lusts get the best of him, that God brought it all back on him in a humiliating and degrading circus of adultery.

When we see our children's rebellion, we would do well to ask ourselves, *Did I teach them this? Is this a reaction to something I did to them in the past?*

Law #2: There Is Almost Always a Delay between the Time You Sow and the Time You Reap

This is why so many people don't think their sin is that big of a deal. They don't see an immediate response. Frankly, if we had immediate consequences to our sins, I think we'd all be more inclined to quickly correct our actions. But God has seen fit to not operate that way with us. And even though there are some incidents in the Bible where people's sins got an immediate reaction from God, most of the time, a lot of water passes over the dam between the time we sow and the time we gather in our harvest.

It was a year after David committed adultery with Bathsheba before God had Nathan confront him with his sins. It was years after that when the harvest of his actions came to full growth in Amnon, Absalom, and Solomon.

Law #3: Whatever You Sow Compounds

The first nine years of my life were spent in western Pennsylvania. At that time, there were a lot of wheat fields checkerboarding Lawrence County. My grandfather leased some of his land to wheat farmers, and I recall numerous occasions when I ventured into those fields around harvest-time. Come early autumn, the heads of the wheat would be heavy and bent over from the weight of the grains, or seeds, on the stalk. I loved to rub my hands together on them, gather a handful of grain, and chew on it. Clearly, quite a multiplication game had taken place since the original seed was sown earlier in the springtime. It could be as much as fifty seeds or more to one.

You can see this principle of multiplication so obviously in David's sad family album. And I've seen it again and again in Christian families. Parents get back exactly what they sow, oftentimes after they've dealt with the problem and thought they had put it behind them. And when it finally revisits them, like that wheat, it's multiplied by a factor of ten or fifty or one hundred.

THE RISK OF ABUSING GRACE

God's grace is supposed to be amazing. It would be a lot more so were it not so abused. Many Christians struggle when it comes to grace by going to one extreme or the other. Either they show too much grace or they show too little. When it comes to our sin coming back to haunt us in our children's rebellion, we're usually guilty on both counts.

Few teachings in the Bible have gotten such poor development as grace. And one of the sinister ways people have grown to abuse grace is in the misunderstanding of their actions' consequences when it comes to grace. They sin. Their sin shocks them. Someone confronts. They repent with a passion. And then they move on with their lives. But they move on under the misguided impression that because God has shown them grace, they will not have any long-term ramifications from their sin.

Let's say a set of parents get off to a rough start in their marriage. Mom cheats on Dad. There's a separation. Then confrontation. Then repentance. Then restoration. They may log twenty years of the sweetest marital harmony a couple could ever experience. And then their daughter gets married and cheats on her husband. Often the parents in these scenarios can't get it all to add up. "How could this be? We repented. God gave us His forgiveness, His mercy, and His *grace*. We have loved Him and served Him passionately ever since He restored our relationship. Why are we having to deal with this in our daughter?"

It's the law of the harvest.

We would all do well to make sure we have a tempered and balanced view of God's grace. Grace does not remove human and earthly consequences from our actions. It simply removes the ultimate consequence. If God responded to us as our sins deserved, we'd be dead. We sense His grace when we realize that Christ is the One who chose to die instead of us. God's grace is also seen in how He helps us recover from our sins as well as process the consequences.

It is the flippant application of God's grace that sets people up for the greater shock when they see their sin and rebellion revisited in their children. Earlier in this book I mentioned that I attended a Christian college. Many of the students had a good working knowledge of Scripture. There is one verse just about everyone on campus knew. I'll bet you know it, too. It is found in 1 John 1:9. John, that wonderful disciple of Jesus, gave us one of the sweetest sentences in the entire New Testament. He said, "If we confess our sins, he is faithful and just and will forgive us our sins and purify us from all unrighteousness."

If we confess—come clean, own up, stop making excuses, assume responsibility for our actions—then Jesus, our redeemer and friend, will forgive us.

He will get out His blood-soaked eraser and scrub away the blot on our record. He will remove our sins—those retched actions we did in secret or out in the open that broke His heart and hurt so many innocent people.

He will purify us by getting out the divine Tide and Clorox and putting us through the double-rinse cycle.

He cleanses us from all unrighteousness—all the muck and vileness of our foolish actions.

It's a wonderful promise that only a God of grace could offer. And He offers it willingly, happily, generously, and consistently. But He doesn't offer it irresponsibly.

I recall a young man who lived in my dormitory that had a very interesting way of applying this precious verse in his life. He saw it more like a magic wand, and he used it like a verb—a verb that he felt gave him permission to sin. He would talk about something he was going to do with his girlfriend later on that night, and then he'd say, "Yeah, we'll *1 John 1:9* it when we're done." That meant they were going to go have some sexual fun with each other, confess it as sin when they were through, and then go on with their lives like everything was just peachy between them and God.

First John 1:9 is not some chemical base we throw into an acidic bucket of sin in our lives just because we *can*. We can't see it as some wholesale neutralizer that has this "undoing" effect on our consequences. First John 1:9 is a tool, not a toy. It is a promise of forgiveness, not a "Get Out of Long-Term Consequences Forever" card.

Therefore, repentance and restoration—although both wonderful outgrowths of God's promise—do not erase the impact or undo the damage of our sins in our children's lives. Just like Jerry at the beginning of our chapter, if we do not get a grip on pockets of sin in our lives, we'll see them come back to us many times over in our kids.

Chuck Swindoll summarizes what I'm saying with much better succinctness than I. He writes, "We reap what we sow, forgiveness notwithstanding. If there is anything we have been duped into believing in our

era of erroneous teachings on grace, it is the thinking that if we will simply confess our sins and claim God's forgiveness, then all consequences
of what we have done will be quickly whisked away."[5]

SO, WHAT DO WE DO NOW?

I'm going to spend the next chapter looking at some things we can do
to handle our children's rebellion properly, but before we close the
pages on this one, I want to give you a few obvious tips. These are
things you should do when you see that your children's rebellion is
either a carbon copy of your own rebellion or is a direct reaction to obvious sins you've committed against them.

Don't Be Passive

When you read those horrible accounts of lust, rape, treachery, and murder among David's children, the thing that is most astounding is David's
response to it all. Nothing. David did—nothing. Well, that's not completely
accurate. You read in 2 Samuel 13:21 that David found out his son Amnon
had raped his daughter Tamar. It says, "He was very angry" (NKJV).

That's it. No action, no response, no consequences, just "He was
very angry." I'm sure that sent chills down Amnon's spine when he
found that out. "Uh-oh! Dad's ticked because I raped Tamar. Shoot, I
hope he doesn't take away my chariot or ground me."

I see David's passivity two ways here. One is in his prayer of confession and repentance. You can find it in the collection of Psalms. It's
the famous Psalm 51. This is one of the most heartrending confessions
you'll read in the Bible.

But I've always had a problem with one line in it. And for a long
time I felt reluctant to say anything about it since the Bible is the inspired
Word of God and all. And then it hit me that although the Bible is the
inspired Word of God, it still contains people's accounts of things, and
those people may not have complete insight. In fact, there are a lot of
those kinds of incidents (think about Job's advisers). And that's exactly
what I think of Psalm 51:4. After David was confronted by Nathan

regarding his adultery, he went to his study and penned these words of lament to God: "Against you, you only, have I sinned and done what is evil in your sight."

Hold it, David. Against God and God *alone*? What about Bathsheba? What about poor Uriah? What about all those aides that take orders from you and were forced into complicity with you in both your sin and then the cover-up? What about all the people of Israel who were counting on you to restore some sense of decency and integrity to the throne? And, David, what about your family? What about that harem of wives you mocked? What about your precious sons and daughters, who were looking to you for leadership in how to live their lives? Where do you get off thinking this was just some infraction that happened between you and God?

The second way David's passivity shows is his unwillingness to do anything personally to blunt the impact of his sins in the lives of the people close to him. He could have, back then—when it happened— sat down with his family and given a full confession to them. They knew about everything he'd done anyway. But he could have diminished its negative impact on them if he would have personally faced them with his confession.

He could have looked all those children in their eyes and said: "Please forgive me. And please know something. What I did was inexcusable. I ruined people's lives. A baby is dead because of my actions (Bathsheba's baby died shortly after it was born). I have brought utter shame on the name of my house and on the name of my Lord. Please, in spite of what I've done, *please* do not follow my example. What I did was utterly foolish. If you follow my example, it will bring you only heartache and ruin as it has brought me. I love each one of you, and I want to spend the rest of my days working to restore the confidence you once had in the God I serve. I don't expect you to ever respect me again. I don't deserve respect. But I want to do whatever I can to help you find the hope in God that my actions may have stolen from you."

David could then have followed that repentance by having ongoing discussions with each individual child. It's interesting to imagine how the story might have unfolded if he had been spending individual time with Amnon, Absalom, and Solomon. All of their actions strike me as the kind of rebellion kids get into in order to get their parents' attention.

I've always believed that Jerry could have saved his daughters and his son a lot of ugly chapters in their adulthood if he had simply acknowledged his legalism and his anger. He could have defused some (certainly not all) of the impact of dragging his daughter out of the pool by her hair if he had melted before her, taken full responsibility for his actions, confessed and apologized to everyone who was there, gone to get counseling for his temper, and made himself accountable to both his family and one very large, mean male friend who would promise to drag him out of the pool by his hair and beat the ever-loving tar out of him if he ever did anything like that again. He could have used what time he had left in his daughter's life to restore what he had stolen from her.

Sure, she still might have rebelled. But somewhere, a person's got to say to him or herself, *Enough!* The point is: Don't be passive about your sin and the impact it has had on your children's lives. Address it when it happens and then work to repair the damage you've done. And keep at it for as long as it takes.

Develop a New and Fresh Relationship with God

David said later in Psalm 51, "Create in me a pure heart, O God . . ." (verse 10). When we have a sinful pattern in our lives or some event has done damage to our children, we can't assume we are going to be able to start over with them until we have first started over with God. The good news is God loves to make things new with us. And when He does, He puts us in the best position to repair some of the damage we've done to our kids.

Get Specific Help with Your Problem

After David asked God to create a pure heart in him again, he said, ". . . and renew a steadfast sprit within me." *Steadfast*. David wanted to make the adjustments in his life necessary to make sure nothing like this ever happened again. Whatever he did, it worked. He just didn't go far enough with it. He failed to realize that his poor example gave his sons permission to do the same. A one-on-one relationship with his children could have preempted much of the pain and ugliness in their futures.

Don't Hide Your Past Mistakes
If They Can Be Used to Save Your Children Future Heartache

David said later in Psalm 51, "Restore to me the joy of your salvation and grant me a willing spirit, to sustain me. Then I will teach transgressors your ways, and sinners will turn back to you" (verses 12–13). It was a nice thought. It just lacked serious implementation.

When we realize that our sinful actions have thrown out seed into the fertile soil of our children's hearts, we need to ask God for wisdom and mercy in using our transparency and contrition as a spiritual herbicide on the weeds that are growing there as a result. We shouldn't wonder if the weeds are there; we need to assume they are.

Maintain an Attitude of
Brokenness about Your Actions to Your Children

Once again, in Psalm 51: "You do not delight in sacrifice, or I would bring it; you do not take pleasure in burnt offerings. The sacrifices of God are a broken spirit; a broken and contrite heart, O God, you will not despise" (verses 16–17). We have a chance to keep our children from rebellion by showing them how God has rescued us from our own rebellion. Humility, graciousness, making full disclosure, and taking full responsibility are attitudes that demonstrate to our children that something genuine and divine is going on inside us.

GRACE THAT IS GREATER THAN ALL OUR SIN

As I said before, I see Christians struggle in two ways with God's grace. They either give too much grace or too little. I've noticed that people tend to use grace on themselves to the point of abuse. They love to overextend the boundaries of God's grace whenever they are the benefactor. If, however, they are inclined to offer too little grace, it's usually when it involves their having to offer it to someone who has sinned against them—like their rebellious kids.

If your child's rebellion is a result of something you've done or something you modeled as a pattern in your own life, offer them the same kindness, patience, and long-suffering that God has extended to you. It may have taken a while for God to turn you around. Give your rebellious child the same measure of grace. Love them, pray for them, stick with them, keep believing in them, and be ready to kill the fattened calf and have a party in their honor when they finally see the error of their ways.

Sometimes it takes years for kids to decide they are tired of emulating our sins. Since we put the seed there in the first place, the least we can do is hang in there with them all the way through to the other side of the process. No moaning! No whining! Just love . . . lots of it . . . unconditionally.

The laws of the harvest work both ways. What we sow we reap. But remember that Paul followed up this point by saying, "The one who sows to please his sinful nature, from that nature will reap destruction; the one who sows to please the Spirit, from the Spirit will reap eternal life."[6] Because of God's grace, God can give you the chance to plant a new garden in your children's hearts. He can help you plant seeds of love, kindness, sobriety, fidelity, honesty, and calm. Just like the bad seed, these seeds take a while to germinate. But be patient. Keep your focus on the Lord and your trust in His ability to work in your children's hearts. Keep watering and cultivating the good seed in your life, and little by little it will grow. You might have angry kids who have long since turned their backs against you. Work to find them. Ask God to show you how to love them—regardless of what they are doing with their lives. Remind them again how much you care for them and how much you regret the harm you've done. And then entrust the seeds of hope to God.

David made a real mess of his life. But that didn't mean God was through with him. In spite of his sin, God used him, and in spite of his children's rebellion, God still passed a seed of hope down through them to their offspring. God had already given David ample reason to know that He was a God of the great "do-over." Do you recall the name of David's great-great-grandmother? It's probably not on the tip of your tongue, and frankly, I had to look it up myself to make sure. It was Rahab, the prostitute that hid the spies Joshua sent out to assess the weaknesses of the city of Jericho. James, in the New Testament, said of her in his letter, "In the same way, was not even Rahab the prostitute considered righteous for what she did when she gave lodging to the spies and sent them off in a different direction?"[7]

Up to that point in her life, Rahab had been sowing some awful seeds in her heart and in her family. But because of her confidence in the God of Israel, He gave her a second chance. In the process, she got to play a role in the royal line of Israel. But there's something even better. God used both Rahab and David to play—in spite of their sin—a redemptive role in the salvation of the entire world. Sure, they may have been bit players in the bigger screenplay, but they still were used by God in a significant way. For it is through their royal line that Jesus came to fulfill the promise of Messiah. It was this ultimate King, of the royal line of David, who brought a solution to rebellious hearts once and for all.

If there's a sin in your life that possibly is casting seeds in your child's heart, deal with it. Deal with it now, today, immediately. Don't be passive. Make a fresh start with God. Get specific help for your sin. Don't hide it; use it to save your children from going down the same path you've been on. Maintain a broken heart about the pain you've caused them. And be steadfast in your love and patience with them as they work through their sins.

Regardless of whether God uses you to spare your children a trip down the wrong side of rebellion or uses you to help them get back on track, don't ever let anyone tell you that you can't make a difference in minimizing the impact of your sin on your kids. Someone has well said, "God uses crooked sticks to draw straight lines all the time." He did it with Rahab. He did it with David. He did it with Solomon. And He can do it with you.

DISCUSSION QUESTIONS

1. Do you think compromised Christian parents radically change the odds that their children will rebel against their Christian faith? Why?

2. Jerry's actions against his daughter put a huge spiritual chip

on her shoulder. What are some things his wife could have done to help minimize the impact of his rage? What could Jerry have done to undo the damage he did to his daughter?

3. Have you seen the laws of the harvest played out in your family of origin when it comes to bad seed sown? How about when it comes to good seed sown?

4. If our children's rebellion is the result of our reaping what we've sown, what are some things we can do to "weed" our kids' hearts of some of our bad seed?

5. Do you think your children tend to magnify your mistakes and use them as excuses to justify their rebellion? What part can you play in reversing this tendency?

6. How does the misapplication of grace (either too little or too much) set our kids up to rebel?

7. Tim outlines five practical steps to take when trying to repair the impact of your sin on a rebellious child. He gleans them from David's prayer of repentance in Psalm 51. Of those five, which one comes easiest for you? Which one is the hardest for you? How could you develop an ability to carry out the ones that come hardest to you?

8. What is the most painful part of having your sins revisit you in your kids? How do you think God can help you move beyond your pain?

9. What is one thing God has taught you through this chapter?

CHAPTER 10

Bridges of Hope

If you reflect on the title of this book, you'll see that I set myself to the job of explaining *why* kids in Christian homes rebel. Throughout these pages I have given you many answers to that question—all with the purpose of explaining the reasons young people, who have been raised in an environment that should yield a strong love for God, sometimes choose to turn away from Him. Perhaps by now, however, you've detected I've had an ulterior motive in writing this material. It has less to do with *why* kids in Christian homes rebel and more to do with *how* to discourage them from rebelling in the first place.

I hope in the process you've been provoked toward some new ways of thinking about how you are raising your child. Maybe along the way you've taken a long, hard look at your style of Christian parenting, making sure it measures up to the demands of your true calling as a parent. Although families of faith embrace different styles of parenting, some of those styles clearly work better than others. And the sad truth is that some hardly work at all.

Passionate Christian parents who live each day with an overwhelming sense of Christ's presence in their lives have a way of transferring more than a belief system to their children. They model a rich and deep faith that only seems to get better and more believable to their kids. This happens because their children are able to see how well their parents' faith holds up, even in the face of life's greatest challenges.

We've talked about the power of the Holy Spirit's presence in a parent's life—a power that starts with a sober and healthy fear of God. It's a fear of God that is so balanced and strong that it frees parents to be unafraid of just about anything they face. These parents don't fear the seductive world system that surrounds their family. They don't fear the defeated enemy that works through forces of darkness. They don't fear sinister philosophies that sometimes use entertainment and public education as their platform. They don't fear their fellowman. They don't fear the inadequacies and fragile nature of their children. And they don't fear public opinion. They don't take their cues from the world system, so it makes little difference to them what the world thinks of them.

I've tried to take an objective look at conventional wisdom when it comes to raising kids. Most people hate to tamper with conventional wisdom. I'm all for leaving it alone, myself, so long as it's producing a good product. But that isn't the case when it comes to the average Christian home. Life within the walls of too many homes of faith is not turning out the way the Bible suggests it should. So many of these homes adhere to the tenets of conventional wisdom. Sadly, these are often the very homes that produce girls and boys who move into adulthood without a clear and exciting goal of making a difference for the kingdom of God.

History demonstrates that conventional wisdom has a bad habit of morphing itself into traditions and organizations whose existence is dependent not on their effectiveness, but on their ability to keep the Christian public (read: consumer) loyal to that particular conventional wisdom. Our religious subculture and the organizations it props up somehow have gained sacred-cow status, enjoying unlimited grazing rights without fear of ever becoming hamburger. And it can often be a bad career move even to question the relevancy of any spiritual sacred cow.

I think it is sad that anything is considered above critique when our children's relationship with their parents and their Creator hangs in the balance. It is equally disheartening if we sacrifice our children's effectiveness as adult Christians in order to guard the health and welfare of any of evangelicalism's sacred cows, regardless of how much money has been invested in it or how many jobs would be jeopardized if its flaws are exposed. With this in mind, I've tried to graciously but firmly put on trial anything and everything that resembles conventional wisdom in the ways Christian parents are encouraged to raise their kids—ways that don't work as effectively as they may be advertised.

My goal is to help parents create a new generation of Christian kids who rebel less and respond more to the promptings of God. I have no delusions about my words or their power—they are just words, and they have no power in and of themselves. But when they are connected with the life-changing power of God, there is no limit on how high they can rise, and there are no boundaries on how far they can go in affecting God's kingdom on earth.

TRADING HEARTACHE FOR HOPE

But you might have picked up this book for other reasons. There is a good chance you were more interested in its subtitle: "Trading Heartache for Hope." That's because either you have a rebellious child on your hands, or you're concerned that you might have one in the making. You are looking for answers to more than the question "Why?" You'd also like to know *what* to do.

I can't blame you. With all the challenges kids can create, it makes sense to get as much help as we can either to turn them from their rebellious ways, or otherwise to keep them from choosing the wrong path.

The good news is that spending all the time you've already spent learning why Christian kids rebel places you way ahead of the game. Answering the question "Why?" is the most important part of figuring out what to do next. A long list of "to-dos" without the context of the philosophies and presuppositions behind them is a great way to find yourself frustrated more than you already are. By just figuring out the "why," you are already way down the path to making wise decisions about the "what" and "how" and "when" in dealing with your child's situation.

Yet, it's still nice to look at a synthesized set of advice. With that in mind, I'd like to close out our discussion on the "why" of childhood rebellion with some final suggestions on what to do when you find rebellion in your home. I want to first suggest a method of communication with a rebellious child, then give you a laundry list of things to do when your child is in the throes of rebellion, and last give you some proven principles for helping restore a rebellious Christian kid.

THE "PROBABLY SO" RULE OF COMMUNICATION

One of the biggest problems of dealing with rebellious children is that it is easy to find yourself fighting and arguing with them. They often dominate these encounters and use them against you, either throwing back at you things you overstated in the heat of the moment, or reminding you of less-than-spiritual behavior that you demonstrated.

The key to conversing with a rebellious child is to maintain an ongoing balance between *consequences* and *sorrow.* Foolish behavior and bad choices should lead to painful consequences. Unless children experience those consequences, there is little reason for them to change the way they are living. We must allow them to bear the consequences of their actions, but at the same time communicate that we gain no joy in seeing their effect. Sincere sorrow should accompany our commitment to allow consequences to run their course.

Foster Cline and Jim Fay have captured this principle well in their helpful book *Parenting Teens with Love and Logic.* Rather than trying to explain it to you, let's look at an excerpt from their book that shows this principle in action. It's what I like to call their "probably so" rule of communication.

Love-and-logic parents know firsthand that *the best solution to any problem lives within the skin of the person who owns the problem.*

For example, Phil's seventeen-year-old daughter, Tiffany, comes home with alcohol on her breath. Should Phil talk to her about it immediately or in the morning? *Morning.* With anger or sadness? *Sadness.*

"Oh, I felt so sorry for you last night," Phil says the following morning. "I smelled alcohol on your breath. I'm starting to worry about you and alcohol. What would you guess about using the family car now?"

"I guess I might not get to use it," Tiffany replies.

"Good thinking," Phil replies.

Did Phil set a limit? Yes. Is Tiffany going to try to talk him out of it? Absolutely. Can she? No. Because no matter what Tiffany says, Phil can say, "Probably so."

"But I won't do it again," Tiffany begs.

"Probably so."

"Well, all the other kids get to do it."

"Probably so."

"Well," says Tiffany, trying to draw her father into an argument, "so you've got a big problem over alcohol, Dad, and now I can't drive and I've got to look like a dork at school because—"

"Probably so."

"Well," she persists, "how am I supposed to get to work at the jewelry shop?"

If Phil gives her an answer, will she like it? No. It would be better for Phil to say, "I don't know. I was going to ask you the same thing."

"Well, I'll get fired!"

"Probably so."[1]

In this scenario, Phil realizes that if he allows his daughter to get the best of him and gets angry, he will neutralize the impact of the natural consequences of her drinking. Anger only muddies the process and draws Phil's emotions into the forefront in such a way that it blocks the logical chain of consequences from taking over. By using Cline and Fay's "probably so" tool, Phil keeps the focus on the consequences of Tiffany's drinking as they affect her access to the car. It makes it difficult for Tiffany to focus her anger on her dad. Rather, the "probably so" exchange keeps forcing her to face the ramifications of the aftermath of her drinking.

The major point here is that you want to be careful not to use either anger or negativity when dealing with your child's bad behavior—it surrenders the high ground to them every time. So much of the will to rebel is lost when a child finds that his parents aren't panicking but are calmly and consistently dealing with him from a balance of consequences and sorrow.

The Top Ten Things to Remember When Dealing with Rebellious Children

1. Never underestimate the power of prayer. Anything supernatural that happens in our children's lives is an act of the Holy Spirit. We can help prepare their hearts, but it is God who is going to change them. Pray for them every day, and don't be afraid or ashamed to recruit others to pray for them also.

2. Remember to ask forgiveness for any ways you've failed them. You want to remove any obstacle that would block them from moving toward forgiveness themselves.

3. Let consequences do their job. Sometimes consequences go on for so long that you want to step in and intervene, and the urge to intervene increases the longer they have to live with their consequences. To the best of your ability, let the chips fall where they may. You don't want to do anything that prolongs their journey to the point of repentance.

4. When in doubt, turn to the Bible. Sometimes the line gets fuzzy between constantly loving kids and letting consequences play out. That's when you need to lean on God for spiritual discernment and divine wisdom. James 1:5 says, "If any of you lacks wisdom, he should ask God, who gives generously to all without finding fault, and it will be given to him."

5. Don't add bitterness to their rebellion. As much as possible, keep all lines of communication open. Enjoy the interaction you have with them outside the times you are forced to deal with their rebellious attitude. Don't let conversations about

their bad behavior dominate so much of your focus that it destroys the foundation of love you established with them before the rebellion began. Keep doing as many fun and interesting things with them as you can. Give them plenty of reasons to believe you not only still love them but also enjoy their company and have great confidence in a hopeful future for them.

6. Don't let your rebellious child ruin your other relationships. Sometimes rebellion requires that you put boundaries in your own life so that it doesn't adversely affect your other children or your marriage.

7. Make sure they know that they always have a place to repent. They need to believe with all their heart that your door is always open to them. Like the father in the story of the prodigal son, your rebellious child needs to have confidence that if or when she comes to her senses, the door to your home is always open, as well as the door to your heart.

8. Be willing to be used of God to help others. Make yourself available to help other people going through similar problems with their kids. As 2 Corinthians 1:3–4 reminds us, "Praise be to the God and Father of our Lord Jesus Christ, the Father of compassion and the God of all comfort, who comforts us in all our troubles, so that we can comfort those in any trouble with the comfort we ourselves have received from God."

9. Make your life more attractive than theirs. Give them a reason to want to turn around. You don't want to exemplify the things that turned them off to the faith. Refuse to allow yourself to get sucked into the trap of compulsory Christianity, cliché Christianity, comfortable Christianity, cocoon Christianity, or compromised Christianity. They need to see that a life of grace-based, passionate faith is so much better than a life of rebellion.

10. Don't give up. You never know when someone's heart is about to turn around.

RESTORING A REBELLIOUS CHILD

When the time comes, be there to help your kids come in from the cold.

A life of rebellion can pull children into a web of regret. Once they are in it, it is hard for them to get out. We need to be there with a well-thought-out plan, ready to help them find their way back into the bosom of the family. It should be our aim, regardless of what our children have done to us, to do everything we can to help restore them to fellowship with God and harmony with their extended family.

Paul says in Philippians 2:1–2, "If you have any encouragement from being united with Christ, if any comfort from his love, if any fellowship with the Spirit, if any tenderness and compassion, then make my joy complete by being like-minded, having the same love, being one in spirit and purpose."

This is no time for accommodating your pride. Your child may have hurt you deeply. Your gut says to get even, exact a toll, and stay mad a little longer. God says, "No!" That's not what He does with us when we want to repent, and He doesn't want us doing it with others, especially members of our own family.

We are called to be peacemakers.[2] Our government sometimes sends out our armed troops to some hot spot in the world to serve as peacekeepers. Jesus didn't say, "Blessed are the peace*keepers*." He said, "Blessed are the peace*makers*." Peacekeepers are simply people with bigger guns and more money in their pockets to keep a rebellion from getting out of hand. Peacekeeping doesn't solve the rebellion; it just keeps it in check.

A peacemaker helps bring rebellion to an end. That's what we're called to do with members of our family who have chosen a life of rebellion. Peacemaking isn't about avoiding conflict or trying to placate someone's anger. In fact, sometimes being a peacekeeper requires you to initiate a confrontation. Peacemaking is about using whatever means is beneficial to bringing another person to a point of reconciliation and restoration. It might mean working to avoid a conflict, instigating a conflict, or bringing a conflict to an end.

If you feel God is leading you to take steps to restore a rebellious child, I want to suggest a few principles to follow when acting on God's lead:[3]

Talk Things Out with God
before You Discuss Them with the Rebellious Child

You want to make sure your heart is right before you attempt to get your child's heart right. God may need to change you first. He probably will have been teaching you things all along. Allow Him to continue to teach you. Talk with Him, but also listen to Him.

Don't be afraid to voice your own despair and frustration to God. You may have a good deal of anger of your own to ventilate with Him. Speak what is on your heart respectfully to Him. But speak it!

God speaks very clearly to us through His Word. Put the Scriptures before you and meditate on them. Ask God to reveal to you the unmet needs in your son or daughter that might have stirred him or her to anger. God may wait days, weeks, or months before He gives you the calm assurance that you are ready to make your approach. Wait for His peace. In the meantime, God may not only be changing your heart; He may also be changing your son's or daughter's heart, too.

Take the First Step

You may have been on the receiving end of a lot of dishonor. Your fragile ego tells you, "It's my kid's job to take the first step. She's the one that administered the bulk of the pain. She should have to initiate peace."

Don't let your flesh do the talking or allow your wounded heart to call the shots. Let God's Spirit take the lead. And remember that holding back only hurts you. The Bible says that refusing to deal with unresolved conflict will block your prayers.[4]

Put forethought into when and where you want to talk with your child. Avoid meeting with him when either of you is unusually fatigued or hungry or in a hurry. Ask God to show you a quiet place that will complement the quiet spirit you want to bring to the rendezvous.

Identify with Their Pain

People don't get angry and rebel for no reason. There may be a lot of pain churning inside them. Listen more than you speak. Ask questions. Ask feeling questions, such as "How did that affect you emotionally? How did you feel when that happened? How has that altered your attitude?"

Go with the goal of sympathizing before attempting to find solutions. The author of Proverbs reminds us, "A man's wisdom gives him patience; it is to his glory to overlook an offense."[5] This is not the time to rehearse the hurts or try to clarify the mistakes your child has made. Nor is it the time to remind him just how much pain he has dished out.

The key at this stage of the restoration process is to communicate that your child has tremendous value to you. Her opinions matter, her feelings matter, and her wounds matter. They all matter . . . to you. *The Living Bible* says, "We must bear the 'burden' of being considerate of the doubts and fears of others . . . Let's please the other fellow, not ourselves, and do what is for his good."[6]

You may have to listen to some accusations and unfounded assaults. Don't get into defending yourself. Let your child get the bile out of his system. When he sees that you aren't rationalizing, explaining, or arguing, it will show him that you are more interested in him than in yourself. And remember, if you have to take some insults you don't deserve, you'll be doing the same thing for your son or daughter that Christ had to do for you.

Own Up to the Negative Part You Played

No parent is perfect. And if you got caught off guard by a child's rebellion, you may have done or said things you shouldn't have. Because your child has been so close to you, you may have unintentionally let him down.

Don't try to explain why you did what you did or said what you said. Just ask for forgiveness. Jesus said, "First take the plank out of your own eye, and then you will see clearly to remove the speck from your brother's eye."[7]

Your attitude of humility and contrition can play a huge role in changing your rebellious child's attitude. It's like opening an exhaust valve on her heart. It diminishes her desire to attack you.

Be thorough, humble, and gentle as you confess the part you played in her decision to turn her back on God's best plans. Ask for forgiveness.

Deal with the Problem, Not the Person

It is very important that you go into this time not accusing your children or convincing them of things they did wrong. God will reveal that to them. This is not the time to attach blame to their actions or to rehearse your hurt.

The book of Proverbs reminds us that "a gentle answer turns away wrath, but a harsh word stirs up anger."[8] Your tone of voice, your posture, and your facial expressions can communicate so much that is in your heart. Just let your child see God's grace and mercy in your eyes and feel it in your voice. The Bible says, "The wise in heart are called discerning, and pleasant words promote instruction."[9]

Regardless of whether they use sarcasm, put-downs, condescension, or insults, don't give back in kind. Paul said, "Do not let any unwholesome talk come out of your mouths, but only what is helpful for building others up according to their needs, that it may benefit those who listen."[10]

Figure Out How You Can Cooperate Rather Than Compete

You may have to eat some crow and swallow some pride. It's not that you are compromising on absolute principles but rather looking for some common ground where you and your child can both agree. The key here is that you're not trying to win a battle. Your goal is unity, not victory.

Don't Aim at Resolving; Aim at Restoring

There's no way both sides of a major conflict are going to agree on everything. Don't even try. Reconciliation isn't about evening scores and fixing all the problems that have occurred. Your goal is the restoration of the relationship between you and your child, not in resolving every difference of opinion. When hearts are brought back together, many of the differences between them become irrelevant.

Not even the best of friends and the healthiest married couples see eye to eye on everything. That's not the goal of love anyway. Grace has room for different perspectives and different interpretations of a situation. Concentrate on bringing your hearts back together and deal with the differences in the future, once God has brought healing to your relationship.

Come to me, all you who are weary and burdened, and I will give you rest. Take my yoke upon you and learn from me, for I am gentle and humble in heart, and you will find rest for your souls. (Matthew 11:28–29)

Cast all your anxiety on him because he cares for you. (1 Peter 5:7)

DISCUSSION QUESTIONS

1. What is some of the "conventional wisdom" of raising kids that this book has helped you rethink? What are some of the "sacred cows" within Christianity that need to be dealt with that could minimize a child's desire to rebel?

2. What are the keys to the "probably so" rule of communication? What are the benefits for you of using consequences and sorrow simultaneously when dealing with your rebellious child? What are the benefits for your child?

3. As you look at "The Top Ten Things to Remember When Dealing with Rebellious Children," which ones were modeled best for you by your parents? Which ones were modeled the least? Which ones do you struggle the most to do? How could you improve your abilities to perform these steps better?

4. Tim drew a contrast between "peacekeepers" and "peacemakers." Why does peacekeeping often make matters worse when it comes to restoring a rebellious Christian kid?

5. Does your pride work with you or against you when it comes to carrying out the seven steps to restoring a rebellious kid? How can an authentic relationship with Jesus Christ help you overcome the natural obstacles that your pride creates when trying to restore the hearts broken by rebellion?

6. Which of the seven steps to restoration comes hardest to you? What can you do to overcome your struggle in this area?

7. What is one thing God has taught you through this chapter?

CHAPTER 11

Echoes of Mercy

There comes a point when, no matter what you've said or wished you'd said, you have to stop talking. For a writer, it means it's time to formulate those last few sentences or two and then walk away.

We've come to that point. It's almost time to place that tiny dot at the end of our journey together and declare it finished.

By now you've seen that this book isn't just about kids in Christian homes who rebel. It's been about all of us. We were all born as rebels without a cause. Without much prompting, we've each figured out how to break God's heart in our own ways. And perhaps your trek through the different corridors of this book not only picked up the echoes of your son's or daughter's anger but your own, too.

A lot of the reasons we are the way we are and do the things we do are because we're still trying to work out our peace. Maybe it's peace with our parents or with some disappointments in our past. Maybe you're still trying to get everything straight between you and God. Don't panic if you haven't figured all that out yet. Few of us have, completely. That's why it's referred to as a faith *walk*, not a *final destination*.

I was trying to do something as I shared my heart with you on this subject. Something more than trying to help you deal with kids who are frustrated with you or God or the world. Obviously, that was the main event. But there was something more important I was trying to slip in through the seams of our discussion, something far better for parents than knowing how to deal with kids who rebel. It was the pos-sibility that *we can raise kids who don't want to rebel and don't need to rebel.*

As I thought of this possibility, a girl named Cammie came to mind. I've never met her personally, but I know all about her. I've been pray-ing for her every morning for the past two years. I've seen her picture; in fact, I keep one in my Bible, but it's not easy to look at. I don't say that because of something unappealing about her features. She's a nice-looking girl. Nor is it because of any thing in her eyes that might betray the deep disappointment she deserves to feel. You could stare at her pic-ture forever and not find that.

I guess what's hard about looking at Cammie is that you can't do it without factoring in all she's been through and is going through and is facing. And it just . . . hurts. It hurts because of the question mark that has hung over her all her life. There's been so little *certainty* about this girl. In fact, I'd say if any child had a right to hold a grudge, perhaps get even, or maybe want to punish some of the people close to her, Cammie might be that child.

Almost since her birth, just about nothing has gone her way. And it had nothing to do with anything she did personally. Little that has hap-pened to her has been under her control. It's just the way life turned out for her. She's simply a young girl trying to get her little piece of the "happy pie," but has been consistently denied.

Her father and I went to seminary together. We played soccer together. We occasionally tried to figure out the Greek and Hebrew languages together. But when it came time to graduate, we went about as opposite directions as two men with the same credentials could go. I went to work for middle-class America in an upscale tourist town in the desert Southwest. He also went to a desert. But there was only one economic class of people he found there—those at the lowest rungs of the inter-national economic ladder. He went to the Sudan.

He took his wife to the southeast corner of this bleak country, to the savanna on the edge of the Sahara. Their goal was to translate the Bible into the local language. It was the best way they knew to bring hope to the masses of people who felt so little hope and to bring help to the myriad who needed a touch of grace. Mostly they wanted these sweet people to know just how much Jesus loved them.

Then along came Cammie—red-haired, fair-skinned, and ready to make her mark.

She was the first of three daughters they would eventually have. Unfortunately, she got a visit from Cancer when she was twenty-two months old.

When you're living in a country that makes third-world countries look like Beverly Hills, cancer isn't a diagnosis you want to hear coming from anyone. Where some countries are equipped to at least put up a fight, the Sudanese doctors simply said the obvious. There was nothing that could be done. "Let nature run its course. She won't last long."

Her family wasn't about to give up on this girl, which required them to head to Houston, Texas, so that the state-of-the-art cancer center at M. D. Anderson Hospital could give them some reason to hope. The battle was fought. The cancer was overwhelmed. It looked like there was reason to assume life could move back onto its original track.

This time, the family was assigned in Kenya. But the battle for Cammie was just beginning. There was a lot of physical damage as a result of the original cancer. Complications kept demanding more and more medical attention. Eventually, the family realized they would have to move back to the States. They settled in Dallas and moved their passion for people to new areas of ministry.

Cancer returned when Cammie was twenty-two, this time with a vengeance.

Cammie is twenty-five now. In spite of all the poking and cutting and chemicals, she's tried to put together some semblance of a normal young girl's life. She's beautiful, actually, but I think she makes most boys nervous. It takes a special young man to fall in love with a girl who has had to live with such uncertainty and so many assaults on her physical features.

Daily life for Cammie is similar to, but worse than, having a bad case of the flu. And it's been that way for more than two decades. There's the ongoing misery of the cancer, the pain from all the tests, and the sheer torture of the treatments. She has made more trips back and forth between her parents' home near Dallas and the M. D. Anderson Cancer Center in Houston than anyone would want to count.

But in spite of having so many reasons to be bitter, Cammie has chosen joy. And it's not some joy she holds close to her vest. Cammie's joy is contagious. It spreads itself through her unquenchable love for God and her overflowing appreciation for everybody else. There are no strangers in this girl's world, just people who either know Jesus or people who need to know Him. And she's just as comfortable with the one as she is with the other. Her attitude toward her fellow human beings could easily be entitled "Love the One You're With."

I recall getting an update on Cammie's health from her father about a year ago. In the process, he wrote about a birthday party the family recently had for her. About fifteen of her friends had been invited for dinner and dessert. Two of them were girlfriends who had shaved off their beautiful hair before the party so they could look like Cammie, who was preparing for yet another fierce round of chemotherapy.

Cammie told her dad she had to run a quick errand and would be back in plenty of time for dinner. When she returned, she brought with her a young girl no one had ever seen before. She simply introduced her as a new friend.

This friend turned out to be a homeless lady that lived under a bridge near the university Cammie attends. Cammie had noticed her as she was driving home one day and had gone back to see if she could turn this homeless woman into another one of her many friends. The poor woman smelled bad; she was wearing clothes layered with months of sweat. After Cammie's mom fixed her a quick snack to hold her over until dinner, Cammie quietly slipped her friend into a private part of the house where she could shed her clothing, get a shower, and wash her hair. Meanwhile, Cammie took the clothes she had been wearing as well as the ones she carried with her and got them turning in the washing machine. She laid out an alternative outfit and made sure there was another place setting at the table for this special guest.

This homeless lady enjoyed a great meal and an evening of laughter and celebration, playing games with Cammie's friends and family. When she walked out of the house several hours later, she smelled new and had a greater sense of hope in her eyes than she had when she first came in. The woman wanted to go "home" to sleep—something Cammie seemed to understand. But before she said good night to her, Cammie reminded her of how much God loved her and how much she loved her, too.

Some kids have so much and seem to appreciate so little. And then there are people like Cammie who have every reason to be bitter but aren't. As I ponder that, I believe the explanation can be found in the way her parents raised her. In spite of all she has struggled with, her parents have not chosen to complain. They've cried plenty—I know that for a fact. And they've wondered and questioned, as any parent would. But they refuse to jump to the conclusion that would be so easy to assume— that God had somehow deliberately shortchanged them and their sweet daughter for no good reason.

Nor did they conclude that Cammie's condition was a reason to protect her from the harsh realities of the world around her. They figured, why deny her a chance to live a full and purposeful life just because she has been denied good health? They not only raised this girl in some of the most hostile and contrary social and moral climates in the world, but they raised her at ground zero in the middle of them.

And she's not an anomaly in the family. Her two sisters were also raised in the midst of the hostile world culture their parents were committed to reaching. And they, too, have developed a passionate love for Jesus. It's a love that shows itself like Cammie's, in a firm desire to impact that culture with the grace and love of God.

As a family, they weren't concentrating on what was around them; they were focused on Who was inside them. Even with cancer as the backdrop, Cammie learned how to love the very people caught up in those hostile settings. Her mom and dad taught her to hold her head high, to fear no one, and to love God with all her heart. And they did all this without having to prod her. In fact, they didn't even really have to mention to her what they expected of her. She already knew it. All she had to do was keep her eyes open and watch them in action.

Cammie's mom and dad have lived a quiet, humble life while maintaining a passionate love for Jesus. It is a love that Cammie has not only seen played out in real time, every day, but it is a love she's felt from

them every waking hour of her life. It's been present in every uncomfortable breath she's taken and has supported her in every unsteady
step she's made.

Cammie hasn't had time to wrap herself in self-pity. She's been too
busy playing the hand she's been dealt. And that has been much more
doable because she is part of a family that defines itself by its relationship to Jesus. There are no substitutes for Him, no evangelical systems
to do His bidding, no Christian bunkers or spiritual attics to hide in from
all the threats—real or imagined—that loom at street level. And in the
process, Cammie has come to the full awareness of God's tender mercies—the assurance that God is real and God is good.

It is a tender mercy to raise your kids in earshot of the battle for the
cross.

It is a tender mercy to show them how to stand when others are
cowering and to charge forward when so many are in retreat.

It is a tender mercy to force your child to a narrow place in life
where all they really have is Jesus.

I know that a lot of Christian kids rebel. But as I said earlier, I'm convinced that most of them don't really want to. They just haven't been
given a better alternative. The only true antidote for a life of rebellion is
a life worth living. It's available to any family that wants it. It's filled with
risks, unknowns, disappointments, and heartaches. You might even have
to put up with the Grim Reaper shadowing you closely. But when you're
in the middle of it, it doesn't seem to matter much. That's what happens
when you get completely wrapped up in the Way, the Truth, and the Life.

Someone has said, "Aim at heaven, and you get earth thrown in. Aim
at earth, and you get neither." Cammie has grown up with parents who
showed her how to keep her focus on something greater than time, bigger than space, better than health, and stronger than pain. Because of
this she has blossomed.

When we give kids something to die for, we free them to live. When
we give kids something to hope for, we free them to face whatever may
come. When we give kids something to love for, we free them to make
a difference. Kids that have all this going for them not only don't need
to rebel, they really and truly don't want to.

As I close this book, I'm going to let Cammie have the last word. This is from a note she sent out to the people who pray for her health. And with these words I close:

I have quite a collection of scars, and though some are more sacred to me than others, they each tell a story. Perhaps in the eyes of some I'd be more beautiful without them, but I've grown to love them—they tell my story and proclaim that my life has been worth fighting for. My newest addition is a five-inch-long incision that runs crosswise along my right side—a souvenir from my last surgery in August.

Each scar is full of little secrets and tenderly reminds me of God's deliverance and healing care. I wouldn't trade them for anything for they have helped me cherish the beauty that lies in the sacred scars of Christ; embedded in His hands, feet, and side. Those precious scars prove His love is more passionate than we could ever imagine—a love that makes it possible for our pain to make sense and grants the potential of fashioning us to be like our beautiful King.[1]

DISCUSSION QUESTIONS

1. As you look at the story of Cammie, what were her parents doing to remove her need to rebel?
2. Some kids feel they need to rebel in order to offset the built-in shortcomings in their parents' parenting style. What are some things you learned from reading this book that can be implemented that would minimize your child's need to rebel?
3. What is the biggest thing you've learned about yourself from reading this book? About your faith? About helping your kids who are rebelling?
4. If you have rebellious children, what is the most important thing you can do to help them get through this time of rebel-

lion? If your children aren't rebelling, what is the most strategic lesson you've learned that would make rebelling unnecessary for them?

5. Of all the lessons you learned in this book, which one do you think will most enhance your relationship with God? With your kids?

Notes

Chapter 1: The Sheer Weight of Rebellion

1. 2 Corinthians 12:9.
2. Exodus 20:5–6.
3. Isaiah 53:6.
4. Jeremiah 17:9.
5. Philippians 2:12.
6. Genesis 4:1–15.
7. Genesis 9:18–25.

Chapter 2: An Overdose of Bad Behavior

1. Stephen Covey, *7 Habits of Highly Effective People* (New York: Simon & Schuster, 1989), 30–31.
2. Romans 3:10.
3. John 8:32.
4. Luke 8:12.
5. Luke 8:13.
6. Luke 8:14.
7. John 10:14, 16.
8. 1 Corinthians 1:18.
9. 1 Corinthians 13:4–8*a*.
10. James 1:13–14.
11. Luke 24:39.
12. John 20:25.
13. John 20:29.

Chapter 3: A Prodigal Primer

1. For an expanded discussion on this style of parenting, see Foster Cline and Jim Fay, *Parenting Teens with Love and Logic* (Colorado Springs: Piñon, 1992), 30–32.
2. Proverbs 3:12; Hebrews 12:6.
3. Hebrews 12:10.
4. Luke 15:8–10.
5. Luke 15:29, emphasis added.
6. Luke 15:29.
7. Phil Waldrep, *Parenting Prodigals* (Friendswood, Tex.: Baxter Press, 2001), 75.
8. Ray Vanderlawn, From the Introduction to *Echoes of His Presence* (Grand Rapids: Zondervan, 1998), 78

Chapter 4: A Lesson from the Italian Stallion

1. James Peterik and Frank Michael Sullivan III, "Eye of the Tiger."
2. Hebrews 12:2.

Chapter 6: Cliché Christianity

1. Josh McDowell and Bob Hostetler, *Beyond Belief to Convictions* (Wheaton: Tyndale, 2002), 14–18.
2. 1 John 1:1.
3. John 8:32.
4. Psalm 119:11 KJV.
5. 1 Corinthians 8:1.
6. James 1:22.
7. 1 Peter 5:8.

Chapter 7: Comfortable Christianity

1. Lamentations 3:22–23.
2. Romans 12:1*b*.
3. Adapted from Lesson 9 in Rick Warren, *The Purpose-Driven Life* (Grand Rapids, Mich.: Zondervan, 2002).
4. Haggai 2:8.
5. 2 Corinthians 12:9.
6. 2 Samuel 5:13.
7. 2 Samuel 18:33.
8. Ecclesiastes 1:9.
9. 1 Samuel 17:45–46*a*.
10. 1 Samuel 17:46*b*–47.
11. 2 Samuel 24:10.
12. 2 Samuel 24:21.
13. 2 Samuel 24:24, emphasis added.

Chapter 8: Cocoon Christianity

1. This story appeared on Matt Drudge's Web site during the autumn of 1999. It was from a newspaper in the former Soviet Union.
2. Matthew 5:16 NKJV.
3. John 16:33 NASB.
4. 1 John 4:4 NASB.
5. James 4:7 NKJV.
6. Numbers 13:1–2.
7. Numbers 13:31–33, emphasis added.
8. Joshua 2:9, 11.
9. Leviticus 26:3, 6–8.

10. Ephesians 6:17.
11. Psalm 119:11.
12. Leviticus 26:12–13.
13. Leviticus 26:14–17, emphasis added.
14. 2 Corinthians 12:9.
15. 1 Corinthians 10:13.
16. Matthew 3:10.
17. Psalm 1:3.
18. Warren, *The Purpose-Driven Life*, 202.
19. Josh McDowell and Dick Day, *Why Wait?* (San Bernardino: Here's Life Publishers, 1987), 79.
20. Romans 5:20 KJV.
21. Charles Colson, *Against the Night* (Ann Arbor: Vine Books, 1989), 181.

Chapter 9: Compromised Christianity

1. Garrison Keillor, "My Cousin Rose," Life These Days. Copyright 1998, Minneapolis Public Radio.
2. Psalm 111:10.
3. See 2 Samuel 13:2.
4. See 2 Samuel 13:6–9.
5. Charles Swindoll, *David: A Man of Passion and Destiny* (Dallas: Word, 1997), 210.
6. Galatians 6:8.
7. James 2:25.

Chapter 10: Bridges of Hope

1. Foster Cline and Jim Fay, *Parenting Teens with Love and Logic*, (Colorado Springs: Piñon Press, 1992), 71–72.
2. See Matthew 5:9.
3. Adapted from Lesson 20 in Warren, *The Purpose-Driven Life*.
4. See 1 Peter 3:7.
5. Proverbs 19:11.
6. Romans 15:2 TLB.
7. Matthew 7:5.
8. Proverbs 15:1.
9. Proverbs 16:21.
10. Ephesians 4:29.

Chapter 11: Echoes of Mercy

1. Cammie VanRooy, "A Note from Cammie This Time," copyright 2003 by Cammie VanRooy. Used by permission.